Karl Shaw trained as a journalist (for *NME* and others) and is the author of several humour books, including *Gross*, *Royal Babylon: An Irreverent History of European Royalty*, and the American bestseller *Five People Who Died During Sex and 100 Other Terribly Tasteless Lists*. He currently works in marketing and lives in North Staffordshire with his family.

Also by Karl Shaw

*Gross*

*Royal Babylon: An Irreverent History of European Royalty*

*Five People Who Died During Sex and 100 Other Terribly Tasteless Lists*

# CURING HICCUPS WITH SMALL FIRES

*A Delightful Miscellany of Great British Eccentrics*

Karl Shaw

BOXTREE

First published 2009 by Boxtree
an imprint of Pan Macmillan Ltd
Pan Macmillan, 20 New Wharf Road, London N1 9RR
Basingstoke and Oxford
Associated companies throughout the world
www.panmacmillan.com

ISBN 978-0-752-22703-0



1 3 5 7 9 8 6 4 2

A CIP catalogue record for this book is available
from the British Library.

Typeset by Ellipsis Books Limited, Glasgow
Printed and bound in the UK by
CPI Mackays, Chatham ME5 8TD

# CONTENTS

# INTRODUCTION

An eighteenth-century French scholar attributed the British talent for eccentricity to a 'mixture of fogs, beef and beer . . . aggravated by the tedium of the English Sunday'. Whatever the reason, for a small nation with a reputation for reserve, the British Isles do seem to have thrown up more than their fair share of oddballs. You could write a dozen books about British eccentrics without mentioning the same person twice. Try searching for 'eccentric' in the online *Oxford Dictionary of National Biography* and you will see what I mean – more than 1,000 results, and those are just the dead ones.

It begs the question, who qualifies as a proper British eccentric? They appear to fall into two camps. On the one hand there are your 'conscious' eccentrics, i.e. people who carefully cultivate their reputation for oddness. This group includes the likes of Lord Berners, who dyed his doves in various pastel shades, and more recently Oliver Reed, among whose many party pieces was a fondness for dropping his trousers and displaying his tattooed penis in public. In this type of contrived eccentric behaviour, the joke is shared by the eccentric and by us. It is self-aware and ironic and demonstrates an ability to laugh at one's self – another trait commonly associated with the British. Some might call it boorish attention-seeking.

The other type are your 'unconscious' eccentrics. The people in this group have absolutely no idea how out of step their behaviour is. They go about their business with a degree of heroic innocence, like the part-time entomologist Colonel Henry Charles Harford, who fought in the Zulu War at Victory Hill in 1879 and in the heat of battle and in full view of the advancing Zulus chased a rare moth with his net, oblivious to the bullets striking the rocks all around him. Or Sir Richard Paget, who developed a sign language for the deaf and tested it on his daughters by stuffing their ears with treacle, then in the spirit of scientific enquiry threw them off the back of a moving bus to test his theory that the force of the air behind them would ensure that they landed on their feet. The latter group, arguably, are your 'true' eccentrics. According to Dr David Weeks, author of the world's only scientific study of eccentricity, 'a true eccentric is never acting'. Unless of course you *are* an actor, like Robert Coates, who thought he could 'improve' Shakespeare by ad-libbing and once tried to enliven a performance of *Romeo and Juliet* by taking a crowbar to Juliet's tomb.

Eccentricity is often linked to madness. Some eccentrics have been wrongly identified as mad, and vice versa. The earliest books about British eccentrics, starting with John Aubrey's *Brief Lives*, which chronicled the oddities of various late-seventeenth-century oddballs, were mostly filled with hermits and religious zealots. Today we would recognize these 'eccentrics' as people suffering from varying degrees of mental illness. Dame Edith Sitwell's *English Eccentrics* were mostly aristocrats, some of whom were undoubtedly mad. It was a question of class; whereas a mentally ill person from the lower orders was mad, a mad aristocrat was merely 'eccentric'. Dame Edith, who was both an aristocrat and eccentric, was writing from considerable personal experience. Always dressed in black, she wore a number of vast topaz and aquamarine rings, which, she would explain as she constantly fingered them, became 'worried' if she didn't give them enough attention, and although massively overdrawn at the bank, gave two parties a day at her favourite restaurant.

Any new collection of 'eccentric biography' of course owes a debt to previous texts in this genre. For my money the best, and an inspiration for this book, is *Brewer's Rogues, Villains, Eccentrics: An A–Z of Roguish Britons Through the Ages* by William Donaldson, another bona fide eccentric, who showed how to do it and make it very funny. In this collection of anecdotes and pen portraits I have covered some familiar ground but have also included some notable Britons from all walks of life who have been overlooked by previous authors in this genre, people not traditionally regarded as full-dress eccentrics but who nevertheless had their moments, such as Charles Babbage, who invented a calculating machine now acknowledged as the forerunner of the computer, but then dedicated much of his spare time working out the statistical probability of the biblical miracles, and Alexander Graham Bell, inventor of the telephone, who was apparently obsessed with nipples on sheep.

As Donaldson points out, eccentricity of course is in the eye of the beholder. One man's charming eccentric with 'a dry sense of humour' is another man's tiresome old bigot (see Prince Philip, Duke of Edinburgh).

# One

# TRAVELLING ECCENTRICS

*'Just speak the Queen's English loud enough and everyone understands'.*

—SEBASTIAN SNOW (1929–2001)

## Three men in a strop

Exploration is the one scientific endeavour that requires no great understanding of the subject; it deals with the unknown. All you need is an enquiring mind and a lot of guts. It tends to attract people who are driven, single-minded and extraordinarily tough. Quite a lot of them have beards; a significant proportion are also quite mad. In the eighteenth and nineteenth centuries Britain had this hairy, robustly peculiar type in abundance, which was fortunate, because the British believed that great feats of geographical exploration were reserved for their countrymen alone, as though by divine appointment.

One of the great obsessions of the age was the course of West Africa's greatest river, the Niger. It had never been mapped and no one knew where it flowed. Speculation was rife. Some insisted that it flowed west to Gambia or Senegal. Others thought the Niger disappeared into a huge swamp called Wangara. There were those who believed it joined the Nile, or that it flowed into the Congo, or that it flowed nowhere at all and simply evaporated under the blazing Saharan sun. Dozens of explorers had died trying to find the answer. In 1822, Britain had another crack at trying to solve the mystery of the Niger with a team of three men. It resulted in the most acrimonious and badly planned expedition in the history of African exploration.

Two of the three chosen for the expedition were Scots: a naval surgeon, Walter Oudney (1790–1824), and a naval officer, Hugh Clapperton (1788–1827). The third member of their party was an English army officer, Major Dixon Denham (1786–1828). It was a disastrous mix of clashing personalities. Denham was high-handed, self-important and treated the other two with barely concealed contempt. Clapperton was huge, red-bearded and quick-tempered. Both Scots bitterly resented Denham's obnoxious, arrogant attitude. The mission was fatally undermined even before they set off by a misunderstanding over who should actually lead the expedition. The two Scots assumed that Clapperton was the leader, because he was the most senior ranking officer. The Colonial Office had told Denham that he was in charge. He knew no more about Africa than Oudney or Clapperton but had used his social connections to be given command. To add to the confusion there was no agreement over where they should even be looking. Oudney and Clapperton were under instructions to find Lake Chad, which had been mentioned in an earlier expedition as a possible outlet, while Denham was ordered to look for the Niger to the south. There was even a huge row over what they should wear. Denham thought they should go native by wearing turbans and robes. Oudney and Clapperton argued that in the interests of national pride they should wear full dress uniforms to remind the Africans how important Britain was. The Scots had their way, and in March 1822, the three men set off from Tripoli across the blazing Sahara in blue frock coats, white waistcoats, breeches and silk stockings. In the event their choice of clothing actually saved Denham's life: at one point he became separated from the main body of the expedition and was captured by marauding tribesmen, who stripped him and started squabbling over his clothes. While his captors were arguing over their catch he was able to slip away; naked, dodging snakes and scrambling through thickets, he crawled, muddied and bleeding, back to camp.

Large portions of their expedition are lost to posterity because, according to their published journal, it was 'wholly uninteresting, and is therefore omitted'. The most remarkable thing about their journey across the Sahara was that all the way to Lake Chad, despite braving treacherous sandstorms, bouts of malaria and travelling for days without water while members of their party dropped dead around them like flies and even the camels were dying from exhaustion, the three men never once stopped arguing. Clapperton and Oudney were goaded by Denham's habit of constantly giving orders. Denham was irritated by Clapperton's mistreatment of, and constant threats to shoot, his native bearers. Denham also accused Clapperton of having sex with one of them. Casual sex with natives during expeditions into Africa was not unusual; Denham himself was not averse to the charms of African ladies. In Clapperton's case, however, the native in question was a man. Clapperton vehemently denied the accusation and Oudney stood by him, but from that point onwards even the faintest hope of unity in the camp was abandoned.

In January 1824, Oudney died from tuberculosis, aggravated by intermittent bouts of fever. Denham and Clapperton stopped arguing just long enough to agree that it was time to go home. This was only a signal, however, to start another row over which route to take. In the end they decided to return the way they had come, and so they bickered and squabbled all the way back to London.

A couple of years later, Clapperton died during yet another attempt at finding the mouth of the Niger. As the only surviving member of the party, Denham came to be regarded as the hero of the expedition and was elected a fellow of the Royal Society. In 1826, he published his *Narrative of Travels and Discoveries in Northern and Central Africa*, in which he left out almost all mention of his companions and took the credit for most of their discoveries.

There was just one footnote to the failed Clapperton–Denham–Oudney expedition – the fate of the menagerie of animals they had brought home with them, including a horse, a sheep, a mongoose, four ostriches, three parrots, a monkey, a shark and three slugs. A home was found for the parrots and the monkey but the fate of the others, including the slugs, is not known. According to the records there was some concern over the fate of the sheep that had become 'so much attached to the horse that their separation might be fatal'. Denham's celebrity was short-lived. The following year he was appointed Governor of Sierra Leone and died of fever five weeks into his new job.

## To Leicester Square and back

Africa was a graveyard for British explorers. In 1806, a Scot, Mungo Park, disappeared while trying to trace the Niger to its mouth. Of the forty-six men who set out on the journey with Park, not one survived. Alexander Keith Johnston was only six months into his expedition to lakes Nyasa and Tanganyika when he died from a double dose of malaria and dysentery in 1879. It left another Scot, twenty-one-year-old Joseph Thomson, in charge. Despite being gored by a buffalo and weak from malaria and subsequently acute dysentery, Thomson completed the mission without further loss of life. At one point he survived an attack from Maasai warriors by persuading them he had magical powers, an illusion he achieved by popping two false teeth in and out of his mouth and whenever danger approached, brewing up a fizzy froth of Eno's Fruit Salts. He returned to London to write his celebrated book *To the Central African Lakes and Back*. The author J. M. Barrie once pressed Thomson to describe the most difficult leg of his incredible, epic journey. The young explorer replied: 'Crossing Piccadilly Circus.'

## Scot of the Sahara

One of the great geographical riddles of the nineteenth century was the location of the fabled African city of Timbuktu. According to legend, it was the seat of great power and learning, home to fabulous palaces and universities on which even the roof tiles were made of gold. In 1809, an English merchant traveller with a vivid imagination called James Jackson published a book called *An Accurate and Interesting Account of Timbuktu, the Great Emporium of Central Africa*. It made extraordinary claims, describing in great detail a city of immense wealth, crawling with beautiful, available women. Jackson's book was a best-seller and Timbuktu became the ultimate prize for every red-blooded explorer. The French government offered 10,000 francs for the first person to bring back information about it. The British, of course, were determined to get their man there first.

Alexander Gordon Laing (1793–1826) was a young Scottish officer serving in the Royal African Colonial Corps in Sierra Leone. He certainly looked the part – tall and handsome, with wild curly hair and an impressive set of mutton-chop sideburns. Unfortunately, he was not particularly well qualified to lead an expedition to the centre of Africa. To start with, his health was described as 'delicate' and his grasp of African geography was hazy. He was also thought to be slightly mad. Laing, however, was not short of self-confidence. More to the point, he was extraordinarily cheap; he offered to find Timbuktu without taking any salary at all from the British Foreign Office, and with a proposed outlay of only £640 10*s.* for expedition set-up costs and annual expenses of £173 7*s.* 6*d.* His proposal was gratefully accepted.

In May 1825, Laing set off for Africa on his cut-price expedition via Tripoli, where he promptly fell in love with and proposed to Emma, daughter of the British Consul Hanmer Warrington. Emma's father, who had no desire to see his daughter marry a madman, much less one who was about to set off on a suicide mission into the world's largest and harshest desert without a clear idea of where he was going, was appalled. Even worse, as British Consul he was the only senior representative of the Church of England in Tripoli and was expected to perform the marriage service himself. Warrington reluctantly agreed to officiate, on the condition that Laing sign an agreement that the marriage would not be consummated until after he had returned from Timbuktu. Mysteriously, Laing agreed to his terms. The couple tied the knot on 14 July 1825, and two days later Laing kissed his new bride goodbye, jumped on his camel and set off into the Sahara. His mission now assumed a new, more manic impetus: frustrated desire for his unobtainable Emma. 'I shall do more than has ever been done before', he wrote home to his parents, 'and shall show myself to be what I have ever considered myself, a man of enterprise and genius.'

As Laing recorded very little in terms of a journal over the coming months, more or less everything we know about his expedition is revealed in a series of highly emotional letters. His despatches revealed more about his gradually unravelling mental state than they did about African countryside. Amid the odd poem and sketch, plus random observations such as, 'I must not meddle with the females of the country,' they were mostly emotional, paranoid and disparaging rants about the efforts of previous African explorers, especially Hugh Clapperton, whom Laing despised. On the subject of clothing, he revealed that unlike Clapperton he had adopted 'plain Turkish dress' – except on Sundays, when he wore his full military uniform. He also regularly begged his father-in-law to send him a miniature portrait of 'my dear, dear Emma'. Without it, he told Warrington a trifle belatedly, 'I might go mad'. When the miniature finally arrived he was shocked to find that the portrait was not flattering to his beloved. To Laing's eyes, Emma looked suspiciously pale and wan – not at all how he remembered her. Half out of his mind with worry, he decided to throw in the towel and return to Tripoli. Receiving this news, Warrington, fearful for his son-in-law's sanity and even more fearful of his early return, wrote to reassure him that all was well with Emma. Laing wavered, then decided to press on to Timbuktu after seeing a large comet. 'I regard it as a happy omen,' he wrote. 'It beckons me on and binds me to the termination of the Niger and to Timbuktu.'

In January 1826, Laing and his small group were attacked by Tuareg tribesmen who stole all of their possessions and left Laing for dead. Writing with great difficulty using the thumb and middle finger of his left hand, he recorded his injuries in a letter to his father-in-law:

> To begin from the top, I have five sabre cuts on the crown of the head and three on the left temple, all fractures from which much bone has come away: one on my left cheek which fractured the jaw bone and had divided the ear, forming a very unsightly wound: one over the right temple and a dreadful gash on the back of the neck, which slightly grazed the windpipe: a musket ball in the hip, which made its way though my back, slightly grazing the backbone: five sabre cuts on my right arm and hand, three of the fingers broken, the hand cut three-fourths across, and the wrist bones cut through; three cuts on the left arm, the bone of which has been broken but is again uniting: one slight wound on the right leg and two with one dreadful gash on the left, to say nothing of a cut across the fingers of my left hand, now healed up.

Laing almost forgot to add that he also had dysentery and was so ill 'that it was presumed, expected and hoped that I would die'.

Having travelled 2,650 miles of unmapped, hostile desert, with horrific multiple injuries, Laing reached his goal and entered the fabled city of Timbuktu on 13 August 1826. He searched everywhere for the glittering palaces and nubile lovelies he had heard of, but found only a poor, run-down frontier town full of mud huts and bandits. To make matters worse, Sultan Bello, the region's powerful ruler, made it clear Laing wasn't welcome. Weirdly, Laing wrote home that Timbuktu 'has completely met my expectations', possibly because he was trying to drum up interest in his forthcoming book. He spent the next five weeks strutting through the streets in full dress uniform announcing himself to everyone he met as the King of England's emissary.

Laing never got to see his beloved Emma again. On 21 September 1826, he wrote to her father saying that Timbuktu had become 'exceedingly unsafe' and it was time to move on. It was the last anyone ever heard of Alexander Gordon Laing. Three days later his northbound caravan was ambushed by Tuaregs. According to an eyewitness, Laing was throttled by two men with his own turban then decapitated and left for the vultures. News of Laing's grisly death destroyed what was left of Emma's health. She died of tuberculosis in October 1829, aged twenty-eight.

## Ujiji mobile library, I presume?

Preparation is the key to any successful expedition. Among David Livingstone's provisions when he started his famous trek across Africa were 73 books weighing a total of 180 pounds. He eventually agreed to discard some of his mobile library, but only after his weary porters had carried them for 300 miles. As the journey continued, his library grew progressively smaller, until only his trusty Bible remained. Not very sensible, but still not quite in the same league as the French explorer Alexander Debaize, who reached Ujiji on the shores of Lake Tanganyika in eastern Africa in 1878 packing twenty-four umbrellas, two suits of armour and a portable organ. Livingstone died in Africa in 1873, after braving illness and years of paddling up and down snake-infested rivers, none of them, alas, leading to the source of the Nile. Along the way the great missionary was only able to convert a single African, who later lapsed.

## Twin piques

To satisfy early nineteenth-century England's craving for exotic conifers, the Scottish botanist David Douglas (1799–1834) braved whirlpools, grizzly bears, robbery, frostbite, snow blindness and near starvation in the Rocky Mountains.

Douglas was renowned for his remarkable courage and tenacity. When his canoe sank in Fort George Canyon and he lost his entire collection of spruce seeds, he simply went back for more. When he found the propagating material of *Pinus lambertiana* out of reach, Douglas shot the cones down with his gun. At one point he was so hungry that he was forced to eat all the berries he had collected to bring home. His diary entries were recorded with scientific precision: 'My feet tonight are very painful and my toes cut with the burned stumps of a strong species of Arundo and Spiraea tomentosa.' He lived off the land and rarely had a tent, preferring to sleep wrapped in a blanket or under a canoe, but always travelled with a complete suit of Stuart tartan which he would slip into whenever the mood struck him, much to the amusement of local natives.

Despite rapidly deteriorating eyesight, Douglas covered over 10,000 miles of Northwest America like a roving, frost-bitten Mr Magoo, literally bumping into trees. This sight impairment led to an epic blunder. Douglas returned home from one of his trips to the Rockies and announced the discovery of two giant peaks, which he named Mount Hooker and Mount Brown after distinguished British botanists. For almost seventy years they were the subject of great excitement and speculation and were listed on every map as the two highest peaks in the Canadian Rocky Mountains, despite defying the very best efforts of experienced mountaineers to find either of them. The search for Douglas's giant peaks was finally brought to a close when someone reread his original journals more carefully and noticed that he had claimed to have climbed both peaks in a single afternoon. In 1834, while looking for plants in Hawaii, the optically challenged Douglas stumbled into a pit that had been excavated to trap wild cattle and was gored to death by a bullock.

## Nuttall's missing

The pioneer Thomas Nuttall (1786–1859) is remembered eponymously in Nuttall's woodpecker, Nuttall's blister beetle, Nuttall's sunflower, Nuttall's evening primrose and *Pica nuttalli*, the yellowbilled magpie.

Nuttall was by trade a typesetter from Yorkshire, who went to America in 1808 to take up a job with a printing company in Philadelphia. He was also an enthusiastic botanist and in 1811, at the age of twenty-five, he jumped at the chance of joining an expedition with John Jacob Astor's Pacific Fur Company, travelling 1,500 miles along the Missouri River. As an explorer, Nuttall's survival skills left something to be desired. His Canadian fellow travellers christened him *le fou*, the fool, after checking his gun before an Indian raid and finding it filled with dirt. He had been using it to dig up plants.

Nuttall spent most of his time completely lost. He kept wandering away from his group while collecting plants and was so engrossed in his work that he couldn't find his way back. One night when Nuttall failed to return a search party was sent out to look for him. He saw them approach in the dark and, mistaking them for Indians, ran off into the bush. The annoyed rescuers chased him for three days without success, until he accidentally wandered back into the camp unassisted. On another occasion in North Dakota, Nuttall somehow strayed a hundred miles away from his group and was so exhausted that he collapsed and lost consciousness. A passing Indian took pity on him, carried him three miles to the river and paddled him home in a canoe. Amazingly, Nuttall somehow found his way back to England, where he spent the next few years at the British Museum of Natural History studying the hundreds of plant specimens he had brought home with him. He came to be regarded as the world's leading authority on the flora and fauna of Northwest America. As Nuttall rarely knew where he was at any given moment, his notes on the locations of some of his discoveries have since been found to be less than trustworthy. For example, he claims to have encountered the Willamette daisy in the Rocky Mountains, however it is now known that he must have found the plant much further west, in the Willamette Valley in Oregon, since it has never been known to grow anywhere else.

## Land of my fathers

Most histories of the mapping of North America overlook the remarkable contribution of a little-known Welsh missionary, John Thomas Evans (1770–99). Evans found inspiration in a local legend, according to which the discovery of the New World was accomplished not by Christopher Columbus or Amerigo Vespucci, but by Madoc, son of the twelfth-century Welsh prince Owen Gwynedd. He sailed from Wales for America in 1170 with three hundred men, who settled and became the progenitors of a tribe of pale-skinned Welsh Indians. The origin of this story is not known. Owen Gwynedd had several sons but none called Madoc, although a seafarer named Madoc, unrelated and possibly mythical, crops up in medieval Welsh literature; one story has him colonizing an unspecified island paradise. The legend of Madoc first appeared in print in 1583, in a document written by Sir George Peckham supporting Queen Elizabeth I's claim to the New World. It was intended to show that, as a Briton had landed in America long before Columbus, Elizabeth, not the King of Spain, had title to all American territories. The story of the lost tribe of Welsh-speaking Indians grew down the years, as reports of Madogwys (Madoc's people) were brought back to Britain from travellers all over America. All told, there were sightings of at least twenty tribes of Welsh-speaking Indians, ranging from Peru to Canada, nearly always in areas hitherto inaccessible to white settlers.

John Thomas Evans was the son of a Methodist preacher from Waunfawr, a village near Caernarvon in north Wales. There was more than a hint of madness in Evans's Methodism. Having grown up with the legend of Madoc, he believed that he had been chosen by God to find the lost Welsh Indians. In 1792, at the age of twenty-two, he set sail for Baltimore to begin his quest, taking with him a Welsh Bible so that he could pray with his long-lost kinsmen in their ancestral language. Informed opinion had it that the wilds of North Dakota would be a good place for Evans to start looking. The local Indian tribe, the Mandan people, had pale skin and spoke a language that sounded very much like Welsh. Mandan women were also very talkative, even in bed – conclusive evidence of Welshness, apparently – although there was no word as to whether the Mandan menfolk played rugby or had a choir.

In March 1793, Evans set out for the frontier from Philadelphia, through the Allegheny mountains and then going by boat up the Mississippi to St Louis. Louisiana was under the flag of Spain, and Evans was quickly arrested as a spy and locked up. After two years, he was released, having agreed to join a Scot called John Mackay who was leading a Spanish expedition to find a route through the Rocky Mountains to the Pacific. At this point no one knew what dangers lay ahead. It was thought that the area was populated with woolly mammoths and had mountains made of salt. Evans agreed to go along because the route took him close to the Mandan settlement, about 1,800 miles from St Louis.

To recap, a Methodist preacher, working for a Scot in the service of Roman Catholic Spain, was now looking for Welsh-speaking Indians on the edge of the known world.

About halfway to the Rockies, the party was frozen in for the winter at Fort Charles in Nebraska. In February, Mackay instructed Evans to strike out alone to find the Mandan settlement, but Evans was attacked by Sioux and fled back to camp. Evans tried again in June and this time actually reached the Mandan village in North Dakota. The Mandan chiefs received him warmly and he got to know them quite well, living with them in their large beehive-shaped dwelling through the bitterest of winters. He spent a total of seven months in their village, but in all that time Evans heard not a single word of Welsh.

With a heavy heart, Evans said *hwyl* to his hosts and returned to civilization after a two-year absence. In 1797, he wrote in his report that 'there is no such people as the Welsh Indians'. His spirit crushed, Evans drank himself to death in a St Louis bar two years later, aged twenty-eight. As for the Mandan tribe, smallpox wiped most of them out a couple of generations later. For all his eccentricity, Evans made a significant contribution to the sum of human knowledge. The map he made of the territories he had travelled through was later used by Meriwether Lewis and William Clark, leaders of the first overland expedition to the Pacific coast.

## Dromedary drama

John Ainsworth Horrocks (1818–46) was arguably Britain's unluckiest explorer ever. His name could have been written large as one of Australia's greatest frontiersmen had his career not been cut tragically short after just six years.

Horrocks was born into a wealthy cotton mill-owning family from Lancashire. When he was twenty-one he emigrated to Australia, where his father had bought him one thousand acres of sheep-farming land near Adelaide. Over time, Horrocks discovered that his true vocation was roaming the outback. Described as 'a young man of splendid physique', he imagined himself as a dashing, romantic, Byronic figure. He named his favourite greyhound Gulnare after a slave-girl in Byron's *The Corsair*. He travelled with a handful of companions, including his faithful butler, but remained aloof, eating alone every night at some distance from the others at a barrel specially set up for him, with a freshly laundered tablecloth and a silver fork and spoon. He found several local geographical features which still bear the names he gave them, including Mount Horrocks and Horrocks Pass. In 1841, he named a plain he passed Gulnare, celebrating his greyhound's success in catching and killing emus for him to eat.

In 1846, Horrocks set out to conquer the hitherto impenetrable hinterland of South Australia with several goats, a bull called Harry and an unnamed camel imported from Tenerife. The addition of the camel to the party was seen as a logistical masterstroke because previous expeditions, equipped with horses and bullocks, had all perished in the fierce heat. The decision turned out to be less of a coup than anticipated when, not long into the journey, the camel attacked their cook, biting a large chunk out of his head. A couple of days later the recalcitrant camel struck again, lurching into Horrocks just as he was loading his gun and causing him accidentally to shoot himself in the lower jaw, knocking out half of his teeth. Horrocks died in agony from his injuries several days later, the first explorer to be shot dead by his own camel. Horrocks was a visionary, because within twenty years camels were considered indispensable to any successful expedition into the outback. It would end in tears for Harry the bull, though, who was sentenced to death for killing his master; Horrocks had in fact suggested it so the good name of camels would not be besmirched by the unfortunate accident. Harry of course was not inclined to go quietly. When the first bullet failed to kill him, he turned and bit the head of an aborigine called Jimmy.

## Strippers with attitude

The mountaineer George Mallory (1887–1924) was one of the most romantic figures in the history of exploration. In 1923, the heroic Mallory was asked by a New York journalist: 'Why do you want to climb Everest?' It produced his historic reply, now a catchphrase in the English language for responding to a formidable challenge: 'Because it is there.' Shortly after noon on 8 June 1924, Mallory, on his third Everest assault, together with his twenty-two-year-old companion Andrew 'Sandy' Irvine, vanished somewhere near the summit. The discovery of Mallory's frozen, bleached corpse seventy-five years later sparked Everest's greatest 'Who got there first?' mystery. It also led to the publication in the British press of some photos of Mallory strolling around the countryside, naked but for his rucksack, shedding new light on the great adventurer's unorthodox approach to mountaineering.

In the best tradition of the upper-middle-class English amateur, Mallory was alarmingly forgetful and careless. On several mountaineering expeditions he took photos at the summit only to find later that he had left the lens cap on his camera. On his fateful Everest ascent he forgot to pack his torch and magnesium flares, equipment which could have saved his life. He also liked to stride around the lower altitudes of Everest stark naked. It wasn't the first time Mallory had climbed a mountain in the buff. In 1912, wearing only plimsolls, he and a friend attempted to climb a steep granite sea cliff near Land's End in Cornwall. Mallory's biographers Peter and Leni Gillman note that 'their lack of clothing posed some interesting technical problems on the abrasive crystalline granite at the top of the route'.

## Turned out nice again

In 1932, Maurice Wilson, manager of a women's clothes shop in Yorkshire, attempted the first ever solo ascent of Mount Everest by crash-landing a plane on the slopes of the world's highest peak at altitude, then walking to the summit. There were, however, a couple of flaws in Wilson's bold plan. He didn't own a plane and had never flown one before, let alone done any mountain climbing; but Wilson was resolute. He went out and bought a three-year-old Gypsy Moth plane and named it the Ever Wrest, then booked himself some flying lessons. Although a less than gifted pilot, after a few sessions he decided he was ready to go on his great adventure. He was planning to fly to his parents' house to say goodbye, but crash-landed the plane en route and was delayed for several weeks while he waited for repairs. By this time the authorities had got wind of Wilson's attempt, and did their best to stop him.

He was forbidden to enter Nepalese airspace and was put under surveillance. In 1933, however, Wilson slipped out of England and flew 5,000 miles to India, where he was forced to abandon his plane and complete the rest of his illegal ascent on foot. Having sold his plane for £500, he hiked overland through Tibet disguised as a monk and on 17 May arrived at the foot of Mount Everest. Wilson was convinced he could surmount any obstacle, including the world's highest peak, via a combination of fasting and prayer. His Sherpas begged to differ and abandoned him at 21,000 feet, but Wilson climbed on, braving yawning crevasses and increasingly desperate weather before dying of exposure. A year later, a British party found his frozen corpse and beside it his diary. Wilson's final entry, for 31 May, was: 'Off again, gorgeous day.'

## Bats and bigotry

The Yorkshireman Charles Waterton (1782–1865) was a pioneer among English naturalists. When he was twenty-two, he left the family seat at Walton Hall to take over the management of his father's sugar estates in British Guiana. He was fascinated by the local wildlife and spent the next twenty years scouring the tropical rainforests of South America, collecting specimens of birds and animals in a series of extraordinary trips into the largely unknown hinterland, and penetrating thousands of miles of unexplored jungle. What made these journeys even more unusual was that he did it in his bare feet, a policy he maintained in spite of the odd painful accident.

He once ripped open one of his feet while chasing a woodpecker and cured the wound by applying hot poultices of boiled cow's dung. On another occasion he was badly injured when he accidentally shot himself while loading his gun. He dressed the wound with dung then bled himself using his lancet. Waterton's faith in bloodletting, a routine he called 'tapping one's claret', was extreme. He bled himself so copiously it was said that he was unattractive even to a vampire bat. Waterton made an important medical discovery when he correctly identified that curare, the mysterious 'flying death' once used by Amazonian tribes to tip their arrows and immobilize their prey, was not, as was thought, a deadly poison, but a powerful muscle-relaxing agent. He proved his point by taking some samples from a native tribe and trying it out on three donkeys. Two died, but the third was resuscitated by means of bellows and lived on. For her work in the cause of science, the surviving donkey earned an obituary in London's popular evening newspaper the *St. James's Chronicle*.

On a single trip Waterton collected hundreds of rare insects, two hundred and thirty birds, two tortoises, five armadillos, two large serpents, a sloth, an ant bear and an alligator. The encounter with the alligator was later sensationally described in his best-selling book *Wanderings in South America*. He snared the thrashing reptile with a hook and rope, then he and his assistants hauled it onto the riverbank, where Waterton advanced to meet it armed with the eight-foot mast from his canoe, which he planned to ram down its throat. Having noted on the alligator's face a look of 'fear and perturbation', according to the author, he changed his mind and threw his weapon away, then jumped onto the alligator's back and rode it Tarzan-style back to his camp, where 'I cut his throat and after breakfast commenced dissection'. He dismissed this stunt as 'no more difficult than riding with the local hunt'.

Waterton always favoured a hands-on approach to his fieldwork. He spent six months sleeping with his foot dangling out of his hammock hoping to be bitten by a vampire bat. He was bitterly disappointed when one failed to take the bait and bit his Indian servant instead. Once, watching as his native guides struggled to capture a large boa constrictor, he ordered them to stand aside and, removing the braces holding up his trousers, tied them around the snake's jaws. He shared his bedroom with a huge snake, 'fourteen feet long, not poisonous, but large enough to have crushed one of us to death', the author noted. Waterton's book did more than record incredible encounters with wildlife and notes on the preservation of dead animals; it also contained idiosyncratic observations on politics, religion and the Hanoverian monarchy.

Waterton came from one of England's oldest and proudest Catholic families, claiming among their ancestors seven saints, including Sir Thomas More. The Watertons held onto their faith and their ancient seat at Walton Hall, despite occasional extreme financial hardship, which they blamed on Hanoverian Protestants. In Charles Waterton, the old family fire of righteous indignation blazed on. He regularly attending meetings of the local Protestant Reformation Society just so he could heckle the speakers.

During his travels Waterton also invented his own method of taxidermy. By marinating his specimens in a cocktail of chemicals, he reduced them to a rubber-like state that allowed him not only to preserve them perfectly but also to manipulate their limbs into various lifelike postures. When he left British Guiana he took with him hundreds of exotic specimens of carefully preserved South American wildlife. On his return to England, a horrified customs officer at Liverpool docks took one look at Waterton's grim shipload of rubbery animal trophies and immediately impounded them. Eventually the Treasury relented and let him bring them in, subject to a punitive 20 per cent import duty. Waterton protested bitterly, but in the end had no choice but to pay up to get his collection home.

Waterton never forgave Britain's 'Hanoverian' Treasury for what he perceived as another deliberate attempt to steal Catholic money. Back at Walton Hall he used his taxidermal know-how to enact hideous revenge in a series of mad, hybrid fantasies. Rubberized monkeys, bats and reptiles were manipulated into horrifying caricatures of members of the Protestant establishment. Animal parts from different species were grafted onto each other in grotesque combinations. A creation he called the 'Noctifer', a combination of bittern and eagle owl, represented 'the Spirit of the Dark Ages, unknown in England before the Reformation'. A monkey with horns represented 'Martin Luther after his fall'. Another hybrid grotesque was called 'John Bull and the National Debt'. The most infamous of Waterton's weird concoctions, the 'Nondescript', had hairy but distinctly humanoid features and was made chiefly from the parts of a howler monkey. Waterton claimed he found it in Guiana and it was the missing link in the evolution of man from an ape-like creature 'according to the theory recently advanced by Mr. Charles Darwin'. Several naturalists were completely taken in and believed that the creature Waterton had killed and mounted was human. In a certain light, however, the Nondescript bore an uncanny resemblance to Waterton's chief adversary, one J. R. Lushington, Secretary to the Treasury. It was rumoured that the Nondescript was Waterton's attempt to 'make a monkey' out of the tax collector, but never proven.

Waterton's flair for self-publicity ensured huge sales for his book and greatly increased his reputation for eccentric behaviour, something he was more than happy to play up to. Defying the formal fashion of his day, he kept his hair very short and wore an old-fashioned swallow-tailed coat and shoes several sizes too large. When he wasn't shocking visitors to Walton Hall in Yorkshire with his ghoulish collection of dead animals (he once surprised his dinner guests by displaying the partially dissected corpse of a primate on his dining table), he would suddenly stand on his head, or go down on all fours and bite his guests' ankles, or demonstrate the benefits of being double-jointed by scratching the back of his head with the big toe of his right foot.

In the 1850s, at a fantastic cost of nearly £10,000, Waterton built the world's first private wildlife sanctuary and nature reserve at Walton Hall and opened it to the public. There was just one animal that wasn't welcome in his sanctuary – the common brown rat, which Waterton was convinced had been introduced to England by the Protestant King George I. The extermination of the 'Hanoverian rat' from the grounds of Walton Hall was an obsession. He kept them at bay with the aid of arsenic, booby traps, owls and a Demerara tiger cat, although he occasionally took time out to fire pot shots with his musket at actual Hanoverians over the walls of his estate. He was once seen dashing a dead rat's brains out against a wall, crying, 'Death to Hanoverians!'

Although he was wealthy and highly eligible, Waterton remained single until he was forty-eight, possibly because of his habit of talking to insects, or the fact that his clothes stank of bichloride of mercury, the substance he used to preserve his infamous specimens from decay. Waterton had apparently been infatuated with a friend's daughter, Anne Edmonstone, from when she was an infant, and had vowed to marry her just as soon as she was old enough. He kept his promise when she turned seventeen, thirty-one years his junior. Waterton's poor teenage bride, having spent two years in a convent to prepare for conversion to Catholicism, died less than twelve months after her wedding day, six days after giving birth to their son Edmund. Waterton was racked with guilt and as a form of penance spent the remaining thirty-five years of his life sleeping on the floor wrapped in a cloak with a block of wood for a pillow. He rose at 3.30 a.m., spent an hour at prayer, breakfasted on dry toast, then for lunch sat down to eat a piece of bread with watercress and a cup of weak tea. He ate so little that he could still get into his old school uniform, a blue-tailed coat with gold buttons and a check waistcoat, which he wore into his eighties. His frugal lifestyle also kept him amazingly fit. He was a dedicated climber and loved to climb trees around his estate. In his late seventies he tried to fly with the aid of a pair of mechanical wings attached to his shoulders. Fortunately a friend arrived just in time to prevent him from jumping off the roof of an outhouse. Waterton was still climbing right up to the age of eighty-three, when he fell from a tree and died from his injuries.

## The cunning linguist

Richard Francis Burton (1821–90), explorer, writer, linguist, expert swordsman and connoisseur of Eastern erotica, burst into the British public consciousness in the early 1850s, when he offered his services to the Royal Geographical Society by volunteering to visit the forbidden Islamic holy cities of Mecca and Medina. It was, on the face of it, a suicide mission; fewer than half a dozen non-Muslims had made the trip and lived. Burton's cunning plan, however, was to make the journey disguised as an Arab pilgrim. The RGS knew he meant business because he had himself circumcised, which is probably taking your travel preparations a bit too far. Burton went to Egypt where he spent several weeks polishing his Arabic before taking on the persona of an Afghan physician. He was so successful in his role that he developed a thriving practice, curing the illnesses of his fellow pilgrims with little more than rosewater and iodine. On 11 September 1853, Burton did something no European had ever done before: he went to the Great Mosque and stood before the Kaaba. His book *A Personal Narrative of a Pilgrimage to Al-Madinah & Meccah* made him internationally famous and became a classic of travel literature.

In April 1855, the RGS called on their man again, this time to solve the greatest geographical mystery of the day: the source of the Nile. The dark, swarthy Burton chose as his travelling companion the blond, boyish and altogether more sensible John Hanning Speke. Their first trip was a disaster. Attacked and overwhelmed by a large party of Africans, Burton and Speke had to fight for their lives and both were badly wounded. Burton was transfixed by a spear that passed through both cheeks, knocking out four of his teeth. A year later Burton and Speke tried again. The time their expedition was marred by desertion and illness. Most of their equipment was either lost or stolen. Speke became deaf after attempting to dig out a beetle from his inner ear with a knife and half a pound of melted butter, and suffered from a severe eye infection that made him temporarily blind, but was in better shape than Burton, who was riddled with tropical disease and being carried everywhere on a litter. With his expedition leader temporarily incapacitated, Speke continued alone, and after trekking for twenty-five days came across a vast blue water which he named Lake Victoria. Speke concluded that this was the Nile's source and dashed back to Burton to give him the news.

Burton was devastated when he realized that he had been scooped by a subordinate. To rub salt in the wound, when they got back to London Speke rushed to the RGS to claim the source of the Nile for himself, breaking a gentleman's agreement that they should report back together. Having shared their momentous experience and braved horrific ordeals together, Burton and Speke spent the rest of their lives hating each other's guts. In September 1864, both men were invited to present their case for priority in a showdown at a meeting of the RGS in Bath. Burton was to argue that Speke had offered no supporting evidence that Lake Victoria was the source of the Nile; Speke planned to stand by his conviction. It was billed as the scientific duel of the decade. On the day before the debate was due to take place, however, Speke shot himself. He could face disease, hostile natives and wild animals in the heart of Africa, but his nerve failed him when he had to face Burton again.

Unlike the other great Victorian explorers, Burton also liked to explore native sexual practices, which he recorded during his various trips to Africa, India and the Middle East in minutely graphic detail. His assiduous hands-on approach to field research gave cause for concern, a clue to which he gave while observing the Wagogo tribeswomen of East Africa, recording in his notes, 'They are well disposed towards strangers of fairer complexion and have no difficulty obtaining the consent of the husbands to be absent for the night.' When the British general in India Sir Charles Napier sent Burton to investigate the homosexual brothels of Karachi, Burton wrote his report in such fine detail, supported by several diagrams, that there was little doubt he was writing from first-hand experience. Burton was rarely far from scandal. He was said to have sampled every available brothel east of Suez and once attempted to kidnap and rape a nun.

Burton had a second career as a writer. He best-known work was a sixteen-volume translation of the *Arabian Nights*. There had been English translations of this series of classic Eastern tales before, but Burton's version was unexpurgated and contained detailed accounts of sex acts, along with passages such as: '. . . he sheathed his steel rod in her scabbard . . . while accompanying her ejaculations of praise and of Glory to Allah! with passionate movements and wrigglings and claspings of his member . . .'. The British public were not quite yet ready to learn about such customs as genital mutilation, birth control, harems and aphrodisiacs, and Burton's frank translations of Eastern pornography shocked Victorian England to the core. His remarkable first-ever translation of the Kama Sutra was dismissed by one important critic as 'scrapings from brothels'.

It was also all a bit much for Burton's wife, Isabel. After his death she collected together twenty-seven of his books, including the master copy of his 1,003-page translation of the classic Eastern sex manual *The Perfumed Garden*, including a chapter on 'Sundry Names Given to the Sexual Organs of Women', along with three decades' worth of notebooks and private journals, and made a bonfire. Strangely enough, the brave Burton admitted to a fear of the dark. When he died in 1890 Isabel had a stone tomb erected with a stained-glass window to allow the light in.

## Snow on the tracks

The source of the Amazon in the Andes was a mystery to Europeans for nearly four hundred years, until 1944, when two French explorers speculated that it might be a glacial lake in southern Peru. It fell to an Old Etonian, Sebastian Edward Farquharson Snow (1929–2001), to confirm their theory seven years later.

Snow was born near Midhurst, Sussex. His father, an eccentric chain-smoker who insisted on lighting up during church services, was the owner of the last private bank in Exeter. Snow broke his thigh playing rugby at Eton and so escaped National Service. He went to work for Lloyd's of London but was dismissed after just six months. In April 1951, aged twenty-two and unemployed, he saw an advertisement in *The Times*: 'Extra gun may be wanted for sporting and exploring expedition. No previous experience necessary'. On a whim Snow applied and, thanks to his father's connections, was accepted. He was only mildly surprised to discover that he had signed up to take part in an expedition to find the source of the Amazon.

Snow made few formal preparations for his epic excursion, such as studying the area in detail or learning the local language. He handled tricky situations by shouting in English, with the occasional Spanish word, mostly *pistola*. 'Just speak the Queen's English loud enough', Snow explained, 'and everyone understands.' Most of the time he was completely oblivious as to his exact location. After bumbling about vast portions of South America singing the 'Eton Boating Song', with the help of strong dyes which they put in the water, and after taking soundings and measurements, Snow and his colleague John Brown confirmed the French finding. After completing their mission Snow and Brown parted company with a cursory exchange: Snow said to his colleague, 'Dinner together on my return,' and with that Brown left for home by the way they had come.

Snow, however, chose the difficult option, single-handedly navigating the 3,505-mile river back to the Atlantic Ocean. After ten months of paddling canoes and bobbing on balsa log rafts, braving ferocious rapids, snakes, headhunters and bouts of malaria and dysentery, he reached Para at the mouth of the Amazon and returned by ship to a hero's welcome in Liverpool. The *Daily Mirror* hailed him as 'a six-foot live hero, straight from the Bumper Book for Boys'. A comic strip about his adventures appeared in a boy's paper, and Snow's own book

*My Amazon Adventure* became a best-seller. When interviewed by the *New York Times*, Snow, then still only twenty-three years old, said he 'found the whole trip a bit dull'. He expanded on the dangers of travelling alone, however, including the possibility of spraining an ankle and being pecked to death by birds of prey. 'That would be a bit trying,' Snow told the American reporter.

There were several more adventures for Snow. After discovering that Sir Edmund Hillary had beat him to the top of Everest, he decided to make do and climb some South American mountains instead. As ever, he was remiss in his preparations, not taking enough food and surviving mostly on roast monkey (which he said tasted 'like stringy beef'), bamboo shoots and snails.

In 1973, wearing a backpack and carrying a briefcase, Snow attempted to walk from Tierra del Fuego to Alaska, a journey of 15,000 miles along the main road, the Pan-American Highway, although experienced friends such as Chris Bonington, with whom he had been on a previous climbing expedition to the Sangay volcano, suggested that a shorter, more sensible route could be taken through the mountains. This time he forgot to take any water with him and had to drink from puddles in the road. After almost two years, over halfway there, he reached Costa Rica and then vanished from sight. Eventually he was rescued and brought back to England, weighing barely seven stones. Three months later, after nearly doubling his weight, he told friends he was ready to go back and do it all again, but was talked out of it. In 1981, Snow returned to Peru to celebrate the thirtieth anniversary of his discovery of the source of the Amazon, planning to retrace his original journey with a photographer, but succumbed to a bout of depression after two days and had to return home. Snow spent his last twenty years living alone in a bed and breakfast in Exeter. In 2001, he phoned friends to inform them that, at the age of eighty-two, he was marrying his landlady. It was a brief affair; he died eight weeks later.

## The jungle Grail

Of all the South American explorers, there was none more quixotic than Colonel Percy Harrison Fawcett (1867 – *c.*1925).

Fawcett was born in Torquay, the son of famous Sussex county cricketer Edward Boyd Fawcett. At the age of nineteen he was given a commission in the Royal Artillery, where he also learned the basics of surveying in the hope of landing a more interesting job involving lots of travel. His ticket to adventure arrived in 1906, when the Royal Geographical Society asked for volunteers to survey Bolivia's frontier with Brazil. It was a difficult and dangerous mission. Disease was rampant and the native tribes had a reputation for savagery, but Fawcett loved his time in South America. In particular, he was obsessed with the local legends, including fanciful tales of hidden Inca cities, fair-skinned tribes and gigantic magic crystals. He found surveying boring, however, and as soon as his secondment was over he resigned from the army and went home to Dorset.

In 1915, Fawcett was back in uniform and was posted to France, where he spent eighteen months in the trenches. In 1916, he took up a new post as Artillery Corps Counter-Battery Colonel, detailed to suppress German heavy guns. Fawcett's subordinates were surprised to learn that their new leader was not in the least bit interested in the innovative work being done on the detection of German guns by flash-spotting and sound ranging. He could detect German targets, he informed them, on his Ouija board. In February 1919, having survived one gassing and risen to the rank of Lieutenant-Colonel, he returned to his family, now settled in the Devon village of Seaton.

After the war Fawcett went back to the uncharted and dangerous Amazon basin several times, all the while pestering the Foreign Office and the Royal Geographical Society for money to fund his trips. In 1920, an irritated John Keltie, secretary of the RGS, noted: 'Fawcett has a reputation of being difficult to get on with, and has a queer manner in many ways, being a mystic and a spiritualist, but all the same he has an extraordinary power of getting through difficulties that would deter anybody else.'

Fawcett wrote up accounts of his journeys in a series of popular books. His stories describing attacks by cannibals on the Amazon and encounters with vampire bats, giant snakes and a killer spider the size of a dinner plate in a hotel bedroom, were prone to embellishment. Take this description of the shooting of a monstrous anaconda in Bolivia:

> I sprang for my rifle as the creature began to make its way up the bank and hardly waiting to aim smashed a .44 soft-nosed bullet into its spine, ten feet below the wicked head. At once there was a flurry of foam, and several heavy thumps against the boat's keel, shaking us as though we had run on a snag. We stepped ashore and approached the creature with caution. As far as it was possible to measure, a length of 45 feet lay out of the water and 17 feet lay in the water, making it a total length of 62 feet.

Fawcett may have trained as a surveyor but his measuring technique was suspect; his monstrous snake was at least double the maximum length of any anaconda ever discovered. There were more strange zoological encounters, including the discovery of a breed of dog with two noses.

Inspired by some of his more romantic ideas about the history of South America, in 1925, at the age of fifty-eight, Fawcett set out with his eldest son Jack and his son's friend Raleigh Rimmell on what he called 'the Quest' – to look for a hidden 'city of gold', known in mythology as 'Z'. Much was made of the younger men's unsuitability for this trip, but physical fitness was seen as less important than the fact that they were not attracted to alcohol, tobacco or girls. The last anyone ever heard of the group was as they crossed the Upper Xingu, a south-eastern tributary of the Amazon. Fawcett's last letter, sent on 29 May 1925, assured his wife Nina: 'You need have no fear of failure.' The party then simply vanished without trace.

Before he set off, Fawcett had left strict instructions that in the event of his failure to return there should be no risky attempts to follow in his footsteps. To date almost one hundred people have died ignoring his advice. The most famous of at least a dozen separate failed expeditions to discover what happened to Fawcett is told in the book *Brazilian Adventure* by the journalist Peter Fleming, published in 1932. The expedition, commanded by an eccentric American Colonel called Pringle, was so badly organized that no one had bothered to learn Portuguese or read the news; if they had, they would have known that Brazil was in the middle of a revolution. The group ended up wandering aimlessly and panic-stricken around the Brazilian hinterland, blazing away with their guns at anything that moved. In the same year Stefan Rattin, a Swiss trapper, emerged from the jungle to claim that the elderly Fawcett was being held captive by Indians. Although his story attracted a great deal of attention from the world's press, Fawcett's surviving son Brian was not inclined to believe that his father, who had been bald for some time, was now the old man with long white hair described by Rattin. Hopes were raised and then dashed again when some human bones discovered in the jungle in 1951 proved on examination not to belong to Fawcett.

In 2004, previously unreleased private papers revealed another possible explanation for Fawcett's post-war vanishing act. The explorer, according to letters he sent to friends, had no intention of returning to Torquay. He was in fact lured by a beautiful native 'she-god', an erotic siren who draws white men into the jungle. There, he planned to set up a commune based on a cult involving the worship of his son, Jack. Was Fawcett eaten by jaguars, or living alone as a native, or starved or murdered by local Kalapalo tribesmen, or was he bunked up in the jungle with a native she-god, retelling tales of unnaturally large serpents to fellow members of a theosophical commune? The question may never be satisfactorily answered.

Percy Fawcett's false teeth and school hat take pride of place in the Explorer's Gallery, Torquay Museum.

# Two
# SPORTING ECCENTRICS

*'Well, the hiccups is gone, by God'.*

– JACK MYTTON (1796–1834)

## Curing hiccups with small fires

'Mad' Jack Mytton (1796–1834), squire of Halston Hall, near Whittington in Shropshire, was the hellraiser's hellraiser. His wild streak had already surfaced by the time he hit his teens. Expelled from both Westminster and Harrow schools for fighting with his teachers, Mytton agreed to go university on condition that he was allowed to study only *The Racing Calendar* and *The Stud Book*. He celebrated his arrival at Oxford by ordering 2,000 bottles of port, then changed his mind at the last minute and decided go on the Grand Tour instead. At the age of twenty-one he inherited the family estate worth £60,000 and an income of £18,000. By his mid-twenties he was drinking six bottles of vintage port a day, the first while he was shaving before breakfast. If alcohol wasn't available he was known to down the odd bottle of *eau de cologne*. It took just fifteen years for Mytton to drink and gamble away his health and his inheritance and lose the Parliamentary seat held by his family for generations.

Jack Mytton's bent for self-destruction mostly revealed itself in his love of dangerous sports. His name was a byword for any sporting activity that was considered excessively dangerous or performed with a recklessness bordering on insanity – it would 'do for Mytton'. He fought dogs and bears with his bare hands, went duck-hunting in winter wearing only his nightshirt and chased rats across frozen ponds on ice skates. His physical endurance was legendary. Although he owned over 150 pairs of riding breeches, 300 riding jackets and 700 pairs of boots, he often went hunting completely naked.

In bad weather, Mytton would knock on the nearest cottage door and ask the occupants if his horse, an old one-eyed steed called Baronet, could dry off in front of their fire. As most of the properties around belonged to him anyway, he was rarely refused. He once tried to warm up one of his horses on a freezing cold day by encouraging it to down a bottle of port; the horse died soon afterwards. Mytton was master of the local hunt and kept two thousand hounds, which he fed on champagne and steak. He also owned sixty cats, which he dressed in fine silk livery. Then there was his bear, called Nell. Once, at a dinner party, he made an entrance by riding into the dining room dressed in hunting pink and mounted on the bear's back. In the havoc that ensued, guests jumped out of the window in terror and the bear bit a large chunk out of Mytton's leg.

He was very handy with his fists. When he was out hunting one day a burly Welsh miner shouted abuse at him as he rode by. Mytton dismounted and challenged him to twenty rounds 'under gentlemen's rules'. He gave the collier a sound beating then offered him ten shillings for his troubles. Most of his money was lost at the races. In a drunken stupor after a rare success at Doncaster, he fell asleep counting his winnings and awoke to find that hundreds of pounds had blown out of the coach window. He couldn't be bothered to stop and go back to look for it.

In 1819, Mytton followed the family tradition and sought election as a Member of Parliament for Shrewsbury. As part of his campaign he went on walkabouts through his constituency with £10 notes attached to his hat. He was elected by a majority of just 97 votes, at a cost of £10,000. Having secured his seat, he attended the House of Commons only once, found it boring and never went there again.

He died aged thirty-eight, a bloated, paralysed and penniless debtor in the King's Bench Prison. After his death, a friend signed an affidavit to the effect that Mytton had been permanently inebriated for the last twelve years of his life. His premature demise was partly attributed to injuries sustained while setting fire to his own night-shirt to try to cure hiccups. Just before the horribly burned Mytton slumped into unconsciousness he said, 'Well, the hiccups is gone, by God.'

## Caught short

The Yorkshire slow left-arm bowler Bobby Peel (1857–1941) played cricket for England from 1884 to 1896. Peel was frequently drunk during matches, a condition tactfully interpreted by the cricketing bible *Wisden* as 'unwell' or 'gone away'. During one county game the Yorkshire captain was forced to suspend Peel from the side for 'running the wrong way' and 'bowling at the pavilion in the belief that it was the batsman'. He was eventually sacked from the Yorkshire team after his performance against Warwickshire at Edgbaston in May 1896. During an unbeaten partnership of 367 with Lord Hawke, Peel urinated on the pitch.

## King of Albania

Charles Burgess Fry (1872–1956), or 'CB' as he was known to friends and fans alike, was arguably the greatest all-rounder in British sporting history. He represented his country at athletics, cricket and soccer and only injury deprived him of international honours at rugby. He equalled the world record long jump of 23 ft 6.5 in., a record that remained intact for well over 20 years. He had arrived for the jump late after a hefty lunch, formally dressed with a whisky in one hand and a cigar in the other. He was also a talented boxer, an excellent golfer, swimmer, sculler, tennis player and javelin thrower. He claimed he only missed out on gold at the Athens Olympics of 1896 because he didn't know they were taking place and he was still running the 110-metre hurdles competitively in his mid-fifties. It is for cricket, however, that Fry is best known. In a remarkable first-class career spanning 30 years, he scored 94 centuries, played 26 Tests for England and with Don Bradman holds the record of six consecutive centuries in first-class cricket.

Fry's near-perfect sporting physique earned him the accolade 'most handsome man in England' and he had a brief career as a nude model. With his clothes on, however, he was a constant source of wonderment. According to the cricket writer Neville Cardus, his wardrobe was 'a confusing variety of clothes of strange dyes, patterns and purposes'. When he was on tour with the England cricket team one of Fry's outfits made him look like 'a deep sea monster' and he turned up for one match 'as though dressed for a South Polar expedition'. Another outfit, featuring a topee and leather shorts, led Cardus to suggest that Fry 'was about to trace the source of the Amazon'. In Australia Fry once waved from the door of his train carriage to cricket fans while dressed as a Chinese mandarin and on another occasion as an Indian rajah. During a later stint as a cricket journalist he turned up wearing a naval uniform, with the obligatory monocle and pipe, and watched his cricket from the grandstand through a telescope. A fellow cricket writer noted that Fry looked like 'something between a retired admiral and an unusually athletic Oxford don'.

Although Fry's talents were many, he liked to embellish his sporting achievements and he was renowned as a great bore. He was capable of speaking at length, with machine-gun rapidity, on almost any subject, no matter how obscure, and without any encouragement; he once treated his cricketing colleagues to an impromptu half-hour lecture on iambics. When he was invited to take part in BBC Radio's discussion group *The Brains Trust*, the chairperson found it almost impossible to shut him up. Hitler had a similar problem in 1934 when he invited Fry to Germany by to explore the possibility of building links between the British Boy Scouts and the Nazi Youth Movement. Fry kept Hitler's interpreter, Ribbentrop, busy for an hour and a quarter. Neville Cardus said later that it was a pity Fry didn't speak German. If he had, war would have been averted because 'Hitler might have died of a fit trying to get a word in'. The starry-eyed sportsman returned home with fulsome praise for the Führer. Later, when Fry heard about the Night of the Long Knives, when Hitler had many of his Nazi colleagues locked up or murdered, he refused to believe 'such a nice man' could have committed anything so brutal.

After Fry's flirtation with Fascism and following his retirement from cricket, he had careers in journalism, diplomacy and politics. He stood three times for Parliament as a Liberal candidate, unsuccessfully, having accused his party of failing to support ballroom dancing. After World War I he had acted as

India's delegate to the League of Nations. It was during this ambassadorial stint in Geneva that the most bizarre episode in Fry's remarkable life had occurred. The new state of Albania, after nearly four hundred years of Ottoman rule, had been granted independence and was on the lookout for a new king. The ideal candidate, the Albanian government decided, would be 'an English gentleman with an income of £10,000 a year'. A three-man delegation approached Fry and offered him the vacant throne of Albania. He was keen to accept, as he later put it, 'on the nail', but declined when he found out that the job was unpaid. The disappointed Albanians turned their attentions to another English gentleman, Lord Inchcape, who was surprised to receive a letter inviting him to accept 'the kingship of Albania', with the footnote: 'In case you turn it down entirely perhaps you would feel called upon to suggest the name of some wealthy Englishman or American with administrative power who would care to take up the cudgels on Albania's behalf.' (Inchcape declined their generous offer because 'it is not in my line'. He later confessed privately that he had no idea where Albania was.) CB Fry reflected years later, upon hearing that Mussolini had invaded Albania, that the Italian invasion would never have happened if he had been king. He would have introduced the Albanians to cricket and 'nobody would have dared to invade Albania with county cricket going on. The British Navy would have been absolutely obliged to step in and prevent it.'

Fry was a lifelong believer in the occult. During a tour of India, he became convinced that a native prince had cast a spell on him and developed a morbid fear of Indians, a confusing state of affairs for his best friend, the legendary cricketer Ranjitsinhji. Fry complained constantly that Indians were stalking him and trying to steal his 'things'. Back in England, he continued to believe that he was being persecuted by Indian thieves and from then on he always kept a paranoid eye on his belongings wherever he went.

For the best part of forty years, Fry and his formidable wife Beatrice ran a 'training ship' for boys aboard the *Mercury*, a floating boarding school to educate boys in a 'classical sense of values'. Beatrice Fry ran the ship with a harsh regimen of lashings and floggings, encouraged the boys to box until they bled, staged 'punishment fights' between small boys and much bigger boys and inspected their pyjama trousers daily for evidence of 'self-abuse'. One boy died during training; another wrote, on joining the Royal Navy, that after the *Mercury* it all seemed 'rather lax'. Fry, meanwhile, had a couple of nervous breakdowns and was occasionally seen in dance halls waltzing with invisible partners, or mounting his horse backwards, or casting a fishing rod out of his bedroom window. A full-time nurse was employed to take care of him after he was caught running naked down the beach in Brighton. Three years later in 1950, however, a rejuvenated Fry re-emerged as the racy raconteur of old and resumed his job on the *Mercury*. After celebrating his seventieth birthday he told a friend that he was looking for a new challenge and was thinking of taking up horse racing. The friend replied: 'What as, CB? Trainer, jockey or horse?' He finished his days in nightclubs with girls young enough to be his great-grandchildren. His biographer John Arlott recalled how Fry took a young girl to a nightclub when he was seventy-eight. She told Arlott: 'Do you know, he didn't have a piss for five hours.'

## Sporting chancer

George Osbaldeston (1787–1866) was a short, muscular country squire known for his fine horsemanship, but he was also a remarkable all-round sportsman. He once played billiards for fifty hours non-stop, won boxing matches despite giving away up to four stone to his opponents, beat the French tennis champion using his hand instead of a racket and once put in a winning performance for Sussex county cricket team despite bowling while drunk and with a broken shoulder. He once felled a hundred pheasants with a hundred shots, but was accidentally shot in the eye himself in the process; he told the errant marksman, 'I said you would hit something eventually.'

Osbaldeston inherited and then gambled away a considerable fortune. He could never resist a bet – the more outlandish the wager, the better. He is chiefly remembered for a famous gamble he made in 1831, when he accepted a bet of 1,000 guineas that he could ride 200 miles in 10 hours. His chances of collecting were slim; at forty-four years old he was long past his prime and limping badly as the result of an old hunting accident. Osbaldeston simply offered to make the bet more interesting by volunteering to do it in nine hours. Fortified by a lunch of partridge washed down with brandy, he completed the 200-mile circuit in 8 hours and 42 minutes, an average speed of 22 miles per hour, then jumped on a fresh horse and galloped off to the Rutland Arms at Newmarket, where he declared himself so hungry he 'could eat an old woman'. Osbaldeston died a few weeks after winning his final bet: unable to walk and confined to a bath chair, he wagered a sovereign that he could sit for twenty-four hours without moving.

## Stonewall Scotton

The Nottinghamshire and England cricketer William Scotton (1856–93) was the most boring batsman in cricketing history. At the 1886 Oval Test he hit 34 runs in 225 minutes, including a spell of over an hour without hitting a run. In another innings he took 155 minutes to hit 17. Following another soporific display in 1890, when Scotton took two hours to hit six runs, *Punch* paid tribute with a piece of verse, a parody on Tennyson called 'Wail of the Weary':

*And the clock's slow hands go round,*
*And you still keep up your sticks:*
*But oh! for the lift of a swiping hand,*
*And the sound of a swipe for six!*

Scotton, however, was no Geoffrey Boycott: he was by all accounts an extraordinarily sensitive man who took criticism of his style of play badly. According to a teammate, he was prone to bursting into tears at the least provocation. It all got a bit too much for him on 9 July 1893, when he was dropped by Nottingham. He retired to his lodgings in St John's Wood and killed himself.

## Foulke hero

The definitive answer to the football chant 'Who ate all the pies?' was William 'Fatty' Foulke (1874–1916), who at 24 stones was the heaviest ever professional footballer. Foulke enjoyed spells as a goalkeeper with Sheffield United, Chelsea and Bradford City. Nicknamed 'Fatty' or 'Colossus' by the fans ('I don't mind what they call me as long as they don't call me late for my lunch'), Foulke stood at 6 ft 3 in. tall, wore shirts with 24-inch collars and could punch the ball as far as some players could kick it. But his size also presented problems. When he got injured it took at least six men to carry him of the pitch. Playing against Accrington Stanley in February

1907, when his jersey clashed with the red shirts of the opposition, no one could find a replacement large enough to fit him, so he played wrapped in a bed sheet borrowed from a nearby house.

Foulke played in an era when centre forwards were allowed to intimidate keepers by shoulder-charging them on the line. In 1898, the Liverpool striker George Allan made the mistake of trying this tactic on Foulke, who seized Allan by the leg, turned him upside down and then bounced him up and down on his head in the goalmouth. Once, while paying for Chelsea against Port Vale, he picked up a Vale player and threw him into the back of the net, conceding a penalty, to the annoyance of his teammates. The referee T. J. Holdcroft noted later: 'I kept a reasonable distance from Foulke for the rest of the game.'

Foulke's temper was unpredictable. At the end of his first Cup Final for Sheffield United in 1902, incensed because the match officials had allowed Southampton's hotly disputed equalizing goal to stand, he charged out of his dressing room naked to track down the referee, Mr Kirkham, who took refuge in a broom cupboard. Foulke was restrained by a group of FA officials while attempting to tear the cupboard door from its hinges. Fortunately, Sheffield United won the replay 2–1, with Foulke making several key saves to keep United in the match.

After a dispute over pay, Foulke left Sheffield for Chelsea for a fee of £50 and was made captain, but stayed for just one season before moving to his final club, Bradford City. In his entire career he won just a single international cap for England against Wales and kept a clean sheet in a 4–0 victory. There would have been many more caps but for Foulke's frequent run-ins with the football authorities, mostly because of his habit of pulling down on the crossbar to make the goals smaller. The *Sheffield Daily Telegraph* recorded: 'It is a pity that Foulke cannot curb the habit of pulling down the crossbar, which on Saturday ended in his breaking it in two. On form, he is well in the running for international honours, but the Selection Committee are sure to prefer a man who plays the game to one who unnecessarily violates the spirit of the rules.' According to one report, Foulke ended his playing career as a sideshow attraction on Blackpool Beach, charging youngsters a penny for a penalty shot at him and offering a threepence reward for every goal scored. He died in May 1916, aged forty-one. There were unsubstantiated reports that he died of pneumonia after catching a chill on the sands, but according to his death certificate the major cause of death was drink-related.

## Seeing red

In 1983, footballer Mike Bagley was so incensed by being sent off for foul and abusive language during a Bristol league game that he ate the referee's notebook. He was banned for six weeks.

## Bible basher

The all-England champion bare-knuckle prize fighter William 'Bendigo' Thompson (1811–80) was such a boxing legend that he had a drink, a racehorse and a town in Australia named after him. Bendigo (a corruption of the Old Testament Abednego, who emerged from the fiery furnace of Babylon) was born in Nottingham, the youngest of twenty-one children. Forced into a workhouse at the age of fifteen when his father died, he got a job as an iron-turner, where he developed his famously powerful physique. By the age of eighteen he was fighting professionally and had defeated his first eight opponents. Although short for a boxer, Bendigo was a tricky customer. An agile southpaw, he bobbed, weaved and hurled insults at his opponents in a style described by a contemporary sports writer as 'full of trickery, treachery and having no ethics'; his favourite tactic was to avoid punishment by going down without being hit. He was also ably supported everywhere he fought by an intimidating gang of local thugs called the Nottingham Lambs.

He is mostly remembered for three epic Ali–Frazier style contests with a boxing blacksmith called Ben Caunt, who at 6 ft 2 in. was six inches taller than Bendigo and weighed 18 stones. The two met for the first time in 1835 for a purse of £25. Early in the fight, Caunt, needled by Bendigo's constant taunting and by his habit of falling down without being hit, tried to break his opponent's back by slamming him against a ring-post, but the smaller man recovered and was able to avoid Caunt's blows, all the while issuing a steady stream of invective, mostly about Caunt's mother. The enraged Caunt ended the fight by nailing his opponent while he was still sitting on his second's knee in the corner and was disqualified.

Over the next couple of years Bendigo steadily built his reputation with wins over notable opponents such as the great John Leachman and Charles Langham. In June 1837, he met the much-feared Liverpudlian Bill Looney for a purse of £500. Again, Bendigo was the much smaller man and had to rely on a combination of agility and merciless taunting. In the third round Looney landed a huge punch over his opponent's ear. Bendigo responded with a hard cross to the forehead and both men dropped to the canvass simultaneously. Bendigo had now added a new trick to his repertoire: dropping onto his backside and flailing his arms and legs in mocking laughter. The fight lasted ninety-two rounds before Bendigo was declared the winner.

April 1838 saw the much-anticipated return fight with Ben Caunt. The rematch was an even less dignified affair than the original fight, with much kicking and throttling. At one point the Nottingham Lambs had to cut the ring-ropes from around Bendigo's neck to save their man from being strangled to death. Pandemonium ensued, during which various weapons including cudgels were applied freely by rival supporters. Bendigo was eventually revived with a large swig of brandy and the match continued. In the seventy-fifth round Bendigo hit the canvas again without a punch being landed, but this time was disqualified. The enraged Nottingham Lambs chased after Caunt, who fled for his life riding bareback on a stolen horse.

Bendigo's next fight was against former British champion James 'Deaf' Burke, who had once been knocked unconscious during a fight but was revived by a second who bit off his ear. Burke was returning from a successful tour of America, where he had recently defeated the Irish champion Sam O'Rourke. Burke laid his title on the line with his charming offer to fight 'any man in the world except niggers'. Although Caunt was the obvious contender, Bendigo was a bigger draw because of his crowd-pleasing antics, and an audience of 15,000 gathered to see the match at No Man's Heath in Leicestershire for a purse of £220. In spite of Burke's immunity to Bendigo's verbal taunts on account of his deafness, the Nottingham fighter still found a way to irritate his opponent so much that Burke was disqualified in the tenth round for headbutting. A few weeks later, Bendigo sustained a badly broken knee at a horse race when he tried to perform a somersault while drunk, and was forced to give up boxing.

Two years later he was tempted out of retirement by popular demand for a third fight with Ben Caunt. On 9 September 1845, a drunken and near-riotous crowd of 10,000 turned out to see the dirtiest of the three Caunt v Thompson encounters, described by a sports writer of the day as 'one of the most scandalous brawls in boxing history'. In the ninety-third round Caunt floored Bendigo with a right hook and, thinking the fight was over, he returned to his corner. Bendigo immediately jumped to his feet and moved towards Caunt. His opponent, hearing a shouted warning from his second, dropped to the canvas in a defensive move to avoid being struck from behind and in an ironic twist was disqualified for going down without being hit.

Bendigo was finally forced to retire due to his injured knee, bragging that although he was not undefeated, he had never once been hit in the nose hard enough to make it bleed. His life went off the rails and he spent the next few years in and out of prison for drunken brawling. After serving his twenty-eighth prison sentence he joined a religious sect, the Good Templars, having fallen under the influence of a Methodist preacher, Dick Weaver, also known as 'Undaunted Dick'.

Bendigo spent the rest of his life touring public houses espousing the virtues of abstinence, although not always convincingly. He was haunted by the presence of the all-seeing Revd Weaver, who, according to Bendigo, kept him on the straight and narrow by following him everywhere he went, staring at him through the windows of pubs. Though illiterate and incapable of reading the Bible, Bendigo had his own way of delivering a sermon. Adopting a southpaw stance, he would point to his trophies and snarl: 'See them belts, see them cups, I used to fight for those. But now I fight for Christ.' His popularity attracted massive crowds and his sermons often got out of hand. At one meeting a rabble of boxing fans were shouting and heckling. Bendigo closed his Bible, put his hands together and said a brief prayer before vaulting the pulpit into the crowd and knocking out four members of the front row. He died in

1880 at the age of sixty-nine, after falling down the stairs of his home in Beeston.

## The demon bowler

John Jackson (1824–1901) played first-class cricket for Nottinghamshire from 1855–66 and was given the nickname 'Foghorn' on account of his habit of blowing his nose loudly after taking a wicket. Six feet tall and weighing over fifteen stone, Jackson was a fearsome fast-bowler with a reputation for injuring batsmen. In 1860, playing against Surrey, he took nine wickets and caused a tenth batsman to retire by bouncing the ball off his head, effectively taking all wickets in the innings. Facing him, many opposing batsmen found that the safest place was the pavilion. One day a particularly hostile delivery struck the Yorkshire batsman Ludd on the foot. Ludd was given not out. 'Maybe not,' said Ludd, leaving the field, 'but I'm going anyway.'

## Getting shirty

The Welsh international goalkeeper Leigh Richmond Roose (1877–1916) was renowned as one of the best keepers of the Edwardian era, with spells at Stoke City, Everton and Sunderland. Signed by Stoke in 1901, he went on to make 144 league appearances and kept 40 clean sheets for the Potteries club, a remarkable record given that Stoke spent most of their time in a relegation battle. Like 'Fatty' Foulke, Roose played in an era when goalkeepers were largely unprotected by referees, but had the presence required to stand up to big strikers on equal terms. According to his biographer, the

Welshman 'enjoyed taunting experienced international forwards, some of whom felt the full force of his fist in goal-mouth melees'. At a time when goalkeepers rarely strayed more than a couple of yards from their goal line, Roose liked to rush out of his penalty area to play sweeper, or occasionally just to clobber opposing forwards. In his first game for Wales he sprinted from his area and shoulder-charged an opposing Irish winger on the touchline, knocking him out of play and unconscious. Roose found his international debut otherwise uneventful and completed the game wearing his overcoat to keep warm.

In 1902, when Stoke were again playing Liverpool at Anfield, Roose and several of his teammates went down with food poisoning after a lunch of tainted fish. By kick-off time most of the Stoke players were feeling the effects. They went a goal down after just eight minutes when Roose suddenly ran from the pitch in search of a toilet and failed to return. By the second half only seven Stoke players were in a fit state to continue and Liverpool won 7–0.

Roose was a great crowd-pleaser. He put on gymnastic displays from his crossbar and whenever a penalty was awarded he would wave to spectators both before and after completing a save. If he got bored he would wander off and sit and chat with the crowd behind the goals. But he wasn't always quite so affable. After a game between Sunderland and Stoke in 1906, one of the spectators, thought to be the guest of a Sunderland director, began calling out insults to the Stoke players, so Roose punched the man in the face.

He was also famously superstitious and wore the same unwashed 'lucky shirt' throughout his career. In 1910, he briefly came out of retirement to play in a game against Stoke for their local rivals Port Vale. He aroused the fury of the home crowd by insisting on playing against his former club in his old

Stoke shirt and was only saved from a ducking in the River Trent by the intervention of the local police. During the fracas, Stoke's chairman, Revd A. E. Hurst, ran onto the pitch to appeal for calm and was knocked unconscious by one of his own forwards. Roose went on to play ninety-two times for Sunderland between 1907 and 1910, until his wrist was broken by a Newcastle United centre forward who tried to kick the ball of out of his hands.

Roose had originally set out on a medical career and was torn between studying for that and playing football. He compromised by remaining amateur throughout his career, playing only for expenses. He interpreted the terms of his expense account liberally, however. He once missed a train that was due to take him to a match at Aston Villa, so he hired a 'private' train to take him in solitary splendour all the way from London to Birmingham, then sent a bill for £31 – a fortune at the time – to his club. On another occasion a puzzled Football League official asked for a copy of the expenses claim Roose had submitted. It listed: 'Pistol to ward off opposition, 4d; coat and gloves to keep warm when not occupied, 3d; using the toilet (twice), 2d . . .'

## Guillotine stopped play

The third Duke of Dorset (1745–99) was a cricket fanatic whose patronage of the game was legendary. He was one of the original members of the MCC (Marylebone Cricket Club) who drew up the laws of the game, and maintained his own team of cricketers at great expense by giving them spurious jobs around his country estate at Knole in Kent.

The Duke was also a cricketing evangelist. In 1784 he was appointed as ambassador to France, although he spent most of the summer hopping back to England to catch up with the cricket. While he was in Paris he hatched an ambitious plan to turn France into a nation of cricket enthusiasts by assembling the first ever international touring side. On 10 August 1789, just as his team was about to leave Dover for Paris, they were surprised to encounter the Duke, who was fleeing in the opposite direction from the French Revolution. He never forgave the French for wrecking his tour, describing them as 'a nation of intriguing, low, artful and cretinous people'.

## The pugilist peer

John Sholto Douglas, ninth Marquess of Queensberry (1844–1900) is remembered eponymously as the sporting gentleman who turned the barbarous activity of bare-knuckle fighting into a civilized contest by supervising the formulation of rules governing professional boxing, thereafter known as the Queensberry Rules. In his private life, ironically, Queensberry was an aggressive bigot who was ready to give anyone a slap who gave him so much as sideways look. His Tourettes-like outbursts of obscenity made him a well-known disrupter of theatrical events. He was once thrown out of the Globe Theatre for threatening and abusive behaviour when he objected to a scene in Tennyson's play *The Promise of May*. In 1895, he was hauled before Marlborough Street magistrates for brawling in the street with his son Percy. The Marquess liked to taunt his sons by telling them he wasn't their real father. His second wife reciprocated by suing for an annulment on the grounds of non-consummation.

Queensberry believed that homosexuality was contagious. When his second son, twenty-seven-year-old Francis, was appointed private secretary to the future Prime Minister

Lord Rosebery, Queensberry, suspecting that Rosebery was, in his own words, a 'snob queer', followed him all the way to a health spa in Germany and threatened to horsewhip him if he didn't stay away from his son. Rosebery was saved by the intervention of the Prince of Wales and the local police. Afterwards Rosebery wrote to Queen Victoria: 'I am unhappy at being pursued by a pugilist of unsound mind.' Queensberry also blamed Rosebery for the infamous relationship between his youngest son Alfred 'Bosie' Douglas and Oscar Wilde, whose trial led to the media furore of the 1890s. The paranoid Marquess died suddenly in 1899, convinced to the end that he was being stalked by 'unknown persons' seeking revenge for his persecution of Wilde. Eccentric to the last, although he once wrote a poem that began, 'When I am dead cremate me', Queensberry stipulated in his will that he was to be buried upright. The gravediggers complied, but are rumoured to have buried him head first.

## Form is temporary, class is permanent

Lionel, Lord Tennyson (1878–1951), aristocratic cricketing grandson of the poet Alfred, was a veteran of the Somme and Ypres, where he was wounded three times and reported dead twice. Off the cricket field he was chiefly famous for his playboy lifestyle, running up substantial gambling losses and seducing women by the dozen. In his spare time he hunted panthers in India and hobnobbed with actors in Hollywood.

Tennyson earned his place in sporting history with his brief but brilliant spell as captain of the England cricket team midway through the home series against Australia in 1921. England had just been defeated inside two days at Trent Bridge and were facing humiliation with their worst ever run of Ashes defeats. Tennyson was then thirty-two and had played in a handful of Test matches with only moderate success, but the selectors decided to take a gamble on the brash, hard-hitting batsman. Tennyson received news of his appointment for the game by telegram only hours before the game was due to start, while partying with friends at the Embassy Club in London. He said later that if he had only heard the news earlier he would have 'knocked off a cigar or two'. Instead, he confidently struck a £50 wager that he would crack a half-century. He went on to hit a swashbuckling 74 not out, returning to the pavilion 'black and blue all over'. England lost, but Tennyson was retained as captain for the next Test at Headingley, where he injured his hand while fielding. Watching his batsmen struggle, he decided to bat one-handed and scored an impressive 63, saving the follow-on. Although the Test was won by Australia, Tennyson's brave innings is remembered as one of the most remarkable ever to grace Headingley.

Although Tennyson had halted the rampaging Aussies, he never played Test cricket again, and his batting heroics were thereafter confined to his captaincy of Hampshire. He was distrusted by the MCC for his swaggering, autocratic behaviour, not least of which was his insistence on using his butler Walter Livsey as wicketkeeper. Livsey had instructions to keep several bottles of champagne handy for his Lordship to celebrate victory or drown the disappointment of defeat. He proved a very loyal manservant. Once, when Tennyson had an appeal for bad light turned down by the umpire, Livsey, who was next man in, pretended to grope his way to the wicket as though blindfolded and called out to his captain: 'Where are you, my Lord? I can hear you but I can't see you.' Livsey once umpired in a charity match Tennyson was playing in and was asked to adjudicate on his master's obvious dismissal. Unable to bring himself to utter the dread word 'out', he summoned up a phrase he had often used when answering the door to unwanted guests: 'I regret, his Lordship is not in.'

Tennyson also had an idiosyncratic method of keeping in touch with his players from the pavilion. One struggling Hampshire batsman was surprised when a boy in a blue post office uniform approached him at the crease bearing an orange envelope. Inside was a note from Tennyson which read: 'For pity's sake, what do you think your bat's for?'

Tennyson's debts and his drinking increased as he got older. He bought himself a black and white Rolls-Royce, then had to sell it three weeks later after losing £7,000 at roulette. He once turned up for a game in Southampton's Hoglands Park the worse for wear, wearing his protective box outside his trousers. He died a virtually penniless alcoholic in 1951 but, according to his biographer, 'in the manner of an English gentleman, sitting up in bed smoking and reading *The Times*'.

## Let the cat see the rabbit

Kenneth Cecil Gandar-Dower (1908–44) was a great sportsman and explorer. He represented England at lawn tennis and squash in the 1930s and was also one of the best-known aviators of his era; in 1932, despite rudimentary navigational techniques, he made the first ever flight from England to India. He also spent two years in Africa, where he scaled several active volcanoes. On his return home he caused uproar at the Queen's Club when he walked into the bar with a male cheetah on a lead.

In 1937, Gandar-Dower was responsible for one of the strangest innovations in British sporting history when he tried to introduce cheetah racing in the UK as an alternative to greyhound racing. Despite cooperation from the White City stadium, the experiment was a total failure. With the scent of a gazelle in its nostrils, a cheetah can reach speeds of up to 63 miles per hour, and in theory could give a greyhound a 30-yard start over a 345-yard track and still win easily. Unfortunately, Gandar-Dower had not taken into account the fact that cheetahs are too intelligent to mistake a piece of rag for a gazelle. At much-publicized events in Haringey and Romford, the eight imported big cats simply wandered around looking for something to eat. The pundits were unimpressed and the project was shelved, to the huge relief of the nation's greyhound breeders.

## Amazing Graces

The cricketing legend Dr William Gilbert 'WG' Grace (1848–1915) was a shameless cheat who blithely ignored umpires' decisions when they didn't suit him. Once given out leg-before, he refused to walk and told the bowler: 'They came to watch me bat, not you bowl.' The innings continued. On another occasion when the ball knocked off a bail, he simply replaced it and told the umpire that the wind had blown it off. The umpire replied: 'Indeed, Doctor, and let us hope the wind helps you on your journey back to the pavilion.' He also developed a sure-fire strategy for winning the toss. In Grace's day the penny had Queen Victoria's profile on one side and Britannia on the other. WG never called heads or tails; instead he shouted, 'Woman!' Another of his game-winning strategies was running with the ball concealed up his jumper or down his pad.

WG intimidated umpires and his opponents by his formidable presence and by his incessant 'sledging' – verbal insults. One of the earliest recorded examples of sledging, however, was at his expense. When his Gloucestershire team took on Essex, he made the mistake of offending Essex's volatile fast-bowler Charles Kortright by referring to Essex as 'rabbits ready to put back in the hutch'. Kortright peppered WG with a series of short balls and clearly dismissed him four or five times, only for the umpire to keep turning down his appeals. Finally, he uprooted two of WG's three stumps. The bearded colossus stood his ground for a second before reluctantly walking off in a huff. As he was leaving, Kortright called after him: 'Surely you're not going, Doctor? There's still one stump standing.'

Although he was lauded as an amateur throughout his career, WG was notoriously grasping when it came to hard cash. On his first tour of Australia in 1873–4, while still a medical student and officially on his honeymoon, he managed to extract a fee of £1,500 from the organizers, the equivalent of more than £100,000 today. On his next tour in 1891–2, a fifth of the entire costs of the tour went into WG's pocket. He collected lucrative testimonials on a regular basis, including one worth £1,458 organized by MCC so he could buy a medical practice. The average annual wage at the time was around £200. He often struggled to reconcile his cricket with his medical commitments. A patient once arrived at his surgery and enquired whether the doctor was in. 'Of course he's in,' the receptionist replied. 'He's been batting since Tuesday lunch time.' WG in fact once saved the life of a player, A. C. M. Croome, by compressing his throat for an hour after he had fallen on spiked railings. On another occasion he was disappointed when the wicketkeeper whose eye he had just stitched up promptly stumped him.

Although WG stole the headlines in terms of cricketing prowess, his older brother Edward Mills 'EM' Grace had more than his share of family eccentricity. Described by *Wisden* as 'the most dangerous bat in England', 'the Coroner', as EM was known, had a famously short fuse. One of his tactics was to rip up the stumps and threaten the umpire with them if a decision went against him. Another was to dive into the crowd and attack, Cantona-style, any spectator who barracked him. Off the field, his private life was similarly chaotic. A relentless womanizer, he had four wives and eighteen children. Once, when a man came out of the crowd to deliver a breach of promise suit, EM casually passed the paper to the umpire and went on to score a fifty.

## Queen of the turf

The racehorse owner Dorothy Paget (1906–60) had over 1,500 winners on the flat and over the jumps during her career. She gambled huge sums of money daily and like many race-goers was highly superstitious, wearing the same shabby old tweed coat and blue felt hat at race meetings for thirty years. It didn't bring her much luck. She ran up vast gambling losses, including in 1948 alone over £108,000 – roughly the equivalent of £3 million today.

Miss Paget was chiefly known for her idiosyncratic lifestyle. She slept all day and came to life at dusk when she lit up the first of her one hundred daily cigarettes, but still found time to eat massive quantities of fish and chips, which caused her weight to balloon to more than twenty stones. She was also renowned as a tyrannical employer, communicating with her staff by memo and referring to them by colour code, except for the colour green, which brought bad luck. She hated company, especially men; she said their presence made her vomit. When she kissed the nose of her horse Golden Miller after his 1934 Grand National win, a race-going wag noted that it was the first time in her life that she had kissed a member of the opposite sex.

Miss Paget was also a fussy traveller. When she went by train she always hired an entire compartment for herself, and she took two seats at the theatre or Wimbledon, including one for her handbag. Once, her Rolls-Royce broke down on the way to a race meeting, so she commandeered her local butcher's Austin for £300. From then on she insisted on taking two Rolls-Royces to every event in case one of them broke down. Horses were not allowed to leave a meeting in the evening until Miss Paget had given the order. They were often unloaded again in the dark so that she could urinate in the privacy of the horsebox before they were reloaded and sent on their way.

Paget phoned her trainers in the middle of the night to berate them if her horses lost. One trainer, Walter Nightingale, lost his patience with her and threatened to set all of her horses loose in Epsom unless she moved them from his stable within twenty-four hours. She fell out spectacularly with her trainer Fulke Walwyn, who had given her five winners in a day at Folkestone, because he had failed to win the sixth. The owner and trainer, no longer on speaking terms, communicated via an intermediary. Having given her final instructions to pass on to Walywn, Paget told the go-between, 'and kick him in the balls while you're at it'.

The 'Queen of the turf' spent her final years a recluse at her mansion in Buckinghamshire, attended only a by a handful of exclusively female employees. Her loathing of the opposite sex extended to firemen. Her mansion caught fire while she was still in bed and she refused to budge until the flames reached her bedroom. She was finally persuaded to leave when smoke began to seep under the door. Observing the blazing wreckage of her home from a deckchair in the garden, she told her assistant: 'Now you can call the fire brigade.'

## Horse sense

James Carr-Boyle, fifth Earl of Glasgow (1792–1869), was the most spectacularly unsuccessful racehorse owner and breeder in the history of the sport, despite owning the largest stable in the UK. The Earl refused to give any of his horses names, oblivious to the general confusion that ensued, especially when it came to identifying which horses came from the best, or worst, bloodlines. If a horse failed to show promise, the Earl had it shot on the spot. After a morning's trial gallop he thought nothing of executing half a dozen horses. As none of them had names, it was anybody's guess if the right ones ended up at the knacker's yard. One that got away was the great Carbine, sensational winner of the Melbourne Cup carrying a record weight of 10 st. 5 lb, and setting a new race record time. On four occasions Carbine won two races on the same day. The Earl intended to have him shot at the age of two, despite his trainer's pleas, but fate intervened when Lord Glasgow died himself.

## The thin man

Fred Archer (1857–86) stood 5 ft 10 in. tall and had a natural winter weight of 11 stones – exactly the right proportions for a light middleweight boxer. Unfortunately, his chosen career was that of a professional flat race jockey. Archer's entire life was a desperate battle against the scales, but his fierce urge to win drove him on to ride a remarkable 2,748 winners, including 21 Classics, and he held the title Champion Jockey for an unbroken thirteen years.

To keep his weight down to 8 st. 6 lb, Archer subjected himself to the most appalling deprivations. He spent his entire adult life on an incredibly strict regime of starvation diets followed by hours on end sweating in steam baths. By the age of eighteen, he was living on a daily intake of hot castor oil and half an orange for breakfast and a sardine and a glass of champagne for dinner. If this failed to get his weight down he took several sherry glasses of his 'special mixture', a devastating purgative prepared by a Dr Wright of Newmarket, so powerful that when a friend tried it he was ill for a week. Off the course, Archer was a walking skeleton with the dress style and the demeanour of an undertaker. Although his success made him very wealthy, he was notoriously tight-fisted, earning him the nickname 'the Tin Man' – tin being Victorian slang for money.

By the time Archer reached his late twenties, as the pressure to keep his weight down and retain his title grew, his dieting became even more manic. The racehorse owner Lord Allington warned him: 'No man can live on two oysters, one prawn, three doses of physic and three Turkish baths daily.' In 1886, his body racked by constant fasting, and feeling depressed after a recent losing run, Archer took a silver-plated pistol awarded to him after winning the Liverpool Cup and shot himself dead in front of his sister. He was twenty-nine years old.

# Three

# RELIGIOUS ECCENTRICS

*'I believe with all my soul that if Christ were born again in London in the present day He would constantly be found walking in Piccadilly.'*

– THE REVD HAROLD DAVIDSON (1875–1937)

## Lost prophets

In 1814, Joanna Southcott, a spinster and self-styled prophet from Devon, announced that she was the expectant mother of a new Messiah, to whom she would give birth on Christmas Day. The fact that she was a virgin and well into her sixties did not deter a small army of followers from camping outside her front door to wait for the impending miracle. Unfortunately the new Son of God failed to arrive on the predicted date and Miss Southcott died ten days later. Her devotees, undismayed by the failure of the prophecy, concluded that the child had gone to heaven and would return later. A post-mortem, however, revealed that Miss Southcott was not with child and that the appearance of pregnancy was the result of a huge cancerous growth. Despite the disappointment, she acquired a cult following in the Panacea Society, a small sect based in Bedford.

In the early 1900s, cult leader Helen Exeter announced that the Messiah would return in 1914, but didn't live to see her forecast fail as she was drowned early that year. The Society pinned their hopes on a large sealed box, once belonging to Southcott, which they believed would reveal the date of Christ's return. In 1927, the box was opened in the presence of the Bishop of Grantham and was found to contain sundry items including a nightcap, an old purse and a lottery ticket. Southcott's followers insisted, however, that they had simply got the wrong box; the true box could only be opened in the presence of twenty-four Bishops of the Church of England, a logistical improbability, but hope springs eternal.

As recently as 1999 the declining membership of the Panacea Society took out a series of newspaper advertisements in the UK national press demanding that the bishops assemble to open the box, warning that otherwise 'Crime and Banditry, Distress and Perplexity will increase in England'. Disappointingly, the requisite number of bishops have yet to step forward.

## Free spirit

There were early, worrying signs that the Revd Edward Drax Free (1764–1843) was not quite cut out for life as a clergyman. During his time at St John's College, Oxford, his generally unpriestlike behaviour, including 'violence against the bursar', almost got him expelled. St John's was only too glad to see the back of him in 1808 when the rectorship of the village of Sutton in Bedfordshire fell vacant.

Revd Free saw his new posting solely as a means of funding his unorthodox lifestyle. He quickly made enemies of his new parishioners by literally turning his churchyard into a pigsty, allowing pigs to roam freely around, defecating and digging up the graves. He sold the lead from the church roof and felled three hundred oak trees which he then sold for timber.

Revd Free was frequently drunk and picked fist fights with anyone who crossed him. He raced through church services, omitting the time-consuming parts such as sermons. He also impregnated every housekeeper foolish enough to work for him and ended up fathering five illegitimate children, most of whom died in infancy. In spite of all this, Revd Free might have held on to his position had he not pushed his luck too far by picking a fight with a powerful member of the local gentry, Sir Montagu Burgoyne.

In 1817, Revd Free tried to fine Sir Montagu £380 for failing to attend church services, citing a largely forgotten Elizabethan statute designed to force Catholics to go to church by making them pay £20 for every month they missed. Sir Montagu refused to pay. He also argued, not unreasonably, that there were no services to attend anyway, because Revd Free was in the habit of locking up his church for months on end while he hid from his creditors. The Burgoynes also hit back by disclosing that Revd Free had consorted with prostitutes. In June 1829, he was brought to trial on charges of immorality and lewdness. He was found guilty, dismissed from his post and told to pay costs. But Revd Free was not disposed to go quietly. Instead, he barricaded himself inside his rectory with his latest mistress and a shotgun. When the Archdeacon of Bedford arrived to turf him out, he took pot shots at him. Eventually, after a ten-day siege, Revd Free was starved into submission. He went to London where, having failed to get a decent reference from his previous employers, he became an unemployed beggar. On 16 February 1843, Revd Free was struck by a stray wheel that had flown off a London street carriage and died of his injuries.

## Our Lord is a shoving leopard

The Revd William Archibald Spooner (1844–1930) spent sixty years at New College, Oxford lecturing in history, philosophy and divinity, serving as Dean from 1876 to 1889 and from 1903 to 1924 as Warden. His name lives on in the bizarre verbal slip now known as the Spoonerism, first recorded in 1900 and defined in the *Oxford English Dictionary* as 'an accidental transposition of the initial sounds, or other parts, of two or more words'.

Spooner was an albino with characteristic white hair and pink complexion and was also small, with very poor eyesight. He had a reputation for extreme absent-mindedness. He once invited a faculty member to tea 'to welcome our new archaeology Fellow'.

'Sir,' the man replied, 'I am our new archaeology Fellow.'

'Never mind,' said Spooner. 'Come all the same.'

After one Sunday service, he turned back to the pulpit and informed his student audience: 'In the sermon I have just preached, whenever I said Aristotle, I meant St Paul.' Spooner once asked an undergraduate he came across in the quad, 'Now let me see. Was it you or your brother who was killed in the war?' He did not acquire the confusing speech mannerism that made him famous until he was well into middle age. According to legend, he stood up one day in the college chapel to announce a hymn, 'Kinquering Congs their Titles Take . . .' and it seems to have taken off from there. Spooner's tendency to get words mixed up could happen at any time, but it happened more often when he was angry or upset. He reprimanded one student for 'fighting a liar in the quadrangle' and another who 'hissed my mystery lecture'. To the latter he allegedly added in disgust, 'You have tasted two worms.'

Many alleged spoonerisms are know known to be apocryphal, including his reference to Queen Victoria as 'the queer old Dean'. Spooner was aware of all the stories attributed to him. At his final college dinner, when the undergraduates called for a speech Spooner stood up and said: 'You want me to say one of those things, but I shan't,' and sat down. The final word on the subject should rest with the great man himself. A couple of years before his death in 1930 at the age of eighty-six, Spooner told an interviewer that he could authenticate only one of his trademark gaffes – the very first one attributed to him while announcing the hymn 'Kinquering Congs . . .'.

## Beyond belief

The Revd Samuel Wesley (1662–1735), rector of Epworth, near Hull, fathered nineteen children, of whom the fifteenth, John, became famous as 'the father of Methodism'. In order to support his huge family, Revd Wesley tried to supplement his meagre stipend by writing reams of poetry. His work was challenging and largely inaccessible, tackling obscure and ambitious subject matter. Titles included 'On a Supper of a Stinking Duck', 'Three Skips of a Louse', 'On the Bear-Fac'd Lady', and 'A Dialogue Between a Frying-Pan and a Chamber-Pot'. His major work, *Maggots: Or, Poems on Several Subjects, Never Before Handled*, published in 1685, was illustrated with a picture of the author with a maggot on his head. Most of his poems were destroyed in a fire; one that was not, 'Behold the Saviour of Mankind', is a staple of Methodist hymnbooks.

## The undergroundologist

In the early nineteenth century, science was largely the plaything of British gentlemen who had the time and the money to indulge their hobby. It tended to attract extraordinary figures. One such gentleman scientist was the Revd William Buckland (1784–1856), the first man to identify and name a dinosaur. Buckland was a vicar's son from Devon, born a stone's throw from the cliffs of Lyme, where he spent his childhood collecting the mysterious fossil shells he found in the local quarries. In 1809 he qualified for a fellowship at Oxford University where he became the first ever Professor of Geology. Revd Buckland was an arresting speaker and his public lectures drew large audiences. He liked to stride about the lecture theatre imitating the giant birds that he believed left their footprints in ancient deposits. One of his students recounted how Buckland

> paced like a Franciscan preacher up and down behind a long showcase . . . he had in his hand a huge hyena's skull. He suddenly dashed down the steps – rushed skull in hand at the first undergraduate on the front bench and shouted, 'What rules the world?' The youth, terrified, answered not a word. He rushed then on to me, pointing the hyena full in my face – 'What rules the world?' 'Haven't an idea,' I said. 'The stomach, sir!' he cried 'rules the world. The great ones eat the less, the less the lesser still!'

These lecture room theatrics, especially the Buckland silly walk, were not universally appreciated. Charles Darwin dismissed him as 'a vulgar and coarse buffoon'.

Buckland's rooms at Oxford were crammed with geological

bric-a-brac. Almost every surface was covered with rocks, fossils, skulls and bones of all types and descriptions. As well as dozens of stuffed animals there were live specimens, including toads trapped in pots to see how long they would live. Other animals were allowed to roam freely around his quarters, including a hyena called Billy. Buckland had imported it from Africa with the intention of dissecting it for its stomach contents, but had lost his nerve when it came to the kill. Billy continued to live a very pampered Oxford life for the next twenty-five years, dining on stray guinea pigs under the family dining table.

Revd Buckland also earned considerable notoriety as an epicure. When visitors to the Buckland household had got over the shock of sharing the dining room with a hyena and a pet donkey, there were many more surprises in store. He had a taste for natural history – quite literally. Buckland was prepared to eat anything that moved; at times his breath variously smelled of crocodile, hedgehog, mole, roast joint of bear and puppy. He admitted that the foulest thing he ever put in his mouth was stewed mole (although he wasn't too keen on bluebottle).

One visitor found Buckland making a rhinoceros pie, a culinary experience he described as 'not unlike very old beef'. Another guest wrote in his diary: 'Dined at the Deanery. Tripe for dinner last night, don't like crocodile for breakfast.' The famous anatomist Richard Owen spent a night over the toilet bowl after a dinner of roast ostrich at the Bucklands'. The art critic John Ruskin regretted having missed the mice on buttered toast. Possibly even more disconcerting for Buckland's dinner guests was the fact that their host was also the leading authority, in fact the world's only authority, on coprolites – fossilized faeces. His dining table was made entirely out of fossilized poo.

Buckland did not limit himself to the palatability of wildlife. His oddest claim to fame was that in the spirit of scientific enquiry he had eaten the heart of King Louis XIV. Allegedly plundered from his grave during the French Revolution, the royal organ had found its way into Buckland's digestive system after it fell into the possession of a friend, the Archbishop of York. Buckland said that the Sun King's heart might have tasted better with gravy made from the blood of a marmoset monkey.

Revd Buckland was convinced that geology would one day confirm the literal truth of the Old Testament and the Book of Genesis. In an attempt to make some sense of the apparently conflicting evidence that was emerging about the earth's history, Revd Buckland set out to make a detailed study of the country's rock formations. Between 1814 and 1821 he produced eight geological maps of the British Isles. Whereas most geologists at that time tended to do their fieldwork dressed in dark suits, as if to underline the seriousness of their work, Buckland did his in a flowing academic gown with bulging pockets stuffed full of rocks. When he was travelling in a coach, if he spotted an interesting looking rock in the road he would drop his top hat or his handkerchief out of the window, forcing the coachman to stop. He often rode his favourite old black mare, laden with hammers, chisels and other rock-breaking tools. The old horse was so accustomed to Buckland's routine that whenever anyone else rode it, every time it came across a rock in the road it would stop and wait for the rider to dismount. As well as his geologist's nose, Buckland had an extraordinarily well-developed sense of smell and taste. One night he was travelling to London by horse with a friend when they got lost. Buckland dismounted, picked up a handful of earth, sniffed it and announced, 'Ah, Uxbridge.' He also once exposed a fake religious relic, a patch of martyr's blood on an Italian cathedral floor that miraculously renewed itself. Buckland licked it and determined that the stain was bat's piss.

Buckland made several important discoveries. In 1822, in *An Assemblage of Fossil Teeth and Bones*, he described a feeding frenzy of ancient hyenas based on some fossil remains he found in a cave. That same year he discovered an ancient human skeleton which he originally identified as male, but then changed his mind and proclaimed the skeleton not only female but probably a witch. He called it the Red Witch, but thought better of it and gave the skeleton the more scientifically plausible name of the Red Lady of Paviland. She later turned out to be a he. Another discovery came when Mrs Buckland was roused at two in the morning by her husband shouting, 'My dear, I believe that cheirotherium's footsteps are undoubtedly testudinal!' They ran downstairs and while his wife prepared a paste to spread over the kitchen table he collected the pet tortoise from the garden. They watched in delight as the tortoise's feet left an impression in the paste similar to that of Buckland's fossil.

For Mrs Buckland there were even more trying times ahead. Their son Frank, who became a famous naturalist, not only inherited, but pushed to new limits his father's indiscriminate eating habits. Frank had an arrangement with London Zoo whereby he would receive a cut of anything that died. Buckland Jr. went on to form the Society for the Acclimatization of Animals in the United Kingdom, ostensibly to teach the British public how they could ease food shortages by eating new types of meat, but mainly an excuse for Frank and his pals at Oxford to sample boiled elephant's trunk, grilled panther, steamed and boiled kangaroo, wild boar, roasted parrot, leporine, garden snails and earwigs. Some culinary experiments were more successful than others. Stewed Japanese sea slug tasted like the contents of a glue pot, while the boiled and fried head of a long-dead porpoise tasted like 'a broiled lamp wick'. In 1868, Frank took part in an eight-course all-horse banquet, served to one hundred and sixty people, to encourage the increased use of horses as food. After munching his way through an entire stud, Frank Buckland conceded: 'In my humble opinion . . . hippophagy has not the slightest chance of success in this country.'

Throughout the eighteenth century a number of giant bones had been discovered in quarries at Stonesfield. Although they were the subject of wild speculation, they had lain in a glass case in the Ashmolean Museum in Oxford for nearly one hundred years, unexplained and unclassified. Revd Buckland began to compare the bones with other fossils to see if he could spot any zoological similarities and worked out that they came from a large reptile, over 40 feet long and as bulky as an elephant.

But Revd Buckland was not in a hurry to publish his findings. There was, after all, no mention of a giant carnivorous lizard in the Old Testament. Besides, this sort of thing was unlikely to impress the people who paid his wages, the Anglican establishment. Buckland's 'undergroundology' was already viewed with deep suspicion by his more conservative colleagues at Oxford. It wasn't befitting a member of the clergy to be digging up dirt on the Creation story, which they held to be a literal truth. He didn't get round to publishing his findings for another seven years, and only then because he thought he was at risk of being upstaged by an unknown, part-time geologist called Gideon Mantell, who had arrived at a similar conclusion. On 20 February 1824, Buckland announced his Stonesfield reptile to a meeting of the Geological Society, which shortly afterwards was published as *Notice on the Megalosaurus or Great Fossil Lizard of Stonesfield.* Never one to miss an opportunity to preach, Buckland argued that the design of his mighty megalosaurus proved the existence of an intelligent, benevolent, highly skilled Divine Creator. He was at a loss, however, to explain why such a benevolent Creator would want to fill the Garden of Eden with such an array of highly dangerous carnivorous beasts equipped with, in his own words, 'organs for the purpose of capturing and killing their prey, instruments formed expressively for destruction'.

In 1845, Buckland was appointed Dean of Westminster, one of the most powerful jobs in the Anglican Church. By this time his position meant he was no longer actively involved in science, but he was still regarded as geology's elder statesman and was so widely respected that he become the government's unofficial general scientific adviser on all manner of subjects.

Buckland spent the last few years of his life poring over the book of Genesis line by line, desperate to find some interpretation that might breach the growing gap between science and religion. By the late 1840s he was showing signs of mental breakdown, possibly aggravated by a head injury he had sustained in a coach accident. The normally mild-mannered Dean began to behave oddly and aggressively and beat himself about the head and scratched himself until he bled – behaviour worrying for his wife and family. In spite of the best efforts of his friends and colleagues to get him medical treatment, his condition deteriorated and it was decided that he should be removed for the safety of his family. By the time of the Great Exhibition of 1851, at which the public could see for the very first time a life-size model of his megalosaurus, Buckland was incarcerated in a lunatic asylum in Clapham, experiencing the very best of nineteenth-century mental healthcare in full, horrifying detail.

## Navel warfare

Revd William Buckland wasn't the only religiously inclined person in the nineteenth century to struggle with the evident contradiction between the fossil record and biblical chronology. The Victorian naturalist Philip Gosse (1810–88) was the author of a number of successful books on zoology and marine biology, but his best known work is his strangest: *Omphalos*, published in 1857. Gosse was a Christian fundamentalist and a member of a strict, unbending sect known as the Plymouth Brethren. He had little time for self-indulgence or, for that matter, his family. An entry in his journal reads: 'Received green swallow from Jamaica. E[mily] delivered of a son.'

Gosse was preoccupied with the knotty problem of whether or not the biblical Adam possessed a belly button. It should go without saying that, strictly speaking, Adam didn't actually need an umbilical cord, having never spent time in a womb, but as the prototype for all men, was he equipped with all the working parts? Gosse's conclusion in *Omphalos* (Greek for navel) was that Adam did indeed have a belly button. God had created Adam's navel – and the fossil record – to create the impression that the world was very old. It was an almighty hoax to tempt humankind and test their faith. Gosse thought his explanation was a work of genius and sat back to enjoy the plaudits, but to his astonishment they didn't come. Scientists scoffed, while fellow Christians really didn't like the implication that God was a practical joker. When thousands of copies of *Omphalos* remained unsold, Gosse was mystified. He convinced himself that the name of the book was the problem, so he reissued it with the more accessible title *Creation*, but it didn't help. Crushed by overwhelming indifference, Gosse gave up science and took up watercolour painting.

## Unfrocked

In 1793, an itinerant preacher called Jane Davison settled in Alnwick in Northumberland and was taken into the home of a kindly Methodist minister, Revd Hastings. Six months later, Revd Hastings was perturbed to discover that his houseguest had mysteriously vanished. Not long after, it was discovered that both of Mr Hastings's unmarried teenage daughters were pregnant. 'Miss' Davison, who was in fact Mr Thomas Heppel, had not only seduced the sisters without either one finding out about the other, but had also planned to elope with both. Having told each of the sisters to meet him at opposite ends of town, he made off with their suitcases, complete with two new sets of women's clothing for his next scam. Heppel was eventually apprehended in York wearing a dress. He was convicted of fraud and theft and was transported to Australia.

## Unholy pursuits

Revd John 'Mad Jack' Alington (1795–1863) was educated at Oxford and followed his BA with an MA and a priesthood in 1822. Shortly afterwards, he inherited a fortune from his maternal grandfather – the small matter of forty-three farms and a million pounds in cash. He also acquired Letchworth Hall in Hertfordshire, where his new duties as landowner made him patron of the local parish church. Alington was a man who took his responsibilities seriously and offered to assist the rector, Samuel Knapp, by taking the occasional service. Revd Knapp generously agreed, a decision he would soon regret. Alington was soon taking all of the services, including weddings and christenings, and leaving the funerals to Knapp.

Alington threw himself into his new job with a great deal of enthusiasm. Unfortunately very little of what he had to say followed the established order of service. A regular feature of his rambling sermons were some of the more risqué passages from the Song of Solomon extolling the pleasures of free love. Knapp complained to the local bishop, who promptly banned Alington from holding services at Letchworth church. Knapp assumed that this would be the end to the matter, but Alington was not a man to give up easily. He simply set up his own church in Letchworth Hall. As most of the people in the village worked for him and lived in his cottages the rebel vicar had little difficulty poaching most of Knapp's regular churchgoers, especially since he also took to handing out free beer and brandy. Occasionally his services got so out of hand that he had to threaten his congregation with his shotgun. He also had several other unorthodox methods of grabbing the undivided attention of his congregation. Instead of the customary vestments he wore a leopard skin and began his services by playing on an old piano. He would begin reading the sermon, usually a story about free love, then disappear behind a screen, then reappear in another part of the hall through a trapdoor, or would occasionally career up and down the aisle, staggeringly drunk, in a four-wheeled cart, propelled by a couple of servants. To signal the end of his service he generally removed his wig and tossed it into the air.

Not content with stealing Revd Knapp's congregation, Alington knew that Knapp's income depended on tithes collected from the Letchworth estate, so he did his best to see that it was farmed as unprofitably as possible. He employed the Letchworth workforce in time-wasting projects, such as digging and refilling holes, or would lay on a barrel of beer for his men and read them Shakespeare. At one point he got them to reshape his pond into a scale model of the world's oceans, then rowed his workers around floating model 'continents' while lecturing them on geography. In 1851, he decided to take his labourers on a day's outing to the Great Exhibition in London. In case they got lost, he spent a week training them in how to find their way from King's Cross station to the Crystal Palace and back with the aid of a giant street plan of London laid out with logs. He lost patience with the project when they made mistakes with the model, so Alington called the trip off. A few years later he got his workers to build a reproduction of the fortifications of Sebastopol so they could get a better understanding of the progress of the Crimean War.

Alington liked to be carried around his garden in an open coffin; he said he was practising for the real thing. When his terminal illness came on at the age of sixty-eight, in December 1863, he refused to take his medicine until his gardener had tested it for three days running. Finally, he refused the medicine and called for a large brandy instead. He drained the glass then fell dead.

## The joy of sects

Revd Henry Prince (1809–99), a vicar from Charlinch, Somerset, came to the attention of the Anglican authorities in 1835 when he began to hear voices in his head that he took to be the word of God, then controversially took it upon himself to divide his congregation into the 'saved' and the 'damned'. His licence to preach was finally revoked by the Bishop of Bath and Wells when Prince took to addressing them naked. The newly defrocked Prince continued to preach, however, and on New Year's Day 1846 he announced that he was the Messiah to a group of people taking tea in a Weymouth café. The incident was brought before the Home Secretary by Dorset county magistrates who complained that Prince was 'impersonating the Almighty'.

Prince shut himself away in a large mansion in the village of Spaxton, just a mile from his old parish, and founded a commune called Church of the Agapemone – Greek for 'abode of love'. It was surrounded by a 12-foot wall and guarded by ferocious bloodhounds, designed to keep prying eyes out and to keep the faithful in. Prince ruled in despotic style over a cult membership that varied in number between sixty and two hundred. His followers, even married ones, were required to live in single-sex quarters, but Prince, now referred to by the faithful as 'the Beloved', made alternative arrangements for himself with a novel take on 'spin the bottle'. Once a week his younger female devotees were seated on a giant revolving stage which the men would then rotate. The girl who faced Prince when the stage came to a stop was his 'Bride of the Week'. He also deflowered teenage virgin Zoe Paterson in his 'chapel', which doubled as Prince's billiard room, while his congregation watched. When Miss Paterson became pregnant despite Prince's reassurance that his 'divine' sperm would produce no offspring, he changed tack and claimed that it was the work of the Devil.

Prince funded his community largely by wheedling money out of several well-heeled spinsters, in particular five impressionable heiresses, the Nottidge sisters, who not only took their turn on the revolving stage but also frequently found notes secreted under their dinner plates with instructions such as 'The Lord hath need of £50'. Prince lived lavishly, surrounded by a bevy of billiard-playing beauties, occasionally driving around Spaxton in a coach attended by liveried outriders who announced his arrival by shouting 'Blessed is he who cometh in the name of the Lord,' while he ran up large bills with local shopkeepers in the name of 'My Lord, the Agapemone'. No one received a penny from Prince for their services, not even the manual labourers who worked the land for him while he slept with their wives; their only reward was the privilege of being made 'saints'.

Despite accusations of brainwashing, sex scandals, dramatic rescues of members by their families and occasional virulent attacks in the popular press, the Abode of Love was allowed to flourish more or less unmolested for the next thirty-odd years.

Prince had declared himself and his followers immortal, but the Agapemonites gradually passed away one by one, until Prince himself died in January 1899. His death came as a genuine shock to the faithful and threw the community into a state of panic. They hurriedly buried him in the front garden in the middle of the night, his body standing upright to facilitate his resurrection. When the expected second coming failed to materialize, instead of arriving at the conclusion that they had been victims of a long and humiliating hoax, Prince's followers stuck together and crowned a new Messiah in the person of his former sidekick, the Revd John Hugh Smyth-Pigott. The new leader of the Agapemonites turned out to be every bit as lecherous as Prince, described by one historian as: 'If not a sexual maniac, at least a man obsessed with sex in his daily life.' Smyth-Pigott sparked a mini-revival for the cult, but after his death in 1927 membership fell away, and the Abode of Love closed its doors shortly afterwards.

## Loose canon

Dublin's most unwelcome dinner guest in the mid-nineteenth century was the absurdly hyperactive Archbishop of Dublin, Richard Whately (1800–90). Whately had several hobbies, including boomerang-throwing and climbing trees. His cure for a headache was to work up a sweat by chopping down a tree. His wayward limbs made him the terror of hostesses and anyone who invited Whately to their homes could expect their furniture to be destroyed, thanks to his habit of whirling chairs around on their legs and lashing out with his feet at anything within reach. In the course of one evening he laid waste to six chairs owned by his host Lord Anglesey, who prepared for Whately's next visit by having a virtually indestructible chair built with legs 'like the balustrades of Dublin castle'. It didn't save Lady Anglesey's best china, however, when Whately decided to prop his feet on the mantelpiece.

One day the Chief Justice was sitting next to Whateley at a Privy Council meeting and, putting his hand into his pocket for his handkerchief, was surprised to find the Archbishop's foot already there. Large crowds turned up for Whately's sermons, but not to hear him preach. One member of his congregation recorded that he 'worked his leg about to such an extent that it glided over the edge of the pulpit and hung there till he had finished'. Whately was also a believer in phrenology, the once fashionable science of studying a person's character by the shape of their head, and had an intense dislike of people with flat-topped heads. He advised a phrenological test of his own: 'Take a handful of peas, drop them on the head of a patient; the amount of the man's dishonesty will depend on the number which remain there. If a large number remain, tell the butler to lock up the plate.'

## When Harry met Freddy

The Revd Harold Davidson (1875–1937) was from a long line of Protestant churchmen. His father, the vicar of Sholing in Hampshire, wanted him to follow the family calling and sent him to study divinity. Harold, however, was bitten by the stage bug after getting a role in a comedy sketch at the end-of-term school entertainments, and dreamed of a career in show business. At the age of nineteen, he toured and played the title role in a production of *Charley's Aunt*, but his acting career soon fizzled out. He completed his studies for holy orders at Exeter College, Oxford and in 1905 was awarded the rectorship of Stiffkey, a tiny fishing village in Norfolk. He had developed a taste for London's theatreland, however, that never really left him.

The new vicar of Stiffkey saw little point in preaching to the converted. Every Monday morning he skipped off to London on the first train to Paddington, returning by the last train on Friday night. His mission was to save fallen women. Revd Davidson's efforts were mostly focused upon attractive young West End waitresses; apparently only the best-looking girls were at risk. 'I like to catch them between the age of 14 and 20,' he explained. 'I believe with all my soul that if Christ were born again in London in the present day He would constantly be found walking in Piccadilly.'

Davidson's technique for chatting up young 'Nippies', as he called them, was generally the same. He would deliver the line, 'Are you not Miss . . . , the famous actress?' and as, inevitably, they were not, he would follow up by introducing his bogus theatrical connections and promising them a job on the stage. Although banned from most of London's tea shops, he managed to 'save' a new girl almost every other weekday for the next two decades. In 1920, he met a twenty-year-old prostitute called Rose Ellis and began a personal rescue mission that would last for ten years. He took her on trips to Paris where he introduced her as 'my secretary, Mrs Malone'. When it was later alleged that Rose was Revd Davidson's mistress, he explained that the purpose of the trip was to get her work as an au pair. In 1930, he found himself in deeper waters after an encounter with a sixteen-year-old prostitute, Barbara Harris, to whom he introduced himself with the line: 'Has anyone ever told you that you look like the film actress Mary Brian?'

The Revd Davidson's unorthodox missionary zeal came to the attention of the Bishop of Norwich, Dr Pollock, when the commuting rector failed to arrive back from soul-saving in London in time for the annual Stiffkey Remembrance Day service. The bishop hired a private detective to look into Davidson's Soho visits. The detective found Barbara Harris, who after a couple of stiff drinks and a down payment of forty shillings, volunteered a fourteen-page statement containing lurid and damning allegations against 'uncle Harold'.

In March 1932, the Church hierarchy moved to defrock Davidson. In the weeks leading to his trial the scandal created a national media frenzy, but the star attraction was far from contrite, insisting loudly from his pulpit every Sunday that he was innocent of all charges. On the day of his hearing he arrived an hour late and, instead of following the bishop to the high altar as decorum required, marched on ahead of him. Revd Davidson denied all charges and put up a spirited defence: had not Prime Minister Gladstone often talked to prostitutes to lead them to salvation?

A succession of witnesses arrived to testify. Some defended his indignant protestations of innocence, others branded Davidson a sex pest. One of his landladies, Mrs Walton, was cross-examined during his trial: 'Did he ever kiss you?'

'Often.'

'What did Mr Walton say to that?'

'He would kiss him too.'

'He kissed your husband?'

'He kissed the milkman too.'

At one point Davidson professed complete ignorance of the word 'buttock'. His case was fatally undermined when the prosecution produced a photograph of Davidson with a naked girl, fifteen-year-old Estelle Douglas. She said she agreed to take her clothes off after Revd Davidson promised he could find her work as a model for bathing suits. He was found guilty and deprived of his living.

Davidson spent the rest of his life protesting his innocence in between preparing various appeals against the court's verdict. He set himself up as an exhibit on Blackpool's Golden Mile, charging twopence a time for people to view him sitting inside a large barrel reading his law books. The queues were so big that he was prosecuted for causing an obstruction. Then he went on hunger strike inside his barrel, refusing to eat until the Church reinstated him. His campaign earned him a great deal of sympathy until it was noticed that he didn't appear to be losing weight; in fact he had a stash of fruit hidden away which he visited every time he took a toilet break. As attempted suicide by starvation was technically a criminal offence, Davidson was arrested, tried and acquitted. His next appointment was to share top billing with a whale carcass on Hampstead Heath. At various other events he would display himself supposedly frozen, or wearing a loincloth on a bed of nails, or roasting in a glass oven while a mechanical Satan jabbed him with a pitchfork.

In 1937, Davidson moved to Skegness, where, billed as 'a modern Daniel in a lion's den', he berated the Anglican hierarchy from inside a cage measuring 14 feet by 8 feet, which he also shared with a large circus lion called Freddy. The publicity stunt went awry when the normally docile cat turned on Davidson and mauled him. He lay fatally wounded in hospital for two days, while the promoter gallantly stuck up a few posters inviting the public to witness 'The lion that injured the Rector'. On the day of Davidson's funeral extra police had to be called in to control a near-stampede of mourners. His long-suffering widow Molly revealed a degree of eccentricity of her own by turning up for her husband's funeral dressed entirely in white.

## Nearer my dog to thee

The famous sculptor, engraver, typographer and postage stamp designer Eric Gill (1882–1940) was the best-known British artist of the 1930s. He produced nearly five hundred sculptures, including Stations of the Cross in Westminster Cathedral, and had a lucrative sideline in carving celebrity tombstones, including those of Oscar Wilde and G. K. Chesterton. Gill was also a pillar of the Roman Catholic community, known as 'the married monk' because of his eccentric choice of workwear: a habit and a girdle of chastity of the order of Saint Dominic. It caused something of a furore in the Catholic Church when, forty years after his death, Gill's secret diaries revealed a highly deviant sex life, chronicled with perverse precision across forty volumes, detailing incestuous relationships with various members of his family, including two of his sisters and his two elder daughters Betty and Petra, not to mention experimental sex with the family dog.

Gill began sleeping with his sisters in his teens and later extended his blandishments to prostitutes and married women, starting with his maid Lizzie during his honeymoon in 1906. One of Gill's life-size sculptures, entitled *Fucking*, was modelled on his younger sister Gladys, with whom he was having an affair, and her husband Ernest. When it was bought for the Tate the work was rechristened *Ecstasy*. On 22 June 1927, Gill wrote in his diary: 'A man's penis and balls are very beautiful things and the power to see this beauty is not confined to the opposite sex. The shape of the head of a man's erect penis is very excellent in the mouth. There is no doubt about this. I have often wondered, now I know.' Gill was also commissioned by the BBC to make a nude sculpture of Prospero and Ariel above the door to Broadcasting House. The head of the BBC, Lord Reith, inspected Gill's finished work from street level and was perplexed by the enormity of Ariel's penis. The BBC promptly sent one of their governors up the scaffolding with a notebook and tape measure. He informed Gill: 'In my view this young man is uncommonly well hung.' To Gill's horror, the organ was chiselled down to a size less likely to be 'objectionable to public morals and decency'. His name lives on in Britain's favourite typeface, Gill Sans.

## Jesus: a fungi to be with

The theologist John Allegro (1923–88) held controversial beliefs that led him to be known as 'the Liberace of biblical scholarship'. In 1953, while a brilliant undergraduate studying Hebrew dialects at Magdalen College, Oxford, he won a place on the team of distinguished scholars working on the Dead Sea Scrolls in Jerusalem. He went on to write a series of authoritative books on the subject, combining his career as an author with his role as a widely respected lecturer in Comparative Semitics and Old Testament Studies at Manchester University.

In the 1960s, Allegro's work took off in an unexpected direction when he declared Christianity to be 'a phallic, drug-taking mystery cult none of us would want anything to do with. They [early Christians] had visions. They went on a trip.' It was around this time that he began to refer to the Bible as 'these tales of this rabbi, Jesus, and his Mum and Dad'. Allegro's academic reputation was further undermined by his obsession with 'magic' mushrooms. In 1970, he published *The Sacred Mushroom and the Cross*, in which he sought to establish that most of the leading characters in the Bible, including Moses and Jesus, were walking mushrooms and that Christ's final utterance on the cross was 'a paean of praise to the god of the mushroom'. The book, wrote a critic, 'gave mushrooms a bad name'. Allegro effectively ended his academic career with the follow-up, the similarly fungi-influenced and prophetically titled *The End of the Road*. He followed it in 1971 with *The Chosen People*, which claimed that Moses and his followers were all high on hallucinogenic mushrooms, and *Lost Gods*, which asserted that the God of the Old Testament was 'a mighty penis in the heavens', who 'in the thunderous climax of the storm, ejaculated semen upon the furrows of Mother Earth'. The latter book prompted the *Sunday Telegraph* to note that it had 'all the freshness and coherence of the conversation of a very tired man in a crowded pub rather late at night'. When challenged, Allegro maintained that he never consumed mushrooms himself: 'I wouldn't be so bloody stupid,' he said.

## Stupid cult

The astrologer, occultist and occasional poet Aleister Crowley (1875–1947), or 'the Beast', as he was known to his mother, was born into a wealthy brewing family. His father, who was a zealot, made the young Aleister study the Bible for hours on end. This early religious instruction turned out to be counter-productive, to put it mildly. Young Crowley found the word of God to be full of inconsistencies. He particularly resented the bits which said that life's most enjoyable experiences, as Crowley saw it, were sinful.

After inheriting a sizeable fortune upon the death of his father, Crowley spent the next few years trying to combat boredom by dabbling in his two favourite activities, namely mysticism and sex. He later combined the two when he discovered 'mystic sodomy', one of the many dubious practices Crowley advocated for self-improvement. He became a member of the Hermetic Order of the Golden Dawn, who held that the world was run by 'Secret Chiefs' perched high in the Himalayas, then he set up his own cult, the Mysteria Mystica Maxima, himself taking the rather grand title Supreme and Holy King of Ireland, Iona and all the Britons within the Sanctuary of Gnosis. The founder of Scientology, L. Ron Hubbard, was one of Crowley's early acolytes, although L. Ron later denied this and claimed he only got involved with Crowley's cult because he was a secret agent trying to infiltrate it so he could break it up. Crowley, meanwhile, seems to have been more sceptical of Hubbard, dismissing him as 'an idiot'.

Crowley first came to the wider attention of the British public when he and a girlfriend performed a sex act with a goat in Italy. The tabloid press in England branded him 'The

Most Evil Man in the World' and 'The Man We'd Most Like to Hang' and he was kicked out of Italy by Mussolini.

Crowley claimed certain magic powers, including the ability to make himself invisible and, less impressively, the ability to make men fall over in the street. Many were said to have died as a result of his sorcery, and perhaps many more grazed their knees. When he wasn't busy raising the spirit of Satan, Crowley, although bald, fat and almost toothless, was also apparently irresistible to men and women. One Crowley-ex, Norman Mudd, was so devastated by being thrown over by the demonic one that he killed himself by walking into the sea off Guernsey with the legs of his trousers filled with stones held in place by bicycle clips.

Crowley had a massive drug habit and became a hopeless addict. By the end of his life he was a rather tragic and pathetic figure, mocked and vilified in the press. In 1934, he tried to sue the author Nina Hamnett for libelling him in her book *The Laughing Torso*, but a judge ruled that it was impossible to libel Crowley because he had no reputation to defend. According to popular myth, the last words of the enigmatic one were: 'I am perplexed.' According to someone at the beside, however, he actually said: 'Sometimes I hate myself.'

# Four

# POLITICAL ECCENTRICS

*'We are a grandmother.'*

– MARGARET HILDA THATCHER,
BRITISH PRIME MINISTER 1979–1990

## Don Quixote of the railways

Colonel Charles Waldo Sibthorp (1783–1855) was the most reactionary figure ever to set foot in Parliament. Long before he became Conservative MP for Lincoln, 'the Colonel' was already a curiosity figure in his local constituency thanks to his luxuriant whiskers and his colourful, anachronistic style of dress, including Regency-style blue frock coat, cravat, antique quizzing glasses and top-boots. He did not become known to the wider public until the elections of 1826, when he stood up to speak at his very first hustings and was felled by a large brick thrown from the crowd, knocking him unconscious.

Sibthorp's constituents got the gist of his political leanings a few days later when he gave an interview in the press. He hated any form of social progress. He was opposed to trains, water closets, taxation, anti-bribery laws, Catholics and 'the lamentable influx into this country of foreigners talking gibberish'. He particularly hated railways – 'the Steam

Humbug' – which he predicted would bring disasters ranging from moral ruin to wholesale slaughter. The trains, he said, were 'run by public frauds and private robbers' and he looked forward to the day when 'the old and happy mode of travelling the turnpike roads, in chaises, carriages and stages, will be restored'. Sibthorp enjoyed the support of at least one important sympathizer, the old Duke of Wellington, who was also suspicious of railways because 'they encourage lower classes to move about'. Sibthorp enjoyed one major triumph when, to the annoyance of Lincoln's businessmen, he stopped the Great Northern Railway from running through his constituency.

Most of all, Sibthorp loathed foreigners. 'It would take ninety-nine foreigners', he informed the House of Commons, 'to make one thorough good Englishman.' The only decent excuse for an Englishman to travel abroad, he said, was to wage war against unruly foreigners. Sibthorp's xenophobia extended to Queen Victoria's husband Albert. As a dyed-in-the-wool Tory he was fiercely pro-monarchist, but the Queen had committed the unpardonable sin of marrying a German – one of those 'nasty foreigners who live on brown bread and sauerkraut'. On the eve of their marriage Sibthorp called for Albert's proposed annual allowance of £50,000 to be halved. To the huge embarrassment of the Tory Prime Minister Lord Melbourne, who had given the Queen his personal assurance that Albert's allowance would go through without a hitch, Sibthorp won the day by 104 votes.

Sibthorp also opposed Prince Albert's most famous project, the 1851 Great Exhibition, on the grounds that it would attract foreign spies and lead to national bankruptcy. 'This unwholesome castle of glass', Sibthorp raged, 'is attracting to our shores a riffraff of swindling foreigners, robbing and murdering us by licence of the Queen's German husband.'

He advised people living near the Crystal Palace 'to keep a sharp lookout after their silver forks and spoons and servant maids'. The Queen vowed never to go anywhere near Lincoln again so long as Sibthorp was MP. She had to wait a long time because his constituents kept re-electing him as their MP right up until his death in 1855. Sibthorp worked himself into a fury for the last time when he rose in the House to accuse his old foe Lord John Russell of fiddling his expenses whilst on a trip to Vienna. He died of a stroke soon after.

## Drag queen

Few in the diplomatic corps have served with as much distinction as Edward Hyde, third Earl of Clarendon (1661–1723), first cousin of Queen Anne, veteran British parliamentarian and Governor of New York. As one portrait of him attests, the heavily built Clarendon was a loud and proud transvestite. Matters came to a head after the opening of the New York legislative assembly in 1702, when the English aristocrat made his entrance in a jaw-dropping off-the-shoulder gown in blue silk with a diamond-studded headdress and satin shoes, and carrying a fan. American businessmen took exception to having to conduct their affairs with a burly Englishman dressed in a frock. When they complained, Clarendon dismissed their 'American stupidity' on the shaky premise that he was a representing the Queen and had a duty to do it as faithfully as he could. It didn't cut any ice with Queen Anne, who quickly had her cousin removed from office.

## Clean bill of health

Britain's first Prime Minister Sir Robert Walpole (1676–1745) stayed awake during debates in the House of Commons by eating apples. He also swallowed about 180 pounds of soap in the last few years of his life in an attempt to get rid of a kidney stone. He died of a ruptured bladder.

## Show business for the ugly

The Belfast MP and pork butcher Joseph Biggar (1828–90) invented filibustering, the tactic of delaying parliamentary business by talking indefinitely. In a highly competitive field, Biggar was thought to be the most unattractive man to ever set foot in the House of Commons. He was short and squat with a hunchback, a 'face like a gargoyle', large bony hands and abnormally large feet and always wore a foul-smelling leather waistcoat. When Biggar rose to make his maiden speech, a startled Benjamin Disraeli turned to a colleague and asked, 'What creature is that?' Surprisingly, Biggar had a reputation as a ladies' man and his amorous adventures got him into several scrapes with the law. He once proposed marriage to a barmaid, Fanny Hyland, sealing the engagement with the gift of a parrot. Biggar broke it off, then compounded his ungentlemanly conduct by suing for the return of his parrot. The disappointed fiancée counter-sued for breach of promise and was awarded £400.

Biggar was also sued for breach of promise by a dancer, Fay Sinclair. When the matter came to court he explained that couldn't marry her because he had four illegitimate children. The judge asked Biggar, 'Is the mother still alive?' Biggar replied, 'Yes, M'lud. All four are.'

## Strange bedfellow

The Norwich Tory MP John Fransham (1730–1810) fought his parliamentary campaign with a promise to ban people from making their beds more than once a week. Fransham believed that daily bed making was 'the height of effeminacy'.

## Too much information

The bibliomaniac MP Richard Heber (1774–1833) rarely bothered to attend Parliament because he was too busy buying books. Almost unlimited wealth gave him a head start with his obsession. He believed that every gentleman should own at least three copies of a book: one for himself, one to lend to friends and one copy for his country house. He had already acquired a large library by the age of eight, which he topped up by buying the entire contents of a library in Paris comprising thirty thousand volumes. Besides his country seat at Hodnet, Shropshire, by the time of his death he owned seven more houses, each of which were crammed to the ceiling with books, overflowing from every room, choking corridors and towering above every available flat surface. Heber resigned his parliamentary seat and fled abroad after he was accused of having an improper relationship with a teenage youth. When he died it took Sotheby's three years to sell all of his 146,827 books – the largest collection of books ever assembled by one person. Also found in his library was a large stash of homoerotic literature including a very rare and extremely valuable copy of the world's first known piece of printed pornography, *Sodom, or The Gentleman Instructed,* ascribed to John Wilmot, second Earl of Rochester. The executors were horrified and quickly destroyed it.

## Be my guest

John William Ward, first Earl of Dudley (1781–1833), served as Foreign Secretary under three British Prime Ministers, including the Duke of Wellington. Ward was often overheard holding conversation with himself in two voices, one gruff and one shrill. He was also highly absent-minded and often forgot where he was. Once when dining at the home of a well-known society hostess he apologized to his fellow guests for the poor quality of the meal. 'I'm sorry,' he explained, 'my cook isn't at all well.' On another occasion he failed to take the hint when his hostess suggested it was late and time for him to leave. 'A pretty enough woman,' he told fellow diners, 'but she stays a devilish long time. I wish she'd go.'

## Tomb raider

The Tory MP William Bankes (1786–1855) was a traveller, archaeologist and thief of Egyptian antiquities. He sent back to his family estate at Kingston Lacy in Dorset numerous artefacts and curiosities that he picked up on his travels to Africa and the Middle East, including a 23-foot-high red granite obelisk he 'rescued' from the Nile valley in 1815. Bankes did not live to enjoy his collection for long. In 1833, while on his way to a late session in the House of Commons, he stopped by at the public lavatory at the corner of St Margaret's, Westminster, and was caught performing 'a lewd act' with a guardsman. He was charged with gross indecency, but acquitted when his powerful friends rallied round to give character references. The Duke of Wellington testified that Bankes was 'utterly incapable of such an offence'. In

1841, Bankes had yet another moment of madness when he was caught *in flagrante* with a guardsman on a bench in Green Park. This time Bankes thought it wise to withdraw and the fled the country for permanent exile in Venice, where he met up with his old Cambridge friend Lord Byron. Bankes was said to have become 'close' to Byron's bearded gondolier Giovanni Falcieri.

## Government Whip

Queen Victoria's three-times Liberal Prime Minister William Gladstone (1809–98) was a legendary bore who could talk at length on just about any subject, no matter how obscure. It was a constant source of irritation to his colleagues, who could find themselves being lectured by the great man for half an hour on the relative benefits of soft and hard boiled eggs, or why it was important to chew every mouthful of food precisely thirty-two times. One day they decided to get their own back. After days of careful research, a couple of his friends sat down to a meal with him at his club and began an in-depth discussion on ancient Chinese music – a subject they were sure was too obscure even for Gladstone. He listened quietly for a while, then said, 'You have evidently read an article I wrote some ten years ago,' then proceeded to monopolize the conversation.

Gladstone also liked to go for long walks, especially when it involved roaming the streets looking for 'fallen' women. His rescue work was not always appreciated by his Cabinet colleagues, who considered that cruising London's red light districts at night was not a healthy pastime for a prominent member of Her Majesty's government. In 1882, ministers Granville and Rosebery flipped a coin to decide who was going to ask their leader to give it up. Granville lost the toss, but his awkward efforts to broach the subject with the PM fell on deaf ears. Nor were London's streetwalkers particularly grateful for the attentions of Gladstone. Those who accepted his offer of hospitality could expect a meal and a bed for the night, but first they had to endure a lecture from Mrs Gladstone, then her husband read them extracts from Tennyson. Help from the long-winded PM was such a depressing prospect that girls who saw him coming generally ran away.

Gladstone used to take to bed with a hot water bottle full of tea; he was an early riser and said the tea was still warm enough to drink when he woke up. There was suspicion that he did more than take tea with the fallen women he set out to rescue, however. The publication of his diaries in 1974 revealed that he secretly read pornography and flogged himself afterwards with a whip.

## Three's company

The first great tabloid-style sex scandal involving a senior British politician destroyed the career of Charles Dilke (1843–1911), Liberal MP for Chelsea and a senior Cabinet minister in William Gladstone's second administration. In July 1885, just as the forty-one-year-old Dilke was being tipped to replace Gladstone as the next Prime Minister, his weakness for married women caught up with him in the form of Virginia Crawford, the twenty-two-year-old wife of a Scottish lawyer. She confessed to her husband that Dilke had persuaded her to take part in a threesome with himself and a housemaid called Fanny Stock, teaching them 'every French vice'. Mrs Crawford added helpfully: 'He used to say that I knew more than most women of 30.' Mr Crawford sued for divorce and cited Dilke as co-respondent. Dilke swore that he never laid a finger on Mrs Crawford, but he was pilloried in the press, mocked in the music halls, dropped from government and permanently ostracized from public life. 'Three-in-a-bed Dilke' spent years trying to clear his name and was successful in having the case reopened in a second hearing, but his efforts backfired. Although he rebutted Mrs Crawford's allegations, he was forced to admit that he had, in fact, slept with Mrs Crawford's mother.

## Titan of tedium

Spencer Cavendish, eighth Duke of Devonshire (1833–1908), was said to be the most boring speaker ever to set foot in the House of Lords. His long-winded monologues were 'the finest example of pile-driving the world has ever known', according to a friend. He was once caught yawning in the middle of one of his own speeches. He apologized immediately: 'I can't help it because what I have to say is so damned dull.' He once related a nightmare he experienced at Westminster: 'I dreamed I was making a speech in the House of Lords and woke up to find I actually was.'

## The wrong trousers

Lord Robert Cecil Salisbury (1830–1903) expressed his gratitude for being elected Prime Minister three times by describing the democratic system as 'a dangerous and irrational creed by which two day-labourers shall outvote Baron Rothschild'. To be fair, Salisbury's disdain for the people who put him in power was matched by his indifference to politics in general. Famously 'laid back', he kept a pen knife in his pocket which he used to jab into his leg to keep himself awake during business in the House of Commons.

As well as being one of Britain's longest-serving Prime Ministers, Salisbury was also the scruffiest. He was so shabbily dressed that he was once arrested by a farmer who thought he was a poacher, and in 1866 was actually refused admission to the Casino at Monte Carlo because he was taken for a tramp. He also incurred the displeasure of the future King Edward VII, who was a stickler for etiquette, by wearing the wrong trousers at a function. Salisbury often wore a skull cap to protect his head from draughts, but when he lost the cap he took to wearing a grey woollen glove on top of his head instead.

Life at Salisbury's home, Hatfield House, was similarly chaotic. He was a keen amateur scientist and liked to dabble in his private laboratory in the basement, connected to his study by a spiral staircase, from where guests heard regular explosions. He once emerged from his lab covered in blood, explaining that he had been 'experimenting with sodium in an insufficiently dried retort'. Hatfield House also happened to be one of the first houses to have electric lighting installed. The overloaded and completely uninsulated wiring ran the length of the ceiling above the dining room table and frequently burst into flame, to the alarm of dinner guests. Salisbury and his family coped by occasionally lobbing a cushion at the ceiling to put out the fire. He was also notoriously vague about remembering names and faces, once mistaking a servant in a fez for the Shah of Persia. On another occasion he was standing behind the throne at a court ceremony when he saw a young man smiling at him. He asked a colleague, 'Who's that?' The reply came, 'He's your eldest son.' Salisbury's appointment of Alfred Austin to the post of Poet Laureate in 1896 was considered one of the worst ever. When asked why he had chosen such a mediocre poet, Salisbury explained, 'I don't think anyone else applied.' Queen Victoria was said to be very fond of Salisbury, despite his 'peculiarities'. He was the only man she ever asked to sit down.

Lord Salisbury's son Lord Hugh Cecil (1869–1956), MP for Greenwich, was known as 'Linky' because his reminded his family of 'the missing link'. Cecil was convinced that his constituency was infested with poisonous snakes. He advised his constituents not to sit in their gardens unless they used very high chairs and recited poetry loudly, because 'I have been told that snakes are afraid of the human voice'. In the House of Commons he avoided the big issues of the day and was chiefly famous for his long-standing crusade against an attempt to repeal the law that made it illegal for a man to marry his dead wife's sister, a situation Cecil denounced as 'an act of sexual vice as immoral as concubinage'. When he discovered that his neighbour in Sussex had married his late wife's sister, Cecil ostracized him. The neighbour took revenge by planting a long line of trees on the boundaries of his property, thereby completely obscuring the Cecils' view of the South Downs.

Cecil also hated air raid shelters, which he thought were a waste of money and a complete overreaction to wartime bombing, a point he made in several letters to *The Times*. 'Would it actually matter', he asked, 'if a theatre full of people were bombed?' When he was appointed Provost of Eton just before the Second World War he fell out with the college's governors, who wanted to build a school air raid shelter. Cecil vehemently disagreed, arguing that it was only the school's job to teach the students, not protect them from German bombers. To Cecil's permanent disgust the matter was settled in favour of the governors after a colleague pointed out that teaching might be difficult if all the pupils were dead. Cecil was asked what he would do if the Luftwaffe bombed the school. He replied that he would ring for Tucker, his butler.

## Members only

Lord Birkenhead, who became Tory Lord Chancellor in 1919, was a regular visitor to the Athenaeum Club in London, of which he was not a member, but used exclusively to visit the men's toilet. One day he was stopped by an irritated member who complained: 'I do wish you wouldn't use this club as a urinal.' The chancellor replied, 'Oh, I see. It's a club as well, is it?'

## Highly strung

Unlike his philosopher father Bertrand Russell, John Conrad, the fourth Earl Russell (1921–1987), was a less than gifted free thinker, renowned for his rambling and often spectacularly confused speeches in the House of Lords. In 1978, during a debate on aid for victims of crime, Russell startled the slumbering peers by demanding the total abolition of law and order and called for the police to 'stop raping young people in their cells'. Russell went on to propose that 'there should be universal leisure for all and a standing wage sufficient to provide life without working ought to be supplied . . . so that everybody becomes a leisured aristocrat . . . aristocrats are Marxists.' He added that 'women's lib would be realized by girls being given a house of their own by the age of twelve and three-quarters of the wealth of the state being given to the girls so that marriage would be abolished and the girl could have as many husbands as she liked'. He finally advised that 'Mr Brezhnev and Mr Carter are really the same person', before suddenly exiting the Chamber without further comment. When the full text of his speech was published in *Hansard* it became a collector's item. Russell retired from politics to take up writing and crocheting. He once made himself a pair of trousers out of string. 'It took a very long time,' he explained later, 'because I didn't have a pattern.'

## Getting the boot

Sir Walter Bromley-Davenport (1903–89) served as Tory MP for Knutsford for forty-two years. A former army light heavy-weight boxing champion, he was known for his intimidating presence, especially his loud, booming voice and was said to be the loudest man ever to sit in the House of Commons. One of his pastimes was wrecking opposition speeches. A favourite tactic was to yawn very loudly in the middle of a speech, or when a new Labour MP stood up to speak he would bawl across the Chamber: 'SIT DOWN!' The trick often worked.

For several years after the war he served as an uncompromising opposition whip. Bromley-Davenport's career as a Tory whip ended abruptly in 1951 when one evening he spotted a well-dressed man leaving the Palace of Westminster. Taking him to be a Conservative MP sneaking off home early, Bromley-Davenport kicked him in the backside, sending him tumbling down a flight of stairs onto the marble floor below. The recalcitrant 'MP' turned out to be the Belgian ambassador.

## Home comforts

William Douglas-Home (1912–92), younger brother of the British Tory Prime Minister Sir Alec Douglas-Home, was dishonourably discharged from the army and spent a year in Wakefield prison for disobeying an order during World War II. In September 1944, while serving as Tank Commander with the Royal Armoured Corps, he was ordered to attack Le Havre, which was full of French civilians. To give himself time to think about the moral implications he drove around a turnip field in his tank twenty-five times before informing his commanding officer that he was unable to obey the order.

William was a three-times unsuccessful candidate for Parliament. Not long before his brother became Tory Prime Minister, William stood as a Liberal in a by-election. During the campaign he took a morning off to go shooting with his brother, who uncharacteristically missed every single bird in the first drive. When William asked Alec if something was wrong, Alec replied, 'I had to speak against some bloody Liberal last night!' – unaware that the 'bloody Liberal' was his own younger brother. William said later, 'I would have given him a lift if I'd known he was going.' After two more political failures William took to writing stage comedies, including *The Cigarette Girl* (1962), reviewed by the *Daily Mail* as 'unspeakable drivel'. Their mother Lillian was also notably eccentric. She had all her teeth removed in one session without anaesthetic, then set off for a formal luncheon engagement ahead of her false set. When the false teeth arrived, they shot out of her mouth as she was greeting an admiral.

William Douglas-Home was also a great practical joker. He once took a stuffed crocodile up to the family home in

Scotland and got a friend to push it out into a stream, where it floated in full view of his mother, who was taking a walk in the grounds with some friends. She remarked, without batting an eyelid, 'I hadn't realized they came this far north.'

## Polls apart

Commander Bill Boaks (1921–86), war hero and road safety campaigner, was the most unsuccessful parliamentary candidate of all time. Over a period of thirty years Boaks contested twenty-one general elections and by-elections. His first candidacy was in the 1951 general election when he fought Walthamstow East as an independent candidate for the Association of Democratic Monarchists Representing All Women. He had actually intended to stand against the Prime Minister Clement Attlee in Walthamstow West but accidentally stood for the wrong seat. In the event Boaks received 174 votes out of 40,001 cast.

His political label changed several times over the years. In one election he stood as the Trains and Boats and Planes candidate, a cunning plan to sway floating voters by adopting the title of a contemporary pop song, but eventually settled for Public Safety Democratic Monarchist White Resident. Boaks cycled around the target constituency wearing a large cardboard box daubed with various slogans airing his main concern: road safety. Later he traded his bike in for a white van painted with black stripes and a large mast and sail on the top. Boaks championed the cause of pedestrians to have the right of way at all times. To reinforce his point he would deliberately hold up traffic at zebra crossings. He stopped his van outside Wembley stadium just before the start of an England–Scotland match and refused to move until all 100,000 football fans had crossed the road in front of him. More dangerously, he once sat in a deckchair in the fast lane of the London Westway.

In the 1950s, Boaks launched a series of private prosecutions against public figures who had been involved in road accidents, including the wife of Prime Minister Clement Attlee, upon whom Attlee relied while he was campaigning. Lady Attlee was a notoriously accident-prone driver (she had seven crashes in five years) and Boaks attempted private prosecutions every time she crashed. When Prince Philip drove his Rover into a Ford Prefect owned by a Mr Cooper of Holyport, Berkshire, Boaks issued a summons against the Queen, as Prince Philip's passenger, for aiding and abetting. In these, as in his electoral campaigns, Boaks was unsuccessful. The litigant was unfazed: 'Cars kill impartially,' he noted. 'I don't care whether the driver is a duke or a bloody dustman.'

In 1958, he applied for the vacant post of Chief Constable of Berkshire, and was disappointed not to get an interview; at the time he was attempting to prosecute the Home Secretary as the accomplice of the police officer who drove him to the House of Commons and, according to Boaks, had committed six traffic offences in Parliament Square.

The nadir of his political career came in 1982, when he contested the Glasgow Hillhead by-election and gained five votes, the lowest ever recorded in a modern British parliamentary election. What made it even more remarkable was that he needed the support of at least ten voters to get his name on the ballot paper in the first place. Boaks remained optimistic in defeat. 'Had I been elected,' he said, 'I think I would have become the next Prime Minister.' He died four years later as a result of head injuries sustained in a traffic accident.

## High dudgeon

Martin Attlee (1927–91), son of Labour Prime Minister Clement Attlee, campaigned vigorously in the House of Lords against drug abuse. He demanded that dealers should be forcibly injected with heroin 'to give them a taste of their own medicine'. Attlee told their lordships he spoke as an authority, having experienced drugs himself. On holiday in Portugal, he had accidentally smoked cannabis and found himself on a 'high' – a sensation he found to be disagreeable. Shortly before he died, Attlee took up another campaign, this time drawing attention to the brutality of the Metropolitan Police force, citing 'horrific stories of police arrogance, especially when it comes to picking up boys with a public school accent'. It later transpired that a couple of days earlier Attlee had fallen asleep on a London underground train and had been bundled into a police cell and charged with being drunk and disorderly.

## Hollow earl theory

William Brinsley Le Poer Trench (1911–95), eighth Earl of Clancarty, spent several years in the House of Lords trying to expose a government cover-up of the existence of UFOs and of beings living in the interior of the Earth.

Lord Clancarty said he could trace his descent from 63,000 BC, around the time beings from other planets had landed on Earth in spaceships. Before he succeeded to the earldom in 1975, however, he sold advertising space for a gardening magazine opposite Waterloo Station. In his spare time he wrote several books about UFOs, including *Secret of the Ages: UFOs from Inside the Earth*, in which he claimed that mankind emerged from inside a hollow Earth. In earlier books he had postulated that a number of the 'Elchim' (gods) had indulged in a breeding experiment. This went wrong and they were expelled, along with the race of Adam. These were the 'fallen angels', 'giants', 'Anunnaki' – the Nephilim of the Bible. 'It is my firm view', he explains, 'that the groundwork has now been prepared for a take over of this planet by those who live inside it.' Most humans were descended from these aliens: 'This accounts for all the different colour skins we've got here.' A few of these early aliens did not come from space, but emerged through tunnels from a civilization which 'still existed beneath the Earth's crust'. There were seven or eight of these tunnels altogether, one at the North Pole, another at the South Pole, and others in such places as Tibet. 'I haven't been down there myself,' he said, 'but from what I gather these beings are very advanced.'

In 1979, Lord Clancarty organized the House of Lords' first ever debate on UFOs. It attracted many speeches on both sides, including one from Lord Gainford, who described a personal sighting of a UFO, and the Bishop of Norwich, who wondered if aliens from other planets had souls. Lord Clancarty confessed disappointment at never having actually spotted a UFO himself, despite having installed a UFO detector in the bedroom of his South Kensington flat.

## Tired and emotional

*Private Eye* coined the euphemism 'tired and emotional' to describe the frequently erratic behaviour of George Brown (1914–85), Labour MP for Belper and Foreign Secretary under Prime Minister Harold Wilson. Brown was chiefly famous for diplomatic gaffes while under the influence of alcohol. He once got only halfway through a dinner in honour of the Turkish President before lurching to his feet and telling his guest: 'You don't want to listen to this bullshit – let's go and have a drink.' Another unfortunate incident occurred shortly after his appointment in 1966 when he was attending a state banquet in Peru where he was expected to dance with the President's wife. After drinking heavily he tapped a lady wearing a red dress on the shoulder. She declined his invitation to take the floor with the response: 'First, you are drunk. Second, this is not a waltz, it is the Peruvian national anthem. And third, I am not a woman, I am the Cardinal Archbishop of Lima.'

## Between a loch and a hard place

David James (1919–86), Conservative MP for Brighton Kemptown, lost his seat in the 1964 general election after a record seven recounts, by just seven votes to Labour's Dennis Hobden, the first ever Labour MP for a Sussex constituency. James, who was also the founder of the Loch Ness Monster Information Bureau, had spent most of the three-week election campaign in Scotland on his annual hunt for 'Nessie'. This is thought to be the only occasion *Nessiteras rhombopteryx* has been pivotal in a general election. Conservative Party Chairman John Hare subsequently blamed James for his party's defeat, since Labour ended up with just a two-seat majority that was soon whittled down to one in a by-election.

# Five
# SCIENTIFIC ECCENTRICS

*'Wild horses were used to eat up the grass, so the lawn is, all over, holes, deep holes. It must be dug, or else filled up. What dreadful work cutting grass is, with scissors. 90 feet by 12, say. Hard work on the back, very.'*

– OLIVER HEAVISIDE (1850–1925)

## Boyle's flaw

Robert Boyle (1627–91) was the seventh son of the first Earl of Cork, one of the richest men in the British Isles. As a young man Boyle wanted to be a writer and composed a series of highly moralistic musings with titles such as *Upon the Sighting of a Fair Milkmaid Singing to Her Cow* and *Upon My Spaniel's Carefulness Not to Lose Me in a Strange Place.* Fortunately for literature, Boyle eventually opted for a career in science instead.

His book *The Sceptical Chymist*, published in 1661, set out his eponymous law, once known to all schoolchildren, relating pressure to the volume of gas. He went on to become a founding member of the Royal Society and is heralded as 'the father of modern chemistry'. But Boyle was also a raging hypochondriac. He commissioned a range of cloaks in various materials to cope with any possible variation in the weather, and decided which one to wear before he went out by consulting the recently invented thermometer. He had been deeply religious ever since he was half-frightened out of his wits by a violent thunderstorm when he was on the Grand Tour. Boyle believed that scientific experimentation was God's work and should only take place on the Sabbath. One of his lesser-known fields of research was interviewing miners to find out how many of them had encountered demons down the pit.

## Newton's neuroses

The eccentricities of Sir Isaac Newton (1642–1727) attracted many legends. As a student he was truly odd. He would wake up, then forget to get out of bed, and sit immobilized for hours as a rush of new ideas came into his head. He wandered the walkways of Trinity College, Cambridge, with his hair wild and uncombed, scratching diagrams in the gravel with his stick, or sat in the great hall in a trance-like state, so lost in thought that he forgot to eat even when food was placed in front of him. On the rare occasions when he had visitors to his rooms he would step into his study to fetch a bottle of wine, forget what he was doing and sit down at his desk to work. Newton's maid walked into his kitchen one day and found him standing in front of a saucepan full of boiling water in which lay his watch, while he was looking with bafflement at an egg in his hand.

Newton was also prone to bizarre self-experimentation. He once stuck a bodkin – a large, blunt needle – into the back of his eye socket between his eyeball and the bone and jiggled it about to see if it would induce optical effects, nearly blinding himself in the process. On another occasion he stared directly into the sun with one eye for as long as he could just to see what might happen. Once again, he was lucky to escape permanent damage but had to lie down in a darkened room for days before his eyesight recovered. He pursued his science like a hermit, cloistered away, hiding his ideas behind conundrums and anagrams, occasionally emerging to engage in priority disputes with fellow scientists such as Robert Hooke over the discovery of gravity, or the long-running feud he had with the German mathematician Gottfried Wilhelm Leibniz over who invented calculus. It is said that Newton laughed only once in his entire life, when someone asked him what use he saw in Euclid.

Newton's mental state was unstable at the best of times, but he went properly mad for a while in 1692, when he was fifty. He experienced a breakdown followed by a period of mental instability that lasted for the best part of eighteen months. A Cambridge colleague described the episode as 'a distemper that much seized his head'. He sent a very strange letter, written in a shaky hand, to the philosopher John Locke, accusing Locke of trying to 'embroil him with women and other means'. In another letter to his friend and colleague Samuel Pepys he wrote:

> Sir, Some time after Mr. Millington . . . had delivered your message, he pressed me to see you the next time I went to London. I was averse; but upon his pressing consented, before I considered what I did, for I am extremely troubled at the embroilment I am in, and have neither ate nor slept well this twelve month, nor have I my former consistency of mind . . . I must withdraw from your acquaintance, and see you nor the rest of my friends any more.

Pepys was completely baffled by the letter. The conversation with Millington that Newton referred to had never taken place.

Newton recovered from his 'black year', wrote a few letters of apology to various people and was soon back at work. His breakdown had a longer-lasting effect, however. Although he had emerged from his period of psychosis with his faculties apparently intact, his work took off in a new and unexpected direction. By the time he was famous, Newton had more or less given up proper science. His research was now focused on a strange and covert enterprise: the study of alchemy.

He had dabbled in it on and off for years, but when he was in his forties and at the peak of his powers alchemy became an obsession. He was anxious to prove that a substance known as 'child of Satan' gave off magnetic rays that would attract the life force of the world. Newton believed that it contained 'God's signature'. He spent a fortune on alchemical books and equipment and built a small furnace in his garden. Bunkered in his laboratory with his assistant Humphrey Newton (no relation) he slogged for up to nineteen hours a day, spending sleepless nights poring over mystical texts, furtively hunched over bubbling retorts of mercury, lead, antimony and sulphur. He often forgot to eat and sometimes went to bed at five or six in the morning. In all, the greatest mind in science spent over thirty of the most productive years of his life trying to change base metals into gold and wrote over 650,000 words on the subject – an exercise in futility and wishful thinking that amounted to so much waste paper. You can't help wondering what Newton might have been if only he had stuck to science.

But Alchemy was not Newton's only professional quirk. He was a deeply religious man; we know this because he severed all relations with a friend who told him a risqué joke about a nun. In fact he was secretly a member of an obscure heretical sect associated with Arius, a third-century priest from Alexandria, whose followers rejected the doctrine of the Holy Trinity – that is, that Christ and God were as one. Newton kept very quiet about his religious beliefs. He was, ironically, a master of Trinity College and if he had been found out he would have lost his job, or worse.

There were, however, slightly more curious aspects to Newton's faith. After completing his monumental *Philosophiae Naturalis Principia Mathematica*, he began to devote more and more of his time to searching for hidden codes in the Bible, which he believed contained God's secret laws for the universe. He claimed that the mathematical formulae in *Principia* were first revealed by God to a group of mystics at the dawn of civilization, a tradition to which Newton had been chosen as heir. He also believed that the Old Testament King Solomon, son of David, was 'the greatest philosopher of the world'. Newton was convinced that Solomon had secretly incorporated the pattern of the universe into the design of his temple. Newton taught himself Hebrew and spent long hours poring over floor plans of Solomon's temple hoping to find mathematical clues to the Second Coming of Christ. He predicted that the world would end in 2060, a calculation he made by studying the Book of Daniel and the date of the foundation of the Holy Roman Empire. The Second Coming of Christ, according to Newton, would follow plagues and war and would precede a thousand-year reign by the saints on earth – of which Newton would be one.

He spent more time and energy writing about biblical history than he did on any of his great scientific works, even his search for alchemy. During the last thirty years of his life he wrote over a million words attempting to establish a new chronology for the Old Testament. He rewrote his

*Chronology of Ancient Kingdoms* at least sixteen times before he was happy with it. When it was finally published, a year after his death, even his most dedicated admirers were puzzled as to why the great man had devoted his unique talent to such an odd subject. When the full extent of Newton's oddball religious beliefs became apparent, years after his death, the matter was quietly swept under the carpet.

When his days as a serious scientist were behind him Newton had two new careers. One was his job as Master of the Mint, the institution that controlled the production of coin for the whole country. Part of this job was to prosecute counterfeiters. A successful prosecution usually meant the death sentence and Newton personally pursued counterfeiters to the gallows with chilling efficiency, with the same ruthless streak he showed when seeing off his scientific rivals. The other was as a very reticent MP for Cambridge University. He spoke in Parliament only once, to ask an usher to close a window to stop a draught.

## Total amnesia

The Yorkshire scientist Sir Neville Mott (1905–96), winner of the 1977 Nobel Prize for Physics, was incredibly absent-minded. Before taking up his post at Cambridge University, Mott spent some time as Professor of Physics at Bristol University. One day after visiting London Mott took the train back from Paddington to Bristol. Just as he was about to arrive, he remembered he was no longer Professor of Physics in Bristol, so he took the next train back to London and from there he caught the next train for Cambridge. Just before he arrived at Cambridge Mott remembered he had travelled up to

London by car. He took the next train back to London, found his car and drove to Cambridge. Just before he arrived, Mott finally remembered that he had been accompanied that morning by his wife.

## There was a crooked man

The name Robert Hooke (1635–1703) crops up regularly in the history of seventeenth-century scientific discovery. He was the first person to describe a cell in his book *Micrographia*, published in 1665. He was involved in everything from air pumps to anatomical dissections to cartography and scientific instrument making. As the first full-time Curator of Experiments for the Royal Society, at any given time you could find him attempting to grow moss on a dead man's skull (the new cure for epilepsy) or blowing bellows into the chest cavity of a live dog to find out how lungs worked, or giving lectures on such wide-ranging subjects as the birth of a dog with no mouth, the remedial properties of cow's urine and the penis of a possum, or the properties of a unicorn's horn. Hooke was much more than just a scientist, he was also the architect of some of London's greatest public buildings. In the years following the Great Fire he helped Christopher Wren rebuild the capital. Yet the only achievement you will find Hooke's name next to in textbooks as his alone is an obscure piece of relatively worthless information about the tension in a spring – Hooke's law of elasticity: 'The power of any spring is in the same proportion with the tension thereof.' Not much for a man now regarded as one of the great intellectual giants of his age.

Hooke was a very little man but he had a towering ego. He was also morbidly secretive, terrified that other scientists would try to steal the credit for his work. Secrecy wasn't unusual among scientists, but in Hooke it was an obsession. He was also in the habit of rubbing fellow scientists up the wrong way by taking credit for ideas that were not necessarily his own. For example, he claimed he invented a pocket watch accurate enough to be used by navigators, but never produced a single working prototype to back it up. This was the recurring pattern of Hooke's career, keeping his own ideas secret, then responding to the discoveries of other scientists by claiming that he had known about them for years. It led to a series of ugly clashes over priority. His biggest mistake was when he argued with the most powerful and the most vindictive man in the history of science, Isaac Newton, over the discovery of the principles of gravity and orbital motion. Hooke continued to press his charge of plagiarism against Newton for years, but he never got the acknowledgement he believed he was due. The rest of Hooke's career, and his life, were overshadowed by his row with Newton.

The second problem for Hooke's reputation was a uniquely scandalous private life. Hooke and his nemesis Newton were the oddest of bachelors, but unlike Newton, Hooke's single status was not out of choice. Even in his smartest periwig, he was not attractive to women. Physical deformities and scars were fairly commonplace at the time, but Hooke was an extreme case, judging by various unflattering contemporary accounts. He is described as 'dwarfish' with a 'twistedness which grew worse with age'. He was so odd-looking that people avoided him in the street or openly laughed. Newton's cruel barb, directed in a letter to Hooke sent on 5 February 1676 – 'If I have seen further it is by standing on the shoulders of giants' – was double-edged. Newton wasn't just mocking Hooke's intellectual pretensions; he was also mocking his disability.

Robert Hooke, however, did have a sex life, although not with the abundant supply of London prostitutes available at the time. Like Samuel Pepys, Hooke was a candid diarist and, like Pepys, his diaries record that he slept with all of his maids. Taking sexual advantage of your female employees was one thing; having sex with your niece, almost a third of your age, was another.

Hooke had a brother, John, who was a grocer on the Isle of Wight. In 1672, John Hooke hanged himself in a fit of depression over financial worries and his ten-year-old daughter Grace was sent up to London to live with her scientist uncle. Robert Hooke's position was that of guardian, but it is clear from his diary that from the outset he was sexually obsessed with his niece. He educated her, showered her with gifts and clothes and, when she reached sixteen, began sleeping with her. He flaunted the relationship and took her out on the town. When the troll-like scientist was seen out and about with a beautiful young girl on his arm, even though the age difference wasn't particularly disgusting by the standards of the day, it caused quite a commotion. Whatever the poor victim of Hooke's urges may have felt privately, she put up with the situation until her premature death from pneumonia in 1687, at the age of twenty-seven. Hooke was devastated by his niece's death and never fully recovered from it.

His peculiarities didn't stop there. Hooke was a hypochondriac and took various alarming self-medications, which he listed meticulously in his diary. There were purgatives, emetics, mercury, tobacco, spirit of wormwood (unfermented absinthe), laudanum and even steel filings. He became addicted to a variety of painkillers and, as the side effects of the drugs worsened, took even more dubious pharmaceutical remedies to dull the pain. In 1689, he delivered a lecture at the Royal Society on a new substance he had discovered, 'a certain plant which grows very common in India' – cannabis. Hooke particularly appreciated its aphrodisiac qualities. Hooke's self-medication took its toll and he became an emaciated wreck, plagued by severe dizzy spells, which he attributed to wearing a heavy wig, and bouts of depression, especially when he suspected that someone was trying to steal one of his ideas. He often complained of a poor memory, which he tried to improve by taking a small pinch of silver filings every now and then, but he never forgot about any of the perceived injustices he had suffered at the hand of Newton and others. As his health and productivity declined, Hooke became an aggressive, paranoid and miserly old crank. His relationships with other scientists, like that with Newton, deteriorated into bitter acrimony over petty priority disputes – such as with Christian Huygens, over the invention of the balance-spring watch. In spite of ill health he kept working, even though by now he had acquired a reputation as an inventor of useless and impractical gadgets and ideas – his suggestion that the day should be divided into twenty-nine hours, for example, or that cancer might be cured by smoking tobacco. In one of his final lectures to the Royal Society he announced that there were people living on the moon.

In his last years Hooke became extremely miserly. He never changed his clothes or washed and refused to spend money on soap. It was widely rumoured that he had actually starved his live-in maidservant to death. The forgotten man of science spent the final year of his life blind and bedridden, before dying alone and broke – or so it was assumed – believing to the last that he, not Newton, had discovered gravity. He was buried at St Helen, Bishopsgate, in an unmarked grave. After his death his executors discovered a treasure chest hidden in his cellar containing a fortune in money and precious stones.

## The reticent genius

One scientist who was uniquely undisturbed by the jealousies and petty arguments within his profession was the singularly peculiar Henry Cavendish (1731–1810). He was beyond doubt the most productive scientist of his generation and arguably one of the greatest who ever lived, but most of his groundbreaking achievements lay hidden in notebooks read by no one but Cavendish during his lifetime. Morbidly taciturn and pathologically reclusive, he was too shy to accept public acclaim or share his genius with the world.

Cavendish had no concept of the value of money in the way that only the seriously rich can. He was born into one of England's wealthiest and most distinguished families; both of his grandfathers were Dukes, respectively of Devonshire and of Kent. When his father Lord Charles Cavendish died in 1783, soon followed by the death of a wealthy, childless aunt, he inherited a substantial fortune. Instead of enjoying his wealth, he chose to live a solitary, frugal existence, working in obscurity in his laboratory in Clapham. His only luxuries were books and laboratory equipment. He refused to discuss money with anyone, as his banker discovered when he made the mistake of asking him what he intended doing with the fortune left to him. Cavendish threatened to remove the whole lot from the bank if he ever bothered him about financial matters again.

He once went to a christening and when told that it was customary to give the nurse a tip on the way out, he dipped into his pocket and gave her a handful of gold sovereigns. On another occasion he was invited to make a contribution for a sick employee on his estate, and chipped in with a staggering £10,000. The only thing Cavendish cared about was the fact that vast inherited wealth gave him free time to pursue a wide variety of scientific interests.

His research spanned chemistry, mechanics, magnetism, optics and geology and he made a series of remarkable discoveries, including the chemical composition of air and water. He invented several astronomical instruments and anticipated Einstein by 120 years in calculating the effect of gravitation on light rays. He pioneered work with condensers and measured the strength of electrical currents, discovering the rules of electrical resistance more than half a century before they were quantified by the German scientist Ohm. Cavendish only ever published a fraction of the experimental evidence he had available to support his theories, to the confusion of fellow scientists, who often found him referring in his papers to experiments he had yet to tell anyone about. His most astonishing achievement was made at the age of sixty-seven, when most scientists were either past their best or had long since retired. From an outbuilding of his home near Clapham Common, he weighed the Earth. By setting up a very simple experiment using a 40-inch rod suspended horizontally from a wire, with a lead sphere fixed at each end, he calculated that the planet had a mass of 6.6 million, million, million tons. His figure was so accurate that it has hardly been altered to this day.

Most of the time Cavendish never left his house. It was only when he was tempted out for the sake of science to attend Royal Society meetings that his eccentricities became apparent to the world. He never sat for a portrait; the only existing likeness of him, sketched secretly from a distance, shows a tall, gaunt, shabby figure in an old-fashioned faded violet velvet frock coat and a three-cornered cocked hat, items of clothing that had been out of date for at least half a century. He owned one suit at a time, wearing it continuously until it fell apart, and only then replacing it with another identical one. He spoke with a shrill voice and a slight stammer, and was terrified of any kind of social interaction. All his fellow scientists were ever able to squeeze out of him was a word or two on technical matters if they were lucky; according to Lord Brougham, Cavendish 'uttered fewer words in the course of his life than any man who ever lived to fourscore years, not at all excepting Trappist monks'. If a stranger came near him he would emit a high-pitched squeak and flee like a frightened animal. New Royal Society members were advised to talk to Cavendish without looking at him. An Austrian visitor once broke the rule and introduced himself; he had travelled all the way from Vienna, he informed the mortified scientist, in the hope of conversing with 'one of the most illustrious philosophers of the age'. Cavendish fled ashen-faced and squeaking from the building and jumped in a cab.

Cavendish was a lifelong bachelor. In fact he was so allergic to women that he couldn't bring himself to talk to or even look at a female. His maids were only tolerated so long as they followed his instruction to keep completely out of his sight on pain of dismissal. At mealtimes he communicated with female staff by leaving notes on the hall table; as he nearly always only ate leg of mutton, the notes were brief. He once accidentally bumped into a housemaid on the stairs and was so upset by the incident that he immediately ordered the construction of a rear servants-only staircase to ensure it could never happen again.

Even as Cavendish lay dying, aged seventy-eight, he couldn't bear the idea of company, and told his manservant that he had something to think about and didn't want to be disturbed. When he returned Cavendish was dead. The bulk of his estate went to his nephew George, who had no idea how much his inheritance was worth, having only ever been granted an annual audience of half an hour with his uncle in his entire life. He was staggered to find that he was now the largest single holder of bank shares in Britain, the owner of a neglected fortune that had grown, unattended, to a value of £1,750,000. It was many years later that the true value of Cavendish's contribution to science became known, by which time much of his research had been wrongly attributed to others.

## The walking thermos flask

Through history some scientists have been so taxed by the business of thinking that they have had to take extreme measures to preserve their health. The most determinedly hypochondriac of them all was the chemist Richard Kirwan (1733–1812), known as 'the Philosopher of Dublin'. Kirwan was a prolific experimenter and made important contributions to mineralogy, meteorology and climatology, including pioneering work in systems for forecasting the weather, many of which are in use to this day. He is also slightly more famous for making one of the most peculiar contributions to eighteenth-century chemistry, as a keen supporter of a theory of combustion based on a mysterious element called phlogiston. His *Essay on Phlogiston*, published to wide acclaim in 1787, was the first general theory of chemistry that appeared to make sense of a wide range of phenomena. When it was translated into French by the wife of the scientist Lavoisier, her husband read it and realized that Kirwan had got it completely wrong; burning was caused by the presence of oxygen and Lavoisier could prove it. When he was shown the evidence Kirwan reluctantly acknowledged his embarrassing mistake, but then lost interest in science and retired to No. 6 Cavendish Row, Dublin, where he spent his time reading the Bible and publishing a series of very odd papers, including one in which he attempted to prove that mankind's first language was ancient Greek. The full and rich variety of Kirwan's eccentricities, however, was only apparent to a chosen few.

Kirwan suffered from the rare throat disorder dysphagia – a chronic difficulty in swallowing. Every time he tried to eat, his efforts were accompanied by violent facial contortions, painful for Kirwan and unsettling for anyone looking on. He was therefore understandably reluctant to eat in company and always dined alone, whether it was in his own home or when he was visiting friends. When he did eat he existed almost exclusively on a diet of ham and milk. The ham was cooked on a Sunday, then reheated and served throughout the rest of the week.

Kirwan was chiefly obsessed with avoiding catching a chill. He kept a blazing fire in his living room all year round and always wore his overcoat indoors. He thought that the body could store heat, like a large thermos flask. He also wore an enormous wide-brimmed hat to prevent heat from escaping through his head. Kirwan shared his home, and eventually, his grave, with a long-suffering manservant called Pope. He was required to sleep in the scientist's bedroom and had instructions to wake his employer every couple of hours and pour hot tea down his throat. The point of this nocturnal tea drinking was to maintain Kirwan's body temperature through the night. There were frequent accidents when Pope 'accidentally' missed his target and poured scalding hot tea in his employer's eyes and nose.

Kirwan also suffered from pteronarcophobia – a fear of flies. He paid Pope a small bounty for every dozen flies he killed. He was, however, fond of big dogs, and kept six large Irish wolfhounds, which he occasionally braved the elements to walk. Before he went out, Kirwan would sit for an hour in front of his blistering fire to absorb the heat. Once outside, the tall, gaunt scientist could be seen loping briskly, with his mouth tightly shut so that no body heat would escape, swathed from head to foot in his huge coat and enormous hat. He also kept a tame pet eagle, which always sat on his shoulder, until a friend who saw it swoop down on Kirwan feared the worst and shot it by mistake.

In spite of Kirwan's neuroses, his home was a regular meeting place for fellow academics and rich acquaintances, whom he received every Thursday and Friday, prone on his couch in front of a roaring fire. There were very strict rules for visitors. The soirées always began promptly at six o'clock and ended at nine o'clock. To ensure that no one arrived or left late he removed the door knocker after the party had begun. Any guest who hadn't taken the hint by nine o'clock was escorted to the door by their pyjama-clad host. Ironically, Kirwan caught a cold in 1812 and died from complications, aged seventy-nine.

## Spaced odyssey

The chemist Thomas Beddoes (1760–1808) was famous for his experiments with newly discovered gases known as 'factitious airs'. He speculated that certain gases such as methane or hydrogen had great therapeutic qualities. Beddoes tested his theory by piping methane gas into a room full of tuberculosis patients; the other end of the pipe was connected to some flatulent cows on a nearby lawn. Fortunately, he was unable to repeat the trick with hydrogen.

At the cutting edge of some of Beddoes's more questionable research was his nineteen-year-old assistant, Humphrey Davy (1778–1829), inventor of the miner's lamp. Beddoes once persuaded Davy to inhale carbon monoxide, with near-fatal consequences. Davy only avoided slipping into a lethal sleep because he dropped the inhaler mouthpiece before collapsing. In 1799, Beddoes got his young assistant to inhale about 32 pints of laughing gas from a used sick bag. Davy recorded that it made him 'dance about the laboratory as madman, and has kept my spirits aglow ever since'. He himself began to inhale nitrous oxide on a recreational basis with friends, including the poets Robert Southey and Samuel Coleridge, and eventually became an addict. He wondered if he could boost the effects of nitrous abuse by binge-drinking wine as a supplement. On Boxing Day 1799, he wrote:

> I drank a bottle of wine in large draughts in less than eight minutes. Whilst I was drinking, I perceived a sense of fullness in the head and throbbing of the arteries, not unanalogous to that produced in the first stage of nitrous oxide excitement. After I had finished the bottle, this fullness increased, the objects around me became dazzling, the power of distinct articulation was lost, and I was unable to walk steadily. At this moment the sensations were rather pleasurable than otherwise, the sense of fullness in the head soon however increased so as to become painful, and in less than an hour I sunk into a state of insensibility. In this situation I must have remained for two hours or two hours and a half.

While completely off his head on nitrous oxide Davy discovered that his experience relieved the pain from a troublesome wisdom tooth, but he never got around to putting his discovery into practical use. Consequently, nitrous oxide would remain unused as an anaesthetic for almost half a century.

Davy was a keen angler and thought he could baffle his quarry by disguising himself as a form of natural greenery by wearing a green coat, green trousers and a green hat. When he went shooting, however, he did exactly the opposite. Not trusting the marksmanship of his fellow sportsmen, he made himself as conspicuous as possible to avoid being shot by mistake, by wearing brightly coloured clothing and a huge wide-rimmed red hat.

## The man who hated buskers

In the Royal College of Surgeons' Hunterian Museum, just behind the Royal Courts of Justice in Lincoln's Inn Fields, London, in a glass case not far from Winston Churchill's false teeth, is an alcohol-filled jar containing the bifurcated brain of Charles Babbage (1791–1871), the man known as 'the father of modern computing'.

Babbage was the quintessential Victorian polymath. He dabbled in half a dozen sciences and published widely on a wide range of topics, from deciphering weather patterns in tree rings to designing railway tunnels and stomach pumps. He was the brains behind black box recorders, railway cowcatchers and skeleton keys, and he more or less invented the Victorian postal system, the flat rate 'penny post', plus countless other schemes that never made it off the drawing board. There was nothing Babbage wasn't prepared to put his mind to. He had himself lowered into Mt Vesuvius so he could closely observe volcanic activity and once allowed himself to be baked in an oven at 265°F for 'five or six minutes without any great discomfort', meanwhile taking notes on his pulse and the quantity of his perspiration. He once invented a pair of shoes for walking on water, but when he tried out his miracle footwear on, or more precisely in, the River Dart in Devon, he nearly drowned.

Above all, Babbage was obsessed with facts, data and statistics. He spent years studying death rates and was very irritated when he read these lines from Alfred Tennyson's poem *The Vision of Sin*:

*Every moment dies a man,*
*Every moment one is born.*

He wrote to Tennyson with a correction to his poem: 'I suggest that in the next edition of your poem you have it read – "Every moment dies a man, Every moment one and a sixteenth is born."' Another Babbage enterprise was to work out the statistical probability of the biblical miracles. He calculated that the chances of a man rising from the dead were 1 in $10^{12}$ – a figure he arrived at by dividing the estimated total number of people who had ever lived, by the number of witnessed accounts of someone being brought back from the dead – i.e. one.

In spite of Babbage's tendency to oddness, no one doubted that he was a visionary and utterly brilliant. And, despite the odd commercial failure, he was also very wealthy. Or at least he was until he sank his personal fortune into his dream of building a giant calculating machine.

It started in 1820, when Babbage was invited by the newly formed Astronomical Society to work on a series of tables, the accuracy of which was particularly important for navigators; one mistake could mean life or death for a seafarer.

Babbage was angered by the discovery that the existing tables of computations included far too many human errors. It would be an understatement to say that tables of mathematical calculations were a Babbage obsession. He was a connoisseur and collector of tables. He owned a private collection of tables running to more than 300 volumes. He even studied the ergonomics of table reading. His idea of a quiet evening in was to draw up tables with various different coloured papers and inks to find out which combination caused the least stress to the reader; just to make sure he had every option covered, he tested green ink on several different shades of green paper. He wrote a letter to the president of the Society describing his plan for a giant steam-driven calculating machine; he called it the Difference Engine. In 1822, he demonstrated a small working model of his device to the Royal Society, who were so impressed they awarded him their very first gold medal. A year later Babbage persuaded the government to give him a grant to build his invention. Unfortunately, he never got anywhere near completing his giant mechanical calculator, his efforts confounded by a lifetime of personal conflict, political confrontations and bizarre vendettas.

To begin with Babbage had completely underestimated the costs involved in building his calculating machine. The apparatus he envisaged was way beyond the limit of nineteenth-century skill and machinery. Most of the precision machine tools needed to shape the wheels, gears and cranks of his engine did not exist, and Babbage and his craftsmen would have to make them. In fact, as no minutes were ever made of his initial meeting with the government, no one could agree how much it was supposed to cost in the first place. With no agreed budget and no delivery date, work on the machine wore on unsuccessfully for years.

The biggest problem was Babbage himself. He got involved in a number of pointless public feuds and wasted his time firing off abusive letters written in green ink on yellow paper at various targets, including publishers of mathematical tables, lambasting them for obscure inaccuracies he had uncovered. The scientific establishment was a favourite subject for his invective. He unleashed a series of highly personal broadsides against leading Royal Society members, including one accusing the great Sir Humphrey Davy of fraud. They were not the only important people to feel the rough edge of Babbage's tongue. He also published a pamphlet called *A Word to the Wise*, a savage attack on the hereditary system of privilege titles, denouncing the British aristocracy as wholly corrupt. As Babbage was hoping for backing for his calculating machine from a government whose membership was still largely drawn from the aristocracy, it was not the best career move.

In the 1830s, Babbage tried his hand at politics, twice, as a Whig parliamentary candidate for the borough of Finsbury, but his efforts at the hustings were a disaster. During both campaigns he was heckled with questions about the public financing of his calculating machine, a touchy subject guaranteed to set him off on a purple-faced rant. As a consequence his speeches were almost completely incoherent. After humiliating defeats in both campaigns he surrendered all further political ambition. He did, however, make one memorable political contribution, the notorious Babbage's Act. He had a bee in his bonnet about street buskers, especially the ones that had sprung up in the area surrounding his London home. He calculated that 25 per cent of his working life had been ruined by buskers, a point he made in regular letters to *The Times*. His campaign and the subsequent enforcement of his Act, which all but banned street entertainers, earned him a great deal of public mockery and the hatred of the London mob. The capital's organ grinders retaliated by serenading under Babbage's window en masse. For the rest of his life he was tormented by an unending parade of buskers and he was followed on the streets everywhere he went by crowds of children who pelted him with missiles, including one dead cat.

Meanwhile, work on Babbage's calculating machine wore on. Each stage of construction posed a new set of technical problems, each requiring a succession of brilliant innovations in mechanical engineering. His original plan was enlarged into a machine of around 25,000 parts. Ten years after the project was first announced, all he had to show for it was one small working section. The government's financial obligations to Babbage's Difference Engine remained unresolved and he was having to pay for the project out of his own pocket. He fell out regularly with his engineer, Joseph Clement, who by all accounts could match Babbage for stubbornness. In March 1833, Clement submitted a bill and Babbage refused to pay, telling him to send it to the Treasury instead. When the Treasury rejected it as 'unreasonable and inadmissible', Clement downed tools. Work on the Difference Engine stopped, never to resume again. By this time costs had spiralled to an astonishing £17,500 – enough to build a couple of battleships. By way of comparison, Robert Stephenson's recently built steam locomotive 'John Bull', commissioned by the United States, had been constructed at fraction of the cost – £785.

Babbage couldn't stop tinkering with his design. Every time it looked as if one means of constructing his device might actually work, he thought of a new and better way of doing it. Every room in his house was filled with abandoned models of his engine. By 1840, he was already committed to an even more ambitious project, the Analytical Engine, a quicker, more advanced machine that could be programmed with punch cards to do computations and store data. Babbage wanted to tell the government all about his exciting Analytical Engine, but they didn't want to hear about an expensive new project. They were already quite sick of the old one; it would be cheaper to build a new navy. It didn't help matters either that he was in the habit of pestering the Prime Minister Sir Robert Peel with letters on the subject of money he thought was owed to him. This was the era known as 'the hungry forties' when some feared the country was actually teetering on the brink of revolution, so the last thing on Peel's mind was the solvency of an obdurate West Country mathematician with a plan for producing steam-driven multiplication tables.

In November 1842, Peel did, however, finally agree to meet Babbage, who was warned in advance not to push his luck; the Prime Minister was in no mood to be lectured. Once again Babbage couldn't resist pushing the self-destruct button and harangued Peel about the government's responsibility for his work. The meeting terminated abruptly with Babbage storming out in a huff. Within days the government, weary of delays and of Babbage's crankiness, gave up on the whole project. Peel offered Babbage a knighthood by way of compensation and in recognition of his work. Babbage refused – anyone could get a knighthood, and he, the most important scientific figure of the age, would only settle for a life peerage. It was never granted.

As his calculating machine schemes ran into the sand, Babbage embarked on increasingly desperate money-making schemes to revive them. He invented a method for mathematically predicting the outcome of handicapped horse races and received hundreds of letters from race-goers who wanted to know more, but unfortunately turned out to be a disastrous tipster. His friend Ada Lovelace, daughter of the poet Lord Byron, took his advice and was almost ruined by gambling debts. Mocked by his critics and abused by the London mob, Babbage became a reclusive misanthrope, spending his final years writing books of varying degrees of eccentricity, including his autobiography, *Passages from the Life of a Philosopher* – largely a rant about his pet hates, especially street buskers. Babbage's wife Georgina is not mentioned at all and there is just a single oblique reference to 1827, the year four members of his immediate family died. He was alone and embittered, suffering from severe headaches and hallucinations. Babbage's biographer Bowden recorded: 'He spoke as if he hated mankind in general, Englishmen in particular, and the English Government and organ grinders most of all.' He died in 1871, two months before his eightieth birthday, his groundbreaking work on computers hidden under a dustsheet in King's College. As Babbage lay on his deathbed, London's buskers played mercilessly on outside his bedroom window.

## The frying game

Public demonstrations of electricity were all the rage in the early nineteenth century. For the inventor, a virtuoso performance was important to attract investors and to give himself and his product a public image. One of the greatest electrical showmen of the age was the British chemist Stephen Gray (1666–1736). Gray was the first person to demonstrate that electricity could flow. He made his point at a Royal Society lecture by taking a boy from the local orphanage, then stringing him up with insulating cords and electrifying him by rubbing him against a glass tube, drawing sparks from the boy's nose.

Similarly disturbing was the work of the Irish priest–physicist Nicholas Joseph Callan (1799–1864), inventor of the induction coil. Hampered by the lack of available instrumentation with which to measure the strength of current or voltage, the ever-resourceful Callan used his students instead. His victims included Charles Russell, later President of Maynooth College, who was put into hospital after receiving several jolts of electricity, and William Walsh, who was knocked unconscious but recovered and later became Archbishop of Dublin. After the mishap with Walsh, Callan was banned from frying junior establishment figures and confined to electrocuting live chickens.

## Darwin's nose

When Charles Darwin (1809–82) returned home from the Galapagos Islands on board the HMS *Beagle* in 1836, the first thing on his mind was not great evolutionary theory. He immediately drew up lists of the benefits and drawbacks of marriage. On the plus side, a wife was 'a constant companion in old age . . . better than a dog'; on the minus side, 'terrible loss of time . . . cannot read in the evenings . . . less money for books'. In the end he settled in favour of matrimony. After a brief and pallid courtship, he married his own first cousin, Emma. It was an odd choice considering that Darwin was the first person ever to elucidate on the dangers of inbreeding. There were also signs of eccentricity on both sides of a family that was, even by the standards of the English upper classes, already considerably inbred.

Throughout the courtship he made notes as though it was some sort of field trip. He recorded that 'sexual desire makes saliva flow' and, when he saw Emma blush, noted 'blood to surface exposed, face of man . . . bosom in woman; like erection'. After the successful wooing of Emma, he noted that the female chooses 'not the male which is most attractive to her, but the one which is least distasteful'. How could she resist?

At first the course of true love did not run smoothly for the newlyweds. Only a year after his return to England, when he was barely out of his twenties, he fell ill with a succession of mysterious illnesses, resulting in boils, flatulence, bouts of vomiting, diarrhoea, headaches and fainting fits, any of which would cause him to withdraw to his sickbed for months on end. He tried every type of quackery available. There were faddish diets, including going for months without sugar, salt, bacon or alcohol. He tried lemon sucking, sipping acid, applying vinegar to his neck, ice-cold baths and cold-water douches. He was wrapped in blankets and heated with a spirit lamp to make him sweat. There was also more technical quackery, involving tying heavy batteries to his stomach and electric chains around his neck. Nothing he did made much difference and for the next forty years the once vigorous young adventurer lived the life of a semi-invalid.

Over the years various authorities have attributed Darwin's mysterious illnesses to tropical infection caught on board the *Beagle*, arsenic poisoning, a bite from a poisonous insect, dyspepsia, 'suppressed gout', ulcers, epilepsy, inner ear disorder and gall-bladder disease, to mention but a few. He always seemed to experience the most severe bouts of illness whenever controversy reared its ugly head. In 1871, for example, when someone published an attack on his book *The Descent of Man* it triggered another two months of Darwinian bed-rest. Whatever the cause of Darwin's health problems, they were also a convenient excuse for him to stay at home and avoid unwanted responsibilities, such as defending his highly controversial theories about natural selection at public debates, for example. It also left him with plenty of time on his hands to pursue his biggest obsession: earthworms.

Although *On the Origin of Species*, published in 1859, was the best-known work of Darwin's professional life, his best-selling book in his lifetime was a volume about the habits of earthworms. Darwin counted the number of earthworms in his garden and arrived at a figure of 53,767 per acre. Then he piled thousands of them onto his billiard table. Nothing exceptionally odd about that, you might think. Except that he then decided to study what happened when he blew tobacco smoke at them, or when his son played a bassoon at them. This is an excerpt from Darwin's much-neglected classic, *The Formation of Vegetable Mould Through the Action of Worms with Observations of their Habits*:

> Worms do not possess any sense of hearing. They took not the least notice of the shrill notes from a metal whistle, which was repeatedly sounded near them; nor did they of the deepest and loudest tones of a bassoon. They were indifferent to shouts, if care was taken that the breath did not strike them. When placed on a table close to the keys of a piano, which was played as loudly as possible, they remained perfectly quiet. Although they are indifferent to undulations in the air audible by us, they are extremely sensitive to vibrations in any solid object. When the pots containing two worms, which had remained quite indifferent to the sound of the piano, were placed on this instrument, and the note C in the bass clef was struck, both instantly retreated into their burrows. After a time

> they emerged, and when G above the line in the treble clef was struck they again retreated. Under similar circumstances on another night one worm dashed into its burrow on a very high note being struck only once, and the other worm when C in the treble clef was struck.

Later Darwin tried a similar experiment, only this time he played a bassoon to his plants; he noted that they were deaf also.

The man who sailed Darwin around the world, Robert FitzRoy (1805–1865), captain of the *Beagle*, was also, it is now generally forgotten, a character of some scientific importance in his own right. FitzRoy was an aristocrat, a direct descendant of the first Duke of Grafton, who was an illegitimate son of Charles II. The third Duke of Grafton, FitzRoy's grandfather, was Prime Minister. Robert FitzRoy was a fifth-generation Grafton, born in 1805, the year of Nelson's death at the Battle of Trafalgar. He was a brilliant if temperamental naval cadet. There was an early test of his seamanship during one of his very first postings on the survey ship *Beagle*, under the command of Captain Pringle Stokes, who was charting the South American coastline. While off Tierra del Fuego, Stokes shot himself in the head, having been suffering from depression. It took twelve days for him to die. FitzRoy steered the ship back to Rio, where he assumed full-time command of the *Beagle* at the age of twenty-three.

In 1831, FitzRoy was assigned to carry out a three-year survey of coastal South America. Having already spent a couple of years on a similar survey with his suicidal predecessor, FitzRoy was wary of the feeling of isolation that such a command could bring. He was also uncomfortably aware of a tendency towards depression and suicide in his own family. His uncle, the statesman Lord Castlereagh, had slit his throat when FitzRoy was fifteen. It made an impression on the boy that he never forgot. The solution, FitzRoy decided, was to take with him some 'gentleman company', someone who could share the captain's table and engage him in intellectual discourse. The young naturalist Charles Darwin seemed to fit the bill. At their first meeting, however, Robert FitzRoy had doubts on account of Darwin's nose. FitzRoy's studies of physiognomy told him that 'people with a broad, squat nose like his don't have the character'. Not that Darwin was particularly qualified, either, for a journey halfway round the world; the longest field trip he had been on up until then was three weeks spent in North Wales collecting insects. FitzRoy's initial reservations about nose shape, however, were outweighed by the fact that the twenty-two-year-old amateur naturalist had also studied divinity. FitzRoy was deeply religious and a fervent believer in the literal truth of the biblical account of Creation. Darwin, FitzRoy thought, would be useful in helping him find data that would reveal God's work. Never in history has an appointment backfired so spectacularly.

FitzRoy had another motive for wanting to go back to South America. On his previous trip to Tierra del Fuego, straying some way beyond his Admiralty brief, he had 'kidnapped' four natives and taken them back to England. His plan was to introduce them to the 'benefit of our habits and language', before returning them to Tierra del Fuego as missionaries.

FitzRoy's great social experiment quickly turned to disaster. Of the four Feugans, one was killed by his smallpox vaccination; the others, York Minster, a twenty-seven-year-old, Jemmy Button, aged fourteen, and Fuego Basket, an eight-year-old girl, were sent to a school in Walthamstow where they were taught English, arithmetic and 'the basic truths of Christianity'. To the deep embarrassment of all concerned, the hulking York Minster fastened his sexual attentions on Fuego Basket. FitzRoy hastily used his powerful family connections to persuade the Admiralty to let him return his Feugans to their native land. They also took with them a few items FitzRoy thought necessary to recreate a piece of England on the wild coast of South America, including chamber pots, tea trays, crockery, beaver hats and white linen.

The *Beagle* was a ten-gun brig of the sort known in the Royal Navy as 'coffins' for their tendency to capsize in heavy weather. Fortunately, FitzRoy was an extraordinary navigator. Despite negotiating some of the most dangerous waters of the world, surviving storms, earthquakes, disease and encounters with hostile natives, the aristocratic young sea captain completed his mission with his ship and most of its crew intact.

Darwin, meanwhile, suffered dreadfully from seasickness, but this was the least of his problems. The man he had to share his meals with three times a day in a tiny cabin was highly unpredictable. FitzRoy had a short fuse and a foul temper, which led to explosive rages, alternating with bouts of deep depression. The two men had terrible rows, according to Darwin, 'bordering on insanity'. In a personal letter home he noted that 'some part of FitzRoy's brain wants mending'. At one point FitzRoy stopped eating and shut himself away for several weeks. He eventually emerged, thin and haggard, and offered his resignation. He told the crew he was suffering from an inherited mental disorder and feared he was going to go the same way as his uncle and his predecessor, Captain Stokes. At this point it seemed that the voyage would have to be cut short. Luckily for science, FitzRoy's loyal second-in-command, Lieutenant Wickham, was able to talk his captain round and to continue the mission.

Following the *Beagle*'s return, it was Robert FitzRoy, not Darwin, who won the initial plaudits. He wrote up his account of this voyage, including masses of detailed weather observations, and was awarded a gold medal by the Royal Geographical Society. In spite of their differences, FitzRoy had been won over by Darwin's charm and they became friends and remained in contact for many years. Darwin was most surprised, therefore, shortly after they got back, by the news that FitzRoy was about to marry a woman to whom he had been engaged for quite some time. FitzRoy had never once spoken a word about his engagement, or his intended bride, Mary, throughout the five-year voyage.

FitzRoy then entered Parliament, serving for two years as Tory MP for Durham. His temper got the better of him and almost resulted in a duel with another Tory candidate – in the end they settled instead for a fist fight in the Mall. In 1843, FitzRoy's life took another unexpected turn when he accepted the position of Governor of New Zealand.

Unfortunately, his tenure as governor was a disaster. His unpredictable mood swings and fanatical sense of religious duty made him deeply unpopular and the Colonial Office swiftly recalled him less than two years later without offering him the customary knighthood. He returned to his naval duties but another bout of morbid depression forced him into retirement.

FitzRoy would probably have remained a footnote in history as the captain of the *Beagle* if the Admiralty had not turned to him for help in 1854. The urgent need for a system for predicting storms at sea was underlined when the passenger ship *Royal Charter* was destroyed by a violent gale off the coast of Anglesey with the loss of 450 lives. The Admiralty asked Fitzroy to investigate the effect of the weather on the British fleet. He immediately set about making weather maps on which he plotted wind, barometric pressure and temperature using symbols to denote clouds, rain and snow. He made the first use of conical storm symbols – the standard gale warning still in use today – and coined the term 'forecast'. Until FitzRoy came along, the weather had only ever been presented retrospectively. *The Times*, for example, would print a report of how the weather had been across Great Britain the previous day. Thanks to FitzRoy's weather maps, on 1 August 1861 *Times* readers could actually read what the weather was going to do over the next two days, based on predictions of the Royal Society's meteorological department. Queen Victoria got into the habit of consulting FitzRoy personally as to when she should make the short boat trip across the Solent to her residence on the Isle of Wight.

In FitzRoy's mind, however, dark clouds were gathering. Marriage had marked a hardening in his religious beliefs, because his new wife Mary was even more zealous than he was. He blamed himself for allowing Darwin to be his personal guest aboard the *Beagle* and, consequently, for the heresy of evolutionary theory. After the publication of *On the Origin of Species* he became a rabid opponent of Darwin and wrote letters to *The Times* explaining that giant animals such as the mastodon had not survived the biblical flood because they were too big to get into Noah's Ark.

Seven months after the publication of *On the Origin of Species*, on Saturday 30 June 1860, science and religion went head-to-head when Darwin's theory was debated at a famous meeting of the British Association for the Advancement of Science at Oxford. Darwin was missing (he was ill again) and was represented by Thomas Huxley and Joseph Hooker. More than a thousand people crowded into the chamber to hear stinging attacks from both sides. According to reports, in the ensuing commotion Lady Brewster fainted and had to be carried out. Meanwhile Robert FitzRoy, who was attending the meeting to present his own paper on weather patterns, walked around the hall brandishing a huge copy of the Bible above his head, shouting, 'The truth is in here!' He was escorted from the building.

FitzRoy was tormented to the end of his days by his misguided decision to take Darwin on board the *Beagle*. To compound his misery, the British public was also largely unappreciative of his pioneering work in meteorology. Almost as soon as his first weather forecasts were made, people began to complain that they were wrong. The newspapers took to printing disclaimers denying responsibility for incorrect weather forecasts. *The Times* apologized to its readers: 'During the last week Nature seems to have taken special pleasure in confounding the conjectures of science.' Questions were asked in Parliament. The strain of criticism became too much for FitzRoy. On the morning of 30 April 1865, he got up early without waking his wife, locked himself in his dressing room and slashed his throat with a razor.

## A well-bred man

Unlike his lazy cousin Charles Darwin, Francis Galton (1822–1911) was an infant prodigy. He could recite the alphabet at eighteen months, was reading Latin at four and knew the *Iliad* and *Odyssey* back to front at the age of six. His IQ was estimated at 200, the highest ever recorded. He grew up to become the ultimate in gentlemanly scientific dilettantism; if it was there to be dabbled in, Galton dabbled in it. He was mathematician, meteorologist, experimental psychologist, anthropologist, inventor and geneticist. He explored unknown regions of Africa, wrote seminal papers on blood transfusions, perfected a form of calculus, deciphered weather patterns, more or less invented modern forensic science and was knighted for his work in applied statistics. The range of his scientific curiosity was astonishing.

Galton's father wanted him to pursue a career in medicine, as his grandfather Erasmus Darwin had, so he was sent to train at a hospital. He proved not to be exactly your average medical student. At the age of sixteen he was using blood to shave the heads of patients injured in brawls because he found it gave a better lather than soap. Given the run of the dispensary, he tried to work his way through the pharmaceutical A–Z by ingesting every drug he could find in alphabetical order; fortunately for Galton, the dispensary was right out of arsenic. His curiosity was sated at the letter C, when castor oil did its predictable best. Galton shortly afterwards packed in medicine because he couldn't bear the screams of unanaesthetized patients, and went to Cambridge to study maths instead. In his third year at university he suffered a nervous breakdown through overwork and collapsed in a fit on the floor. He thought it was the result of 'an overheated cranium'. To keep his head cool and prevent further fits, he invented a self-ventilating top hat with hinged lid that could be raised and lowered by squeezing a rubber bulb.

The death of his banker father endowed Galton at the age of twenty-two with a substantial inheritance, enough for him to drop out of university. In 1845, he went to Africa with a couple of wealthy pals to shoot the local wildlife. Unfortunately, Galton was such a poor shot that he couldn't hit a hippopotamus at close range, despite using hundreds of rounds of ammunition. Embarrassed by his failure he practised, at the expense of the lives of thousands of game birds, until he was able to shoot (and eat) a giraffe. Somewhere along the way he also experienced a casual sexual encounter that left him with such a dire dose of venereal disease that it dampened his ardour for several decades to come.

It didn't put him off travelling though. In 1850, Galton set sail for southern Africa, after stopping by a costume shop in Drury Lane to buy a theatrical crown, which he planned to place 'on the head of the greatest or most distant potentate I should meet with'. Battling against searing heat and marauding lions, he ventured into parts of the African interior never before seen by a European. To assist him on his journey through Damaraland he employed native guides, but was frustrated by their inability to tell him how long it would take to get anywhere, despite the odd whipping, because the Damarans could count no higher than three. Galton noted with some irritation, however, that they had more than a thousand words to describe the markings on cattle. Later, after encountering some voluptuous Hottentot tribeswomen he turned his analytical mind to the measurement of black African ladies' breasts. Quite what the buxom natives made of Galton, as he whipped out his sextant and measuring tape, we will never know because, as the scientist confessed in his full account of the expedition, 'I did not know a word of Hottentot and could never therefore have explained to the lady what the object of my footrule could be, and I really dared not ask my worthy missionary host to interpret for me.'

He pressed on to Ovamboland, where a misunderstanding with a tribal chief, King Nangoro, resulted in Galton's accidental betrothal to the king's daughter, Princess Chipanga. Nangoro was so pleased with Galton's gift of a fake stage crown that he despatched his daughter to his guest's tent for her honeymoon wearing nothing but red ochre and butter. Galton, who was wearing his only clean white linen suit, saw the naked princess and realized with horror that 'she was as capable of leaving a mark on anything she touched as a well-inked printer's roller . . . so I had her ejected with scant ceremony'.

When Galton returned to London the story of his thousand-mile journey through the bush, grippingly told before the Royal Geographical Society, earned him overnight celebrity. He followed up with a 366-page book, *The Art of Travel.* It was packed with such useful tips as how to stay afloat by using an inflated antelope skin; how to keep your clothes dry in a rainstorm (take them off and sit on them, in case you were wondering); how to avoid blisters (break a raw egg into each boot and fill your socks with soapsuds); how to get rid of lice (make yourself a necklace out of mercury, old tea leaves and saliva); and how to prevent your teeth from falling out if you catch scurvy (spread treacle and lime juice on your gums). In a chapter titled 'Revolting Food that May Save the Lives of Men', Galton advises that 'bones contain a great deal of nourishment which is got at by boiling them, pounding their ends between two sticks, and sucking them'. He tells us what to do in the event of shipwreck: 'A half-drowned man must be put to bed in dry, heated clothes . . . All rough treatment is not only ridiculous but full of harm.' Galton's book was a tour de force of Victorian political correctness. In a section on 'The Management of Savages' he notes: 'If a savage does mischief, look at him as you would a kicking mule, or a wild animal whose nature it is to be unruly and vicious, and keep your temper quite unruffled . . . a savage cannot endure the steady labour that we Anglo-Saxons have been bred to support. His nature is adapted to alternatives of laziness and severe exertion . . . a skulking negro may sometimes be smelt out like a fox.' A critic reviewing *Art of Travel* complained that it contained few tips useful to the casual tourist on a tour up the Rhine or a visit to Paris, but it might come in useful 'if you were marching through the interior of Africa where the wanderer may have to catch a wild boar for dinner in a pitfall and then boil it in its own skin'. *Art of Travel* was a best-seller, reprinted seven times and became standard reading for the British Army.

Galton was an inveterate inventor of cranky devices known as 'Galton's toys'. His bicycle speedometer required the cyclist to measure the diameter of his wheels and count and time their revolutions with a hand-held hourglass as he rode. It didn't catch on; nor did his submarine spectacles, designed to allow people to read a newspaper underwater – Galton nearly drowned while testing them in the bath. Another reading aid, Galton's Gumption Reviver, was designed to keep people awake during long periods of study. It comprised a jar fitted with a stopcock on top of a tall stand that dripped cold water onto the reader's head at regular intervals. Yet another that never got off the ground, literally, was his steam-driven flying machine. Prompted by a near-approach of the planet Mars to Earth, he also devised a celestial signalling system to permit communication with Martians. Less ambitiously, there was the Galton Whistle, a device that could produce very high-pitched notes designed to test for human and animal sensitivity to sound. It was hidden inside a hollow walking stick and operated by squeezing a rubber bulb on the handle. His modus operandi was to walk down the street with his stick and point it an unsuspecting passer-by. If he got a reaction, he knew they had heard it. On a trip through Regent's Park he acquired little useful data, although he managed to annoy some lions. Further afield, Galton noted: 'At Berne, where there appear to be more lazy dogs lying idly about the streets than in other towns in Europe, I have tried the whistle for hours on a great many large dogs, but could not find one that heard it. I once frightened a pony with one of these whistles in the middle of a large field. My attempts on insect hearing have been failures.'

Galton was obsessed with statistics. He wrote down, logged, cross-referenced and quantified anything and everything he came across. He never stopped measuring: it might be the length of a man's nose, or the strength of his hand grip, or the number of brush strokes on a painting (the results of which he reported in his article 'Number of Strokes of the Brush in a Picture', *Nature*, 1905). In 1897, he published a paper on the precise length of rope required by a hangman to break a criminal's neck without decapitation, in which he triumphantly revealed an error in previously used calculations that did not take into account the bigger neck muscles in fat men. He also wrote a thesis demonstrating that prayer was a waste of time, citing statistical proof that frequent public prayer for kings, queens and other heads of state was ineffective because the average age of royals at death was lower than that of commoners. Galton's research showed that God appeared to protect priests and axe murderers equally. His cousin Darwin, despite his own reticence on the subject of religion in public, quietly approved. A select bibliography of some of Galton's more esoteric works might include 'Arithmetic by Smell' (*Psychological Review*, 1884), 'Intelligible Signals between Neighbouring Stars' (*Fortnightly Review*, 1896), 'Gregariousness in Cattle and in Men' (*Macmillan's Magazine*, 1861), 'Note on Fitting Normal Curves to Distribution of Speeds of Old Homing Pigeons' (*Homing News and Pigeon Fanciers Journal*, 1894), not forgetting his seminal 'Cutting a Round Cake on Scientific Principles' (*Nature*, 1906). Inevitably, this great English scientist also developed a complex formula for determining the best way to make a cup of tea.

In order to work out the proportion of optimists to pessimists he randomly stopped complete strangers on the street and asked them how they liked the weather. He also made a 'beauty map' of the British Isles compiled from a statistical assessment of females he passed on the street. Using his latest invention, a strategically concealed pocket calculator, Galton rated girls on a scale ranging from 'attractive' to 'repellent'. After many months of pocket-fiddling, his observations led him to conclude that Britain's ugliest women lived in Aberdeen.

In *The Art of Travel* Galton expanded upon his limited knowledge of the fairer sex. He wrote:

> It is the nature of women to be fond of carrying weights. You may see them in omnibuses and carriages, always preferring to hold their baskets or their babies on their knees to setting them down on the seats by their sides. A woman whose modern dress includes, I know not how many cubic feet of space, has hardly ever pockets of sufficient size to carry small articles, for she prefers to load her hands with a bag or other weighty object.

This was written, incidentally, by a man who regularly carried around with him a brick wrapped in brown paper and tied to a length of rope so he could stand on it to see over people's heads in a crowd.

Galton's attitude to women, even those who were not Aberdonian, was described by his biographer D. W. Forrest as 'one of polite indifference', but in 1853 he took the plunge and married Louisa Butler, daughter of the Dean of Peterborough. Mrs Galton was a committed hypochondriac; she prepared for her impending death so regularly that the phrase 'Aunt Louisa's dying again' became the family catchphrase. Their illnesses were synchronized; whenever Mr Galton was in good health, Mrs Galton was ill, and vice versa.

Although wealthy and famous, Galton was an uncomfortable host. He and his wife had a complex system of secret hand signals, which she used to let him know if he was boring people, or talking too loudly, or too quickly. At dinner parties he placed pressure sensors under the chairs to record the body movements of his guests. He theorized that if the party was going well, the guests would incline their chairs towards one other. Galton also thoughtfully installed a warning signal in his dining room to let his guests know when the lavatory was engaged.

It was his cousin's great opus *On the Origin of Species* that took Galton in an entirely new intellectual direction, the one he is largely remembered for today, as a pioneer of the pseudo-science of eugenics. Heredity, Galton was convinced, determined everything. 'The brains of our nation', he wrote, 'lie in the higher of our classes.' The English alone, and his own family in particular, apparently possessed this attribute in abundance – far more than any other European nation, let alone the 'swarms of coloured folk with their constant unintelligible jabbering'. Over the years Galton refined his arguments, developing statistical procedures, in horrifically prejudiced detail, to bolster them. For example, he studied court cases in various countries to work out which race was the most honest. He concluded that the British could be relied upon more than any other race to tell the truth, while 'the centre of gravity for lying' was Greece.

Galton also amassed a welter of human physical data to back his theories. In 1884, he set up an Anthropometric Laboratory in South Kensington where thousands of people paid threepence to submit themselves to seventeen different tests and measurements, including weight, height, shoulder width, reaction times, eyesight, eye colour, the length of stride and, crucially, their thumb prints. One of Galton's preoccupations was the measurement of craniums; he thought that large skulls indicated higher intelligence and good breeding. The Prime Minister William Gladstone, who was quite proud of his own heritage, visited Galton's laboratory and challenged him to find a better skull. Galton obliged and revealed that there was nothing very special about the PM's cranium at all; his own huge bald dome was much nobler.

It was only a matter of time before Galton's obsessive measurement-taking turned up something that was actually useful. For several years he annoyed his acquaintances by pestering them for their thumbprints, which he recorded with another of his pocket devices, a little inky pad and roller. It was after studying 2,500 sets of prints that he realized that they were all different. He published a 200-page essay, titled *Fingerprints*. To his frustration, he could find no correlation between fingerprint patterns and race or religion, despite redoubling his efforts by taking prints of Welsh, blacks, Basques and Jews. He was surprised to note: 'I have prints of eminent thinkers and eminent statesmen that can be matched by those of congenital idiots.'

His final work was an unpublished novel called *Kantsaywhere* about a fictional society, where tall, intelligent, healthy men and buxom women were treated and paid well and encouraged to have plenty of children. In Galton's utopia, social undesirables were only tolerated if they worked hard and stayed celibate, neatly anticipating Nazi racial policy by at least a quarter of a century. Ironically, Galton would not have passed muster in his own eugenics utopia. His frequent nervous breakdowns alone would have been considered grounds for sterilization. In any event, neither his brand of arrogant elitism, nor his hereditary male pattern baldness was passed down the line. In contrast to his prolific cousin Charles, who fathered ten children, Francis Galton produced none.

Like his cousin Darwin, Galton was plagued with various illnesses and regularly took to the spas in continental Europe to recover. His health was probably not improved by his diet, prescribed by a Dr Clark, which restricted him to a pint of claret at dinner plus cakes, spices and coffee, or his cure for deafness and asthma, which he treated by smoking hashish. In 1911, after a harsh winter and another severe asthma attack, Galton fell terminally ill at the age of eighty-nine, and was given oxygen on his deathbed. Barely able to breathe or speak, he died struggling to explain to his doctor that he had once written a paper about breathing apparatus.

## Inventing the dog and bone

Alexander Graham Bell (1847–1922) and his brother Melville were obsessed with the mechanics of speech from their early teens. One day they made a speaking apparatus using the voice box of a dead sheep. Using a set of bellows, they were able to make their model cry 'Ma-ma' in such a lifelike manner that the neighbours thought it was a child in distress. Encouraged by this success, they tried to teach their family dog to talk by manipulating its mouth and vocal cords. They claimed that they had persuaded the dog to growl 'How are you, grandmother,' although to impartial listeners it sounded a very much like 'Bow-wow-wow-grrrr.' Eventually they gave up on this idea and decided to dissect their pet cat to study its vocal cords in more detail instead, much to the relief of their dog.

Alexander Bell was both neurotic and depressive and had erratic working habits. He didn't go to bed until four or five in the morning. He was such a fussy eater that he refused to eat from plates that had the wrong pattern on them. While struggling to patent his telephone he more or less forgot to eat anything at all, and his weight dropped to under nine stones. He suffered from intense headaches and, claiming he was abnormally sensitive to light, he kept his windows covered to keep out the 'harmful rays' of the full moon. His work on the telephone was partly motivated by his desire to communicate with his prematurely deceased elder brother Melville, who had died of tuberculosis aged twenty-five. He and Melville had a pact whereby whoever died first would try to contact the other. His research into the mechanics of sound took some odd directions. At one point Bell constructed a device he called the 'phonautograph', which comprised a dead man's ear attached to a lever. He spoke into the disembodied ear and caused its membrane to vibrate, thus moving the lever, which then drew a wavelike pattern on a piece of smoked glass.

Bell's patent for a telephone system, filed on 14 February 1876 under the title 'Improvements in telegraphy', would become the most valuable ever issued, and the creation of the Bell Telephone Company in 1877 with Bell the owner of a third of the 5,000 shares made him extremely rich. He carried on inventing, but with considerably less success. He made peculiar aircraft with wings based on kites, experimented with hydrofoils and built a prototype iron lung, none of which was either practical or commercially viable. One of his less competent experiments helped kill US President James Garfield.

In 1881, just three months after he was sworn in, Garfield was felled by two bullets fired by the assassin Charles Guiteau: one grazed Garfield's arm but the other lodged itself somewhere inside his body. Various doctors and surgeons poked and prodded around inside the President's body for the bullet but couldn't find it. The US government called upon Bell to assist them with his latest invention, a crude metal detector, to help locate the offending missile. After several passes with his device Bell announced triumphantly that he had found the bullet. When the physicians set about cutting Garfield open to remove it they realized with horror that Bell's equipment had actually located the metal springing under the mattress; the bullet continued to elude them. Ten weeks after the shooting, the deep and by now badly infected wound caused Garfield to have a massive and fatal heart attack. At his trial, Charles Guiteau, a lawyer with a history of mental illness, claimed that God had told him to shoot the President, but argued that it was the incompetence of Bell and the doctors, not he, who actually killed Garfield. Worth a try, but he was hanged anyway on 30 June 1882.

Less dangerous but no less embarrassing were Bell's experiments with sheep. In 1870, the Bell family had moved to America and in 1886, while they were on holiday in Nova Scotia, he bought a ewe for his children to play with. When they returned the following year the ewe had given birth to a lamb. Bell was pleased with this modest increase in his flock, but thought the ewe could do better; after all, if young pigs were produced in dozens and kittens and puppies in half-dozens, why not lambs? Bell was convinced that the answer was sheep with extra nipples. He set about breeding a flock of multi-nippled super sheep that were guaranteed to have twin births. Bell built a huge village of sheep pens and spent the next thirty years counting sheep nipples. In the end, foxes, dogs and harsh winters, not to mention an eager assistant who slaughtered and slit open one of his best ewes to get a sneak preview if she was bearing twins, saw off most of his flock. By the time the US State Department ruled that extra nipples were not linked with extra lambs, the experiment had cost Bell $250,000.

## Happiness is a slab of warm granite

The mathematical physicist Oliver Heaviside (1850–1925) lacked the one qualification that usually allowed you to take up a career in science in nineteenth-century Britain: inherited wealth. Born into the London slums depicted by Charles Dickens's novels of the period, he died in poverty a recluse, but in between made extraordinary advances in mathematics and physics, including the foundation of modern electric circuit design, and made possible, amongst many other things, long-distance telephone calls.

Heaviside was the youngest of four sons, raised in semi-squalor in Camden Town by an abusive father who beat him regularly with a leather strap. His unhappy childhood was made even more difficult by an early bout of scarlet fever that left him partially deaf. He left school at sixteen and got a job as a telegraph operator, but in his spare time taught himself the principles of electricity and higher mathematics. It was the only paid job he ever held down. At the age of twenty-four he 'retired' and went to live with his parents in Devon. Heaviside spent the next fifteen years more or less shut away in a darkened room working on electrical theory. His family were stunned by his decision to give up paid work and although they could ill afford it they did their best to support him, usually by leaving trays of food outside his bedroom door. He survived for weeks on bowls of milk. Fortunately, Heaviside's 'retirement' was productive, because when he emerged from his seclusion he had written a series of groundbreaking papers on the theory of the electric telegraph.

Unfortunately, hardly anyone could understand a word of what he had written. Heaviside was literally the most misunderstood scientist of his generation. He revelled in obscurity, deliberately making his work difficult just for the sake of it. When a fellow scientist politely pointed out that his brilliant articles on electromagnetic theory might benefit from a little editing because they were 'hard to read', Heaviside replied curtly, 'They were harder to write.' It was an odd way to achieve recognition. In a review of one of Heaviside's books, the editor of the *Electrician* wrote: 'May the fact that I cannot understand nineteen twentieths of your book *Electromagnetic Theory* prevent me from congratulating you on the completed Volume II?'

Heaviside's unrivalled reputation as an author of almost completely indecipherable scientific papers meant that he made little money out of his epoch-making discoveries. He was well past middle age before the scientific community finally recognized his worth. By this time, however, he was already in bitter retreat, living the last seventeen years of his life in poverty as a hermit in a rented house in Newton Abbot. Increasingly deaf and dotty in equal measure, he became dirty and dishevelled, except for his hair, which he dyed black, and perfectly manicured fingernails, which he painted cherry pink. He also replaced all of his comfortable furniture with granite blocks. Heaviside was a raging hypochondriac and suffered from what he called 'hot and cold disease'. He spent most of his time indoors wrapped in several layers of blankets with a tea cosy worn over his dyed black hair. He rarely left his sparse, tightly closed room and spent what little money he had on gas to keep his home in sweltering heat, a condition described by a rare visitor as 'hotter than hell'. He spent his last years in a running battle with the gas board – the 'gas barbarians', Heaviside called them – over unpaid bills, once going without heat or light for almost a whole year because he refused to pay his gas bill. He narrowly escaped with his life when he opened up a mains gas pipe and ignited it, causing a huge jet of flame to singe his hair and clothing.

Heaviside's neighbours, mostly unaware of his great scientific achievements, shunned him as a lunatic. Boys threw bricks at his windows and plugged the sewage outtake to his home, causing the surrounding area to stink so much that it was reported in the local newspaper. He filled up his day writing to friends, who found his correspondence increasingly incoherent and mostly full of baffling trivia about his health and the minutiae of his daily life. In 1897, he wrote to a friend about his lawn: 'Wild horses were used to eat up the grass, so the lawn is, all over, holes, deep holes. It must be dug, or else filled up. What dreadful work cutting grass is, with scissors. 90 feet by 12, say. Hard work on the back, very.' He also wrote copious letters about his diet, which generally consisted of bowls of milk, with no minor detail overlooked. The recipients were puzzled to find that he always signed his correspondence 'W. O. R. M.' It wasn't an acronym – it stood for nothing but worm.

In 1908, Heaviside fell ill and his brother Charles, concerned that he wouldn't be able to take care of himself, arranged for him to lodge with his unmarried sister-in-law Mary Way at her house in Torquay. Bizarrely, Heaviside kept his host and full-time carer a virtual prisoner in her own home. He wouldn't let her leave the house without his permission and made her sign a series of contracts that effectively controlled her movements, cutting her off completely from the outside world. One agreement read, 'MW agrees to wear warm woollen underclothes and keep herself warm in winter'. She remained a virtual slave for almost eight years until she was rescued by her niece, who visited one day without warning and, finding her aunt in a pitiful state of neglect, drove her away, leaving behind most of her belongings. When Heaviside was asked later to explain her disappearance he replied that she was mad and had to be put away. Mary Way eventually agreed to sell the house to Heaviside, and from 1916 until just before his death in 1925 he lived there alone.

In 1922, the Institute of Electrical Engineers tried to make amends for years of neglect by the scientific community by presenting Heaviside with its highest honour, the Faraday Medal. When told to expect a deputation of four who were to travel to his home to present him with the award, Heaviside refused to see them all at once and wrote back insisting that they came one at a time on four successive days. In the end they agreed to send just one delegate, the president of the institution, J. S. Highfield. It was the last time the outside world had any contact with Oliver Heaviside. Three years later he fell from the top of a ladder at the age of seventy-four and died from complications a few weeks later. His trip by ambulance to the Mount Stuart Nursing Home, Torquay, was the first and last he ever made in a motorized vehicle. Several unpublished, characteristically brilliant papers written by Heaviside were later discovered stuffed under the floorboards of his house. He had put them there to act as insulation.

## Martyrs to science

Jack Burden Scott 'JBS' Haldane (1892–1964) was one of the most eccentric figures in modern science, but he was only maintaining a family tradition of academic weirdness. His father, John Scott Haldane, was the archetypal absent-minded professor. He was famous for his dishevelled and slightly moth-eaten appearance. For several years he continued to use a wristwatch after the minute hand had fallen off, estimating the time by the fractional movements of the hour hand alone. Once he and his wife were hosting a dinner party when Mrs Haldane sent her husband upstairs to get changed into something more suitable. He failed to return and was discovered fast asleep in bed in his pyjamas. Once roused, he explained to his wife that he had found himself getting undressed and assumed it was bedtime.

Haldane Senior saved many lives thanks to his special interest: 'bad air' in mines. He discovered that most mining fatalities were caused not by the actual explosion but by exposure to lethal gases such as carbon monoxide or nitrogen. He came up with the idea of the canary in a box – an indicator of the presence of carbon monoxide. Before he did that, he actually placed himself in a box, or rather, a sealed container, to see what would happen. He noted the side effects of being starved of oxygen in horrifying detail: '10 minutes, lips turn blue . . . 20 minutes, blinding headache and knocking feebly on glass, mouthing, "Get me out of here" . . .'.

He was never happier than when he was down a coal mine testing his newly invented breathing equipment. With every new mining explosion he would grab his miner's helmet and rush to investigate. One of the effects of serious carbon monoxide poisoning is that it addles the brain and the victim tends to repeat himself. Haldane would send a reassuring telegram home to his wife – 'I'M ALRIGHT' – then ruin the effect by sending identical messages at half-hour intervals. He didn't just sample the poisonous gases he found down mines; he also tried them out on himself in the laboratory. He once inhaled an almost lethal dose of carbon monoxide, all the while taking readings and blood samples. He quit when he could no longer stand up, just before he lost all control of his muscles. One evening after a similar experiment he was observed staggering home from his laboratory and was stopped by a policeman. Haldane explained that he was not under the influence of alcohol, but gas. His housekeeper offered her sympathies to his wife, Kathleen: 'I knows how you feel, Ma'am. My husband's just the same on a Friday night.'

Haldane was hired by the Admiralty to find out how deep-sea divers could safely ascend without getting 'the bends'. Although he never learned to swim, Haldane jumped overboard in a full diving suit to experience the effects of 'the bends' for himself. On another occasion he filled a ship's hold full of rats and pumped the sealed area full of sulphur dioxide to test its effectiveness as a rat poison. He then ran around the ship holding his breath to see how many dead rats he could collect before he passed out.

On this, as with many other experiments, his son Jack was expected to accompany him. In one experiment, father and son crawled for miles along a narrow coal seam until they found a pocket of methane gas. The younger Haldane was instructed to stand up and recite a passage from Shakespeare, which he gamely attempted to do before passing out. He recovered consciousness to hear his father inform him, 'You have just learned that gas, being lighter than air, always rises.'

When the first gas attacks of World War I came in 1915, the British were taken completely by surprise and Haldane was sent to France to investigate. He decided to try out one of the 90,000 gas masks that had already been dished out to the British troops. He and his son took it in turns to sit inside a chamber into which lethal chlorine gas was pumped. Father and son alternately took notes while the other ran around and did press-ups inside the chamber. After almost killing them both Haldane concluded that the gas masks were not fit for purpose. Father and son returned home and rigged up some home-made gas masks out of stockings, vests and various items of knitwear. Mrs Haldane could tell from the sound of coughing and retching from her husband's study whether or not the experiments were going well.

John Scott Haldane's lungs were permanently damaged by his various experiments. He died at the age of seventy-five while investigating the effects of heat stroke on oil rig workers in the Middle East. Enigmatic to the end, his dying words were, 'I've had a telegram to say that Priestley was dying too, but I think it was an imaginary telegram.'

Jack 'JBS' Haldane's childhood was not a normal one. Family holidays were taken in Cornwall so that his father could examine hookworm in tin miners. By the age of eight he was helping his dad with difficult gas analysis experiments. In 1914, he left university to go straight into the army, and was posted to France, where he threw himself into the fray with more than average enthusiasm. Unlike most of his generation, JBS found the Great War 'a very enjoyable experience'. He described April 1915, a month spent under constant shelling, as 'one of the happiest months of my life' and said he was 'grateful to have been given the opportunity to kill people'. His exploits at the front were hair-raising, especially his reckless nightly raids into no-man's land to deliver bombs by hand. He was wounded twice, the second time by 'friendly fire', and was taken away in a field ambulance driven by the Prince of Wales, the future King Edward VIII. At one point Haldane neglected to remove his boots for three weeks, which caused General Haig to observe that he was 'the bravest and the dirtiest soldier in the army'.

After the war, JBS returned to his first love, science. He took the Haldane family motto – 'Suffer' – to extremes. He once drank a bottle of hydrochloric acid then cycled home to see what effect it would have. He noted laconically, 'concentrated HCl [hydrochloric acid] dissolves one's blood'. There was a thirteen-day experiment during which JBS swallowed a near-fatal dose of calcium chloride which resulted in 'intense diarrhoea, followed by constipation due to the formation of a large hard faecal mass. There was great general discomfort, pains in the head, limbs and back, and disturbed nights.' To test his lung capacity he swallowed one and a half ounces of bicarbonate of soda then ran up and down a one hundred and fifty-foot flight of stairs twenty times. A colleague once found him apparently dead drunk on a staircase and rushed to help. Haldane reassured him, 'It's nothing. It's just that I'm only 80 per cent sodium haldanate at the present moment.'

JBS was given another opportunity to serve his country just before World War II, when Britain's new submarine *Thetis* sank in the Mersey with the loss of many lives. He was asked to look at ways of improving the escape gear installed in submarines, so he built a decompression chamber he called 'the pressure pot'. It was an enclosed steel tube, eight feet long and four feet in diameter, big enough to fit two or three people sitting. There followed a series of highly dangerous and extremely painful experiments in which he exposed himself and a few colleagues to high pressure and high concentrations of carbon dioxide and oxygen. The tests resulted in seizures, vomiting and nosebleeds: on one occasion JBS decompressed the chamber to the point where the fillings in his teeth exploded. While investigating the poisoning effects of elevated levels of oxygen he had a violent fit, which resulted in several crushed vertebrae. A similar experiment later left him without any sensation or feeling in his lower back for six years. Collapsed lungs and perforated eardrums were commonplace occurrences. He noted in one of his papers after a relatively light day at the office: 'The eardrum generally heals up, and if a hole remains in it, although one is somewhat deaf, one can blow tobacco smoke out of the ear in question, which is a social accomplishment.'

As well as his willingness to serve as his own chief guinea pig, JBS was happy to experiment on others. He once casually subjected his wife Kathleen to a simulated descent in his pressure chamber, which caused her to have a fit lasting thirteen minutes. She recovered and was sent home to cook JBS's dinner. He didn't always ask for permission. While lecturing at a public meeting on the dangers of gas in trench warfare, the unwitting audience watched in curious silence as JBS vaporized a spoonful of pepper over a spirit lamp. As the hall filled with pungent smoke they fled for the exits with their eyes streaming, gasping for air. 'If that upsets you,' JBS shouted after his fleeing audience, 'how would you like a deluge of poison gas from an air fleet in real war?'

JBS was never afraid to speak his own mind and his love of conflict made him enemies, but it was his deep involvement in left-wing politics that cost him most dearly. He put his physically imposing 200 pounds to use as a bouncer at Labour Party rallies, until his habit of removing hecklers by sticking a finger up each nostril then hauling them backwards up the aisle 'like hooked trout' got him sacked. He also wrote a science column for several years in the *Daily Worker*, in which he mixed observations about biology and the cosmos with quotes from Engels and Lenin.

By the end of the 1930s, Haldane was a card-holding member of the Communist Party, and by the onset of World

War II openly and unswervingly loyal to his hero, Josef Stalin. Although the British government valued his scientific advice, not to mention his generous habit of subjecting himself to prolonged confinement in submarines, Haldane was now considered a security risk. He found to his irritation that the military had overlooked some of his various schemes to defeat Hitler, including the release of thousands of fish equipped with tiny magnets to trigger magnetic mines. In 1956, he went to live in India in protest against 'Western imperialism', announcing, 'It is entirely possible that within the next two or three years European civilization will largely destroy itself.' A couple of years later he was diagnosed with terminal rectal cancer. He bore the news with characteristic fortitude and a mordant sense of humour, signalling his impending demise in a poem called 'Cancer's a Funny Thing'. It began:

*I wish I had the voice of Homer*
*To sing of rectal carcinoma*
*Which kills a lot more chaps, in fact*
*Than were bumped off when Troy was sacked.*

## The IT factor

Alan Mathison Turing (1912–54) studied and taught mathematics at Cambridge University where he developed a concept for what became known as the Turing machine, now considered the basis for the modern computer. He put his area of expertise to practical use in 1939 when he was put in charge of a code-cracking team at Bletchley Park, 60 miles north of London, tasked with a top-secret project to crack the secret Nazi Enigma code machine. For the code-breaking team in

'Hut 8' at Bletchley Park, their new leader was the biggest enigma of all.

By the time Turing arrived at Bletchley he was twenty-seven years old but retained the appearance of a very scruffy schoolboy. His hair looked as though he had been sleeping rough, his fingernails were filthy and his trousers were held up with his old school tie. In the best tradition of absent-minded professors he was also highly neglectful of his personal hygiene. He had long since given up shaving on a regular basis after cutting himself with his razor and then fainting at the sight of blood.

Turing's social skills were limited. He was prone to long silences followed by bursts of cackling laughter. When he spoke it was in a curious high-pitched stutter. He tended to ignore anyone he considered his intellectual inferior, including the entire military staff at Bletchley, but in the evenings he liked to relax by listening to the children's BBC radio show *Larry the Lamb.*

Although awkward and flat-footed, Turing was surprisingly good at the non-team sport of long-distance running. Several times a week he would set off on punishing cross-country runs through the local fields, bemusing the locals by grabbing handfuls of grass and eating them as he ran – Turing's way of making up for vitamin deficiency in his wartime diet. He would often arrive at meetings in Whitehall to face a committee of civil servants in a state of sweaty disarray, having just run ten miles across London wearing old flannels and a vest with an alarm clock tied with binder tape around his waist. Little wonder that some people didn't always take the dishevelled egghead seriously.

At the outbreak of war Turing had been convinced that Britain would be invaded. With great difficulty, he managed to have his life savings converted into silver bars and secretly buried them in the woods near Bletchley, committing the location to memory. After the war, however, the world's most brilliant code-cracker couldn't remember where he had buried them. He never recovered his silver bars, in spite of conducting several thorough treasure hunts and even inventing his own metal detector. Turing moved north to take up a post as deputy director of the computer laboratory at Manchester University, to work on the Manchester Automatic Digital Machine. It was the first ever electronic stored-programme computer to actually function, a gigantic machine known as MADAM. It was a huge advance in technological achievement, but for now, Turing's fellow team members were frustrated to learn, their deputy director would be spending all of his time teaching his brainchild how to play chess.

Turing was openly gay at a time when homosexuality in Britain carried a prison sentence, a situation quietly ignored by the authorities because of his incalculable contribution to the war effort, although he was still careful to keep it from his mother, a complicated ruse he was able to sustain to the end of his life. He surprised everyone (except his mum), therefore, when he suddenly got engaged to a female cryptanalyst. The engagement lasted six months, just long enough for her to teach him how to knit gloves. His undoing was a fumble with a Mancunian rent boy. By the end of the 1940s, Turing was at the peak of his powers and internationally respected. He had also taken up residence in Wilmslow, an affluent suburb on the outskirts of Manchester. Shortly before Christmas 1951, he met nineteen-year-old Arnold Murray, who spent the night at Turing's Wilmslow home. A few weeks later, while Turing was away taking part in a BBC radio debate entitled 'Can Automatic Calculating Machines Be Said to Think?' one of Murray's friends broke into Turing's home and stole a shirt, two pairs of shoes and some silver fish knives. Turing reported the theft to the local police, who were quick to seize on the homosexual subplot. The scientist was arrested and charged with gross indecency. Turing's trial in March 1952 was not widely reported in the newspapers, apart from a piece in the *News of the World* under the banner headline 'ACCUSED HAD POWERFUL BRAIN'. He was forced to agree to a course of hormone treatment, effectively a form of chemical castration to 'cure' him of his homosexual urges. For twelve months he was given injections of oestrogen which reduced the former fitness fanatic to an impotent physical wreck. He confided to a friend that he was growing breasts.

By now the British government considered their wartime saviour a serious security risk. In 1953, Turing went to Norway where he befriended a youth called Kjell. The British police force, acting on a tip-off that a Norwegian homosexual was about to enter the country to corrupt their top scientific mind, were put on a farcical heightened state of security alert, but in the event Kjell never showed. Homosexual persecution by the ungrateful authorities led to Turing's suicide. On 8 June 1954, ten years after the D-Day landings he made possible, he was found dead in bed by his housekeeper; by the bedside was his customary bedtime apple, generously laced with cyanide. As the existence of the British code-breaking effort was still a secret, Turing's death went largely unnoticed, his brilliant contribution to the evolution of the computer recognized only by a handful of experts. Even Turing's parents didn't know about Enigma; as far as they were concerned he had spent the war in the Foreign Office.

## Silence of the dons

The Bristol-born physicist Paul Dirac (1902–84) is considered by many of his peers to be the most important physicist of the twentieth century, greater even than Einstein. He once said he got his ideas by lying on his back with his legs in the air so that the blood ran to his head. The most remarkable thing about that statement is that Dirac said it at all. His father, French teacher Charles Dirac, had two strict rules: the first was that family members were only allowed to speak in perfect French at the dining table; the second was 'never start a sentence until you know how to finish it'. His son Paul, brilliant at maths but not particularly gifted at French, got into the habit of saying nothing at all. For the rest of his life his spoken vocabulary was said to have been limited to three replies: 'Yes, 'No,' and 'I don't know.'

Dirac went on to teach maths at Cambridge University, then physics at Florida University. His students found his answers so monosyllabic that they named a unit after him: the Dirac unit of volubility, equal to one word per year. He was so reticent that some of his colleagues believed that he was actually dumb. When he did have something to say it was precise, as the many anecdotes about his social interaction, or lack of it, attest. His colleague Jagdish Mehra recalled attempting to strike up a conversation with him about the weather. He got as far as far as his opening gambit, 'It is very windy, Professor.' Dirac said nothing at all but a few seconds later he got up and left. Mehra was horrified, convinced that he had somehow inadvertently offended him. Dirac went to the door, looked out, came back, sat down, and said, 'Yes.'

An unexpected side to Dirac was his love of fast cars and

enthusiasm for mountain climbing. He scaled several well-known peaks, including Mount Elbruz in the Caucasus; he prepared by climbing trees in Cambridgeshire, wearing the same black suit he wore to lectures. He also took everyone by surprise when he got married to the sister of the famous Hungarian theoretical physicist Eugene Wigner. Shortly after their wedding the couple bumped into an old friend of Dirac's who had not yet heard about the marriage. Dirac's friend wondered who the attractive woman with the professor might be. 'Sorry,' replied Dirac. 'I forgot to introduce you. This is Wigner's sister.'

## Cosmic crank

It was an argumentative Yorkshireman, Fred Hoyle (1915–2001), who first coined the expression 'big bang' to describe the theory that the universe was created by a huge explosion. Hoyle was one of the most important cosmologists of the twentieth century and made major contributions to several branches of astrophysics, including the origin of the solar system, the evolution of stars, the origin of cosmic rays, the mystery of dust in interstellar space, the formation of the Milky Way, radio sources, pulsars and quasars. Unfortunately, as his obituary in the journal *Nature* pointed out, he also 'put his name to much rubbish'.

Hoyle believed that the 'big bang' theory was complete nonsense and was ready to argue with anyone who said otherwise. When he first came up with 'big bang' during a radio talk on the BBC, it was flippant remark intended to mock the theory. Hoyle clung stubbornly to his belief that the universe had always existed to his death. Unfortunately, in 'big bang' he had created such a memorable soundbite that most people thought he created the original theory himself – annoying for Hoyle, to say the least.

His views were controversial and often baffling. During a radio broadcast in the early 1950s, at a time when Australia was dominating England at cricket, listeners were puzzled to hear Hoyle remark that somewhere in the Milky Way there was a cricket team who could beat the Australians. He also raised a few hackles when he claimed, without any evidence, that the famous archaeopteryx fossil in the Natural History Museum was a fake and had been created by pressing bird feathers into a tub of cement. Palaeontologists were outraged by Hoyle's outrageous claim; even less impressed were the museum staff who had to spend days fielding phone calls from the world's press. In his later years, Hoyle's reputation went further into eclipse when he said that life on Earth evolved from microbes falling from cometary tails about four billion years ago. According to Hoyle, the AIDS virus arrived from space in the mid-1970s and was originally passed to humans from rainwater via cuts on their feet. Hoyle went on to claim that humans had evolved protruding noses with downward pointing nostrils to stop alien pandemics from falling into them from the sky. Hoyle finally lost all credibility as a serious scientist when he embarked on a successful second controversial career as writer of TV science fiction. Financially, at least, he had the last laugh; when his seven-part television series *A for Andromeda* was shown in the US the early 1960s, a quarter of the population tuned in to watch.

# Six
# LITERARY ECCENTRICS

*'Thrippy Pilliwinx — Inkly tinky, pobblebockle able squaks? Flosky! Beebul trimble flosky! Okul scratch abibble-bongibo, viddle squibble tog-tog, ferry moyasitty amsky flamsky crocklefether squiggs. Flinsky wisty pomm.'*

– EDWARD LEAR (1812–88),
LETTER TO EVELYN BARING, 1850

## Doctor Strangelove

Dr Samuel Johnson (1709–84) was once asked by the famous actor David Garrick to name his greatest pleasure in life, to which the great man of letters replied, 'Fucking.' Unfortunately, Dr Johnson was desperately unsuccessful with women, most of them put off by his bizarre facial tick, his appalling table manners, his chronic flatulence and his failure to wash. When Johnson was twenty-five he married Elizabeth 'Tetty' Porter, a short, dumpy widow almost twice his age. They were married for seventeen years and, although Johnson always spoke of her affectionately, she refused to have sex with him on health grounds. Johnson's friends commiserated with him on this 'conjugal infelicity'. Meanwhile, Dr Johnson was haunted by sexual fantasies.

Late in his career Johnson suffered a mental breakdown and was nursed back to health by Hester Thrale, wife of a well-to-do brewer, Henry Thrale. According to a mysterious diary entry, Johnson gave Mrs Thrale a set of padlocks and had 'insane thoughts about leg iron and handcuffs'. According to another entry he shaved off all his body hair to see how long it would take to grow back. He often fought off his sexual urges by taking strenuous exercise – walking thirty miles a day, swimming, or by rolling down hills.

He was a messy, often frenzied eater, even in front of royalty. His biographer James Boswell said Johnson ate like a wild animal, gorging himself until his veins swelled and sweat poured from his head. Johnson also had a number of obsessive-compulsive disorders. He had a morbid fear of certain streets and alleys and would make elaborate detours to avoid them. He never stepped on the cracks in paving stones and touched every post along the road as he walked; if he missed a post by accident he would make his companions wait while he went back to touch it. Boswell got used to Johnson's strange habits, but there was one that baffled even him. The doctor had an extraordinary routine whenever he passed through a doorway. According to Boswell, Johnson would leap through the gap from a precise number of steps away. Although academically brilliant, Johnson was also incapable of telling the time from a clock.

Johnson's *Dictionary of the English Language* established him as the world authority on his mother tongue, but it earned him a relatively small amount of money and he lived mostly in poverty. He tried to supplement his income by teaching from home, but found only three students, most put off by his weird behaviour. He complained that he lived 'a life radically wretched', but his sense of humour was never in doubt. Johnson's *Dictionary* was full of idiosyncratic entries which gave insight into his personality, for example:

*fart: Wind from behind.*
*'Love is the fart*
*Of every heart;*
*It pains a man when 'tis kept close;*
*And others doth offend, when 'tis let loose.'*

## The Bard of Dundee

*Oh! It was a most gorgeous sight to be seen*
*Numerous foreign magnates were there for to see the Queen*
*And to the vast multitude there of women and men*
*Her Majesty for two hours showed herself to them.*

– W. McGonagall,
*The Queen's Diamond Jubilee Celebrations*

No one followed their muse with quite the same heroic dedication as the poetic Scot William Topaz McGonagall (1825–1902). He was born in Edinburgh, the son of an Irish cotton weaver who settled in Scotland. Long before he became a poet, McGonagall unleashed his remarkable creative talents on the world as an actor. In 1858, he and a few friends bribed the manager of Dundee's Theatre Royal to let him play the leading role for a remarkable two-act version of Macbeth. In the combat scene, after being run through by the sword of Macduff, McGonagall stayed on his feet and brandished his weapon about the ears of his adversary with such enthusiasm that the performance nearly ended in real bloodshed. The actor playing the part of Macduff repeatedly told McGonagall to 'die or else', and eventually had to disarm him with a well-aimed kick, but the weaponless McGonagall continued to dodge round Macduff like a prize fighter. In the end Macduff threw his sword away, grabbed hold of McGonagall by the neck and wrestled him to the ground. McGonagall retired from the stage at the age of forty-seven (or possibly fifty-two; he was never clear about his birthdate) when, in his own words, a 'divine inspiration' urged him to 'Write! Write!'

His choice of subject matter was eclectic and often inspired by contemporary news events. An example of his deftness of touch is shown in these lines from his 'Calamity in London; Family of Ten Burned to Death':

*Oh, Heaven! it was a frightful and pitiful sight to see*
*Seven bodies charred of the Jarvis family;*
*And Mrs. Jarvis was found with her child, and both carbonised,*
*And as the searchers gazed thereon they were surprised.*
*And these were lying beside the fragments of the bed,*
*And in a chair the tenth victim was sitting dead;*
*Oh Horrible! Oh Horrible! What a sight to behold*
*The charred and burnt bodies of young and old.*

McGonagall was prolific, often at the expense of his health. In 'A Tribute to Dr. Murison' he explains how his life was saved by a physician's advice:

H*e told me at once what was ailing me;*
*He said I had been writing too much poetry,*
*And from writing poetry I would have to refrain,*
*Because I was suffering from inflammation of the brain.*

McGonagall's public readings were often halted by the police on the grounds that they constituted a breach of the peace, because his audiences often rioted and pelted him with rotten vegetables. He was unaffected by the reaction to his work. The literary critic William Power saw McGonagall wearing full Highland dress, wielding a broadsword, oblivious to catcalls and laughter from the audience. Power left the hall early, 'saddened and disgusted'.

Many of McGonagall's best-known offerings were dedicated to Queen Victoria. He sent her reams of dire verse and whenever she visited Scotland he travelled to Balmoral hoping to deliver a personal recitation of his latest work, but never succeeded in getting beyond the castle gates. Eventually he elicited a frosty letter of acknowledgement from the Queen's private secretary, Lord Biddulph, stating that Her Majesty did not wish to receive samples of his work. This near brush with royalty went to McGonagall's head and he had some business cards printed, on which he had restyled himself 'Poet to Her Majesty'. In his lifetime McGonagall sold just one piece of work, for which he received two guineas: a rhyme to promote Sunlight Soap.

*You can use it with great pleasure and ease*
*Without wasting any elbow grease;*
*And when washing the most dirty clothes*
*The sweat won't be dripping off your nose*
*You can wash your clothes with little rubbing*
*And without scarcely any scrubbing;*
*And I tell you once again without any joke*
*There's no soap can surpass Sunlight Soap;*
*And believe me, charwomen one and all,*
*I remain yours truly, the Poet McGonagall.*

The legacy of McGonagall's work lives on. In May 2008, an original folio of his poems sold at auction for £6,600, putting his work at a similar value to first edition signed copies of J. K. Rowling's *Harry Potter* novels.

## On a fried kitten

The poet Percy Bysshe Shelley loathed cats. He once tied one to a kite in a thunder storm to see if it would be electrocuted.

## Chips with everything

Queen Victoria had the misfortune of being pursued by two talentless but patriotic poets. Joseph Gwyer (1835–90), the 'McGonagall of Penge', was a potato salesman who followed his two great obsessions, poetry and potato growing, with roughly equal enthusiasm. He often combined the two, as seen in his 1875 volume, *Sketches of the Life of Joseph Gwyer (Potato Salesman) with His Poems (Commended by Royalty)*. The title was optimistic, given that at no time in his career was any of Gwyer's work ever commended by anyone, especially not royalty, even though he had volunteered his services as unofficial Poet Laureate on several occasions over a period of twenty years. When sales of his book proved slow, Gwyer offered to throw in a sack of potatoes and a photograph of the author and his horse with every copy. The potato theme looms large throughout Gwyer's work. In 'Love and Matrimony' the poet points out that the most important thing a man should look for in his choice of bride is an ability to cook and roast POTATOES (in Gwyer's work, the word 'potatoes' was always underlined or written in capitals). Gwyer's potato theme often baffled his public but was not lost on his critics. *Punch* began a review of his work 'The Alexandra Palace, Muswell Hill, Destroyed by Fire', 'We consider this work no small potatoes.'

## Cats and doggerel

The reclusive Anglo-American T. S. Eliot (1888–1965) was regarded as one of the giants of twentieth-century poetry thanks to such works as *The Waste Land.* He also wrote a number of verses about cats, the basis for the longest-running show in Broadway history, plus several obscene poems, the 'Columbo and Bolo verses', largely about defecation and violent sex, as yet undiscovered by Sir Tim Rice or Lord Andrew Lloyd-Webber.

## My heart will go on

The literary classics of Thomas Hardy (1840–1928), including *Far From the Madding Crowd, Tess of the D'Urbervilles* and *Jude the Obscure*, received poor reviews when they were first published. Critics picked up on his obsession with full lips and heaving breasts and concluded that Hardy was 'sex mad'. He unfortunately destroyed most of the letters, diaries and notebooks which may have shed some light on his unusually complicated private life.

When Hardy was twenty-six he fell in love with and was briefly engaged to his cousin, sixteen-year-old Tryphena Sparks. In the 1960s the Hardy Society was shaken by the disturbing but as yet unsubstantiated claim that Tryphena was in fact Hardy's niece, something Hardy was apparently unaware of the time, and that the affair resulted in a secret love-child called Randle. The incestuous Tryphena, it is alleged, was to resurface in many Hardy love poems and was the inspiration for some of his most famous heroines. In 1874, he married a girl he was not already related to, Emma Gifford. He neglected his wife badly for work and other women (mostly other women), and after a long and childless marriage Emma died in 1912. Hardy was unexpectedly grief-stricken after the death of his wife. He had her body placed in the coffin at the foot of his bed where it remained for three days until her funeral, and later expressed his bitter regrets at his rotten treatment of her in an extraordinary outpouring of poetry – considered the finest he ever wrote – which continued until his death fifteen years later. Although Hardy loved many women, including one peasant girl whom he only glimpsed in passing from horseback and whose memory haunted him for years afterwards, in the end he lost his heart to a cat. His ashes were buried with impressive ceremony in Poet's Corner in Westminster Abbey, but his heart went home to Stinsford, his birthplace. According to tradition, his cat Cobby snatched the heart from the kitchen table and ran off with it.

## Courting the miaows

The Victorian 'nonsense poet' Edward Lear (1812–88) wrote his best-known work *The Owl and the Pussycat* for the three-year-old daughter of a friend. The pussycat was based on his own beloved tabby cat, Foss, who was Lear's constant companion for seventeen years. When Lear moved to San Remo, Italy, he instructed his architect to build an exact replica of his old home in England so Foss would not be too stressed by the change in scenery. Throughout his adult life, Lear suffered from 'the morbids', a state of mind which he attributed to excessive masturbation.

## Unhappily ever after

The marriage of Thomas Carlyle (1795–1881) and Jane Walsh was one of the strangest unions in literary history, an arrangement famously defended by Tennyson on the grounds that 'otherwise four people would have been unhappy instead of two', had each of them married someone else. The problems began on their wedding night when the shaggy-bearded Sage of Chelsea refused to sleep in the marital bed, complaining that he felt ill. A few days into the honeymoon, he wrote a letter to his mum, to whom he was said to be 'abnormally attached', explaining that he had not yet slept with his wife because (a) he was suffering from insomnia, and (b) their bed was too narrow. His highly strung wife meanwhile was quite open about (a) the fact that she carried a torch for her husband's best friend, the preacher Edward Irving, and (b) she couldn't cope with her husband's constant farting. For the next forty years of their marriage the Carlyles rarely shared a bedroom; in between frequent and violent rows, he took refuge almost round the clock locked in a soundproof study writing wordy histories, including six volumes of *Frederick the Great*. Against all odds, the marriage lasted until Jane's death aged sixty-four, at which Carlyle was unaccountably stricken with grief.

## Royal paean

The post of Poet Laureate has been held by a handful of greats (including Dryden, Wordsworth and Tennyson), several mediocre poets and two truly terrible ones. In the latter category was Henry James Pye (1745–1813). Pye was given the job by Prime Minister William Pitt the Younger, evidently as compensation for losing his parliamentary seat. Away from poetry, he had a chronically dull prose style and specialized in rambling dirges on largely agricultural themes, including his extraordinary *The Effect of Music on Animals*. His position was further hampered by the fact that his patron King George III had gone completely and irretrievably mad during his laureateship. Pye did his best to avoid or to manfully circumnavigate the subject, a tricky business at the best of times, especially when it came to the obligatory annual 'King's Birthday Ode'.

The worst ever Poet Laureate was Alfred Austin (1835–1913). He was the leader writer in the *Standard* and known for his hard-line right-wing politics, and had twice failed to be elected to Parliament when he was mysteriously awarded the laureateship by the Prime Minister Lord Salisbury. Although Austin had no track record as a poet, he was cheerfully ignorant of his limitations and took his appointment as proof that he was officially, in his own words, 'at the head of English literature'. Austin quickly became known for his overblown epics and political insensitivity. One of his most infamous works, a poem about the Jameson raid of 1895 (when a group of British privateers made an abortive attempt to overthrow the Transvaal government), in which Austin acclaimed Jameson as a hero, was considered so inappropriate that it even earned a reprimand from Queen Victoria. His efforts were universally panned by the critics who followed his career with mounting disbelief, but Austin struck a pose of lofty indifference, continuing to churn out rubbish and to lecture his public about the literary deficiencies of his contemporaries and how all critics were idiots. He interpreted the scathing attacks on his efforts as jealousy. When it was pointed out to him that his poems were full of basic grammatical errors, Austin replied, 'I dare not alter these things. They come to me from above.' Austin complained to Lord Young that he was always broke, but added, 'I manage to keep the wolf from the door.'

'How?' Young enquired. 'By reading your poems to him?'

## Grave reviews

The poet and Pre-Raphaelite artist Dante Gabriel Rossetti (1828–82) lost his beautiful wife and model Elizabeth when she accidentally overdosed on the laudanum she was taking for her neuralgia. Rossetti was heartbroken and as a token of his love had a pile of his unpublished manuscripts wrapped in her long, golden hair and buried with her in her coffin. Seven years later, however, he had a change of heart, and decided he wanted them back. Up came Elizabeth, and the poems were dusted off and published to critical acclaim.

Rossetti was a close friend of the famous Victorian interior designer William Morris, but he had designs on another Morris interior, that of his wife Jane. He painted her portrait and wrote an erotic poem about her, a preamble to a passionate affair, then moved into the Morris household on a full-time basis. William Morris, who was more worried about the social disgrace that divorce would bring than the fact that one of his best friends was bedding his wife, simply bought a bigger house where he and his children and his wife and her lover could all live together. To the end of his life, Rossetti was haunted by the terrible secret of the exhumed manuscripts and he became an alcoholic and morphine addict. Ravaged by drugs, he filled his home with a menagerie of exotic wild animals, including several wombats, which regularly fought, killed and occasionally ate each other. The only pet he regretted not having, he said, was an elephant, because it could help him clean his windows by squirting water through its trunk.

## Absent friends

G. K. Chesterton (1874–1936) was preoccupied with writing to the exclusion of almost everything else. He never learned how to knot a tie (his wife claimed he didn't even know how to take it out of the drawer), and never came to terms with the telephone. The flowing cloak and broad-brimmed hat which became his trademarks were tactfully employed by his wife to hide the fact that he would often turn up at lectures with items of clothing missing or accidentally stolen from a friend half his size. He was notoriously absent-minded when it came to appointments and relied on his wife in all practical matters. Once on a lecture tour he sent her a telegram: 'Am in Market Harborough. Where ought I to be?' She wired back: 'Home.'

## Clear as Maud

Alfred Lord Tennyson (1809–92) was Queen Victoria's favourite poet and succeeded Wordsworth as Poet Laureate in 1850, but he wasn't to everyone's taste, and was the target of much critical abuse. When *Maud* was published in 1855, one reviewer noted that its title contained too many vowels and that the removal of either one would be equally satisfactory. Tennyson was plagued by imagined illness and went for ten years without writing a single line of poetry; he sought a cure through hydropathy, a method of treatment where the patient is doused with cold water. He was also known for his eccentric choice of clothing, especially the long Spanish cloak and massive sombrero he wore every time he went out. One of his young admirers, Elspeth Thompson, once accompanied him as he marched through the streets of London, oblivious to the strange looks he drew from passers-by. 'Child, your mother should dress you less conspicuously,' Tennyson grumbled. 'People are staring at us.'

## Love of the lash

When the job of Poet Laureate fell vacant upon the death of Tennyson in 1892, Queen Victoria remarked, 'I understand Mr Swinburne is the best of my poets.' She was referring to the controversial Algernon Charles Swinburne (1837–1909), poet, dramatist and critic. She was possibly unaware at the time of his reputation for cross-dressing and flagellation, not to mention the verses he had penned about Her Majesty's presumed sex life, especially the one about how she had been shagged by Wordsworth. Five feet tall, ginger-haired and with an enormous head, Swinburne had an obsession with flogging that could be traced back to his schooling at Eton, where the headmaster of the day was so notorious for birchings that he was said to be more familiar with his pupils' backsides than their faces. To be fair, there were clues to Swinburne's predilection in his works ('The Flogging Block', 'Arthur's Flogging', 'Reginald's Flogging', 'A Boy's First Flogging',

'Charlie Collingwood's Flogging' and 'The Whippingham Papers'). Swinburne said his idea of heaven was to be 'the powerless victim of the furious rage of a beautiful woman'. When a beautiful woman was not at hand Swinburne wasn't terribly fussy; he claimed he had once copulated with a monkey dressed as a woman.

## Word flu

The Scottish Royalist Sir Thomas Urquhart (1611–60) was taken prisoner by Roundheads during the English Civil War and locked up in the Tower of London. During his imprisonment he tried to save his neck by writing a book called *Pantochronochanon: A Peculiar Promptuary of Time*, which set out to prove that Urquhart was directly descended from Adam (153rd on his father's side) and Eve (147th on his mother's side).

Urquhart was chiefly known for writing impenetrably obscure books. His lengthy, complicated prose made him one of the most difficult writers in the English language. One of his pet projects was a proposal for a universal language – a forerunner of Esperanto. It was predictably complex: verbs had four voices, seven moods and eleven tenses; nouns and pronouns had eleven cases, four numbers and eleven genders, and 'every word in this language signifieth as well backward and forward, and however you invert the letter, still shall you fall upon significant words'. Urquhart boasted that his new language had sixty-four advantages over every other language in existence but, sadly, he never got round to proving it as he couldn't find a publisher. Another Urquhart work was a translation of Rabelais's *Gargantua and Pantagruel*, in which he described seventy-one hitherto unknown animal noises, including the 'curking' of quails and the 'boing' of buffaloes. According to tradition, he died in a fit of laughter when he heard about the restoration of the monarchy.

## Stranger than fiction

Amanda McKittrick Ros (1860–1939) died largely forgotten, but now enjoys cult status as arguably the world's worst ever novelist. She was born in 1860 at Drumaness, County Down, Ireland, the fourth child of a headmaster. She developed a highly unique style which she attributed to never having read a book in her life. It showed, agreed her critics. Ros wrote a series of quite unfathomable romantic novels in which nearly all of the characters had alliterative names. Her first novel, *Irene Iddesleigh*, was published in 1897; her second, *Delina Delaney*, was published a year later. In the posthumously published *Helen Huddlestone* all the characters are named after fruit and vegetables. There is a Lily Lentil, a Lord Raspberry who has a sister called Cherry, a Duke of Greengage and a Madam Pear, who 'had a swell staff of sweet-faced helpers swathed in stratagem, whose members and garments glowed with the lust of the loose, sparkled with the tears of the tortured, shone with the sunlight of bribery, dangled with the diamonds of distrust, slashed with sapphires of scandal and rubies wrested from the dainty persons of the pure'. You get the drift. Her poems, meanwhile, were reminiscent of McGonagall at his finest. 'Visiting Westminster Abbey' begins:

*Holy Moses! Have a look!*
*Flesh decayed in every nook!*
*Some rare bits of brain lie here,*
*Mortal loads of beef and beer,*

*Some of whom are turned to dust,*
*Every one bids lost to lust;*
*Royal flesh so tinged with 'blue'*
*Undergoes the same as you.*

Ros's career was marked by lengthy and vitriolic feuds. She wrote a torrent of mostly abusive verse on her pet subjects – lawyers, fashion, the Kaiser, the abandonment of moral standards, clerics and, inevitably, critics. She never recovered from what she took to be the massive snub of failing to secure a nomination for the Nobel Prize for Literature in 1930. By way of consolation, her works are now much sought after by connoisseurs of kitsch, and she has her own appreciation society.

## Prude awakening

The art critic and author John Ruskin (1819–1900) was twenty-eight when he married his cousin Effie Gray. Their wedding night did not go well. No one is quite sure exactly what happened when Effie removed her nightie, but Ruskin evidently found his bride's nakedness so shocking that he decided never to sleep with her again. Some suggest it was his first sight of womanly pubic hair that put him off; others have it that he was freaked by the discovery of menstruation. Suffice to say that the couple spent a sexless honeymoon in Venice where Ruskin painted, took copious notes on the local architecture and generally mused on such higher matters as the decline of the Venetian empire. He later relented and promised to sleep with Effie again in three years' time, on her twenty-fifth birthday, but when her birthday came around he simply extended the deadline. Meanwhile, the frustrated

Mrs Ruskin met the artist John Everett Millais, who was painting her husband's portrait. Millais was able to enlighten her on a few points, including the fact that a sexless marriage was grounds for divorce. The Ruskin marriage was annulled on the grounds of his 'incurable impotence'. Ruskin's fear of naked ladies never left him. In 1871, he founded the Ruskin School of Art, where, bizarrely, students were forbidden to draw or paint nude women.

## Brief encounters

James Joyce (1882–1941) was an underwear fetishist. He was turned on by the sight of his wife Nora's dirty knickers and kept a tiny pair of doll's panties in his pocket: his party trick in public bars was to slip them over his fingers and 'walk' them across the table top. Around the time of the publication of *Ulysses* he began an affair with a much younger woman he met in a unisex public lavatory in Zurich. He fell for her, he informed a friend, 'at the very moment she was in the act of pulling the chain'. Joyce overcame writer's block by masturbating. One day a fan approached him and said, 'Let me shake the hand that wrote *Ulysses*.' Joyce thought for a while and replied, 'No, best not, it's done a few other things as well.'

## Faecal matters

Before he wrote *Gulliver's Travels*, the satirist Jonathan Swift (1667–1745) was rector of a small Irish parish, where his odd appearance and strange behaviour earned him the nickname 'the mad parson'. Swift had obsessive-compulsive disorder and counted every step he walked. The journey from his apartment in Chelsea to the centre of London, he informed baffled acquaintances, was exactly 5,748 paces. He was also obsessed with exercise and dieting and took to eating his meals while walking round the room.

Swift had a well-earned reputation for extreme rudeness. His irritability was partly because of a painful gallstone problem which caused gritty matter to accumulate in his bladder. One day he was sitting in a coffee house when he was approached by Dr Arbuthnot, who had no idea who Swift was. Arbuthnot had just finished writing a letter. He politely asked Swift if he had any sand he could use to dry the ink. 'No, Sir,' Swift replied, 'but I have the gravel and if you will give me your letter I will piss upon it.' Swift especially hated Scots, children and women; the latter were 'a sort of species hardly a degree above a monkey' and 'not worth giving up the middle of your bed for'.

Towards the end of his writing career Swift became obsessed with bodily functions. He wrote a treatise on excrement in 1733 called *Human Ordure* under the pen-name 'Dr Shit', and two books about flatulence, *The Benefit of Farting Explained* (1722) and *Arse Musica; or, The Lady's Back Report,* under the name Countess of Fizzlerumpf (1722). Swift wrote under many pseudonyms, including Isaac Bickerstaff, T. Tinker, Andrew Tripe, Simon Wagstaff, Martinus Scribberus and SPAM. (The copywriter working on an advertisement for the manufacture of the canned ham product of the same name claimed he came up with it after communicating with Swift in a dream.)

Swift dreaded old age and foresaw the prolonged illness and terrible consequences of dementia. He told a friend, 'I shall die like a tree, from the top.' This was prophetic; before he died senile at the age of seventy-eight, Swift's manservant showed him off to members of the public for a fee.

## Alice in numberland

Charles Dodgson (1832–98), writing under the pen name Lewis Carroll, produced the classic of children's literature *Alice's Adventures in Wonderland*. Dodgson was first and foremost a professional mathematician who lectured at Christ Church, Oxford, for forty years. His students knew him as a tall, timid man who had a stammer and would flee the lecture room if he overheard a remark he thought was off-colour or slightly indecent. Dodgson was obsessed with random calculations. He calculated how long it took him to write a page, assuming that he could manage about 20 words a minute and a page represented about 150 words. Another Dodgson calculation of a slightly more unsettling nature came when he worked out how long it would take his 'child-friends' to give him 'millions of hugs and kisses', assuming that 'millions must mean 2 millions at least and that their rate of kissing probably wouldn't exceed 20 times a minute'. Queen Victoria loved *Alice's Adventures in Wonderland* so much that she demanded that his next book be sent to her the moment it appeared. When the eagerly awaited follow-up arrived it was called *An Elementary Treatise on Determinants.*

## The shape of things to come . . .

The science fiction writer H. G. Wells (1866–1946) had his first sexual experience with a prostitute when he was twenty-two, around the time he wrote *The Time Machine*. It was such a massive disappointment to him that he didn't see a naked female body again until his own honeymoon five years later – another major let-down – with his frigid wife Isabel. Wells afterwards made up for lost time with an endless string of extramarital affairs. He was an unlikely Lothario, being a short, fat, balding diabetic, with an overly large head and a high-pitched, squeaky voice. Perhaps the secret of his success was that, according to one lover, his body 'smelled of honey'. One of his more famous conquests was the novelist Dorothy M. Richardson, whom he later declared 'most interestingly hairy'. Wells, although diabetic and toothless, was still bothering prostitutes right up until his death a month before his eightieth birthday.

## Chick lit

The poet William Butler Yeats (1865–1939) had a lifelong obsession with magic and was a member of an obscure cult called the Hermetic Order of the Golden Dawn. He often composed his poems in a trance-like state he called 'spirit writing'. When he was riding the bus he would go off into a 'compositional trance' and stare straight ahead, uttering a low hum and beating time with his hands, to the amusement of other passengers. Almost unprecedented in literary history, and in spite of the fact that he couldn't spell, Yeats produced his greatest work when he was in his fifties. The newly famous poet suddenly found himself surrounded by adoring young women, but to his great frustration also found himself temporarily plagued with impotence and writer's block. Unable to compose poetry or to get it up, he experimented with a number of quack impotence cures. In 1934, he underwent a vasectomy, a procedure known as 'Steinaching', performed by a Viennese doctor, Eugene Steinach. He also tried injections of monkey glands, after which the Irish press dubbed him 'the Gland Old Man of Poetry'. In between writing poetry, seducing young women and dabbling in the occult, Yeats was also in the habit of trying to hypnotize hens.

## News of the weird

The Fleet Street journalist William Comyns Beaumont (1873–1956) held a variety of controversial beliefs which he expounded on in three lengthy books. *The Riddle of Prehistoric Britain*, published in 1946, set forth Beaumont's firmly held conviction that there was a Jewish conspiracy to overthrow the British Empire. He believed that the actual location of the Holy Land was Britain and part of Scandinavia. The lost world of Atlantis had also been one of the British Isles; it was from Atlantis that a race of giant Aryans had populated the earth, colonizing it as they spread from country to country. He was convinced that Egypt, the seat of the mighty Pharaohs, had in fact been situated in western Scotland. Moreover, London was actually Damascus, York was Babylon and Glastonbury was the garden of Eden. According to Beaumont, Earth had experienced a direct hit by a giant meteor somewhere near Edinburgh – or, more correctly, Jerusalem, as it was in those days – an event which led to Noah's flood and caused Britain to lose its subtropical climate and become cold and damp. Thereafter, the Roman Emperor Hadrian and the well-known Yorkshireman Constantine the Great had been responsible for perpetuating the malicious and wholly ridiculous myth that the Holy Land was not in Britain, but somewhere in the Middle East. None of these extreme views, however, was considered in any way incompatible with Beaumont's day job as leading staff writer with the *Daily Mail*.

## The great dictator

Dame Barbara Cartland (1901–2000) was the most prolific author in history. Dictating from a chaise longue at breakneck speed, she 'wrote' 723 romantic novels, selling an estimated one billion books. Her plots were generally very similar, featuring virginal heroines, dashing heroes, villainous female rivals, happy endings and a mysterious absence of sex.

Despite evidence to the contrary, she claimed that her own private life had given her exclusive knowledge of the 'secrets of love'. Her first brush with men came in her teens when a randy army major invited her to his bedroom to show her 'how his revolver worked'. She said she once received three proposals of marriage in a single fortnight, although in later versions of this account it had risen to around fifty. There was one actual engagement to an officer in the Life Guards, but she was appalled when her mother explained to her the mechanics of sexual intercourse and broke it off. The jilted fiancé threatened to shoot himself with his service revolver outside the coffee stall in Hyde Park. He didn't carry out his threat, but it came in very useful as a storyline (or two or three) later on.

In between writing fiction she still found time to champion various causes, especially the curative qualities of honey and vitamins (she once sent the actor Patrick Campbell a bottle of vitamins to 'cure' his stutter) and the colour pink. In later life she took to pulling her cheeks back with visible bits of sticking plaster and piling on cakes of white make-up and mascara, a look described by Clive James as 'like two crows that had crashed into a chalk cliff'.

Dame Barbara was an utter snob, and never afraid of reminding people that her daughter, Raine, had married into the Spencer family and become Princess Diana's stepmother. A BBC Radio 4 interviewer once asked her if she thought class barriers had disappeared. 'Of course,' she replied. 'Otherwise, why on earth do you suppose someone like me would be talking to someone like you?' She attributed her phenomenal literary output to twenty-nine different kinds of vitamin pills, and to Lord Beaverbrook, who advised her to keep the paragraphs in her novels to three lines or less. When she died aged ninety-eight she was laid to rest in a cardboard box in the grounds of her mansion home near Hatfield, Hertfordshire, while mourners joined in singing the Perry Como ballad 'I Believe'. Her number one fan is Colonel Gaddafi of Libya.

# Seven
# ARISTOCRATIC ECCENTRICS

*'Those comfortable padded lunatic asylums which are known, euphemistically, as the stately homes of England'.*

– VIRGINIA WOOLF (1882–1941)

## Have egg, will travel

Sir George Reresby Sitwell (1860–1943) had three talented children, Osbert, Sacheverell and Edith, each of whom became writers of note. Edith Sitwell, in her book *English Eccentrics*, made only a passing a reference to her father Sir George, but he deserved at least a chapter of his own.

Visitors to Sir George's family mansion, Renishaw Hall at Eckington in Derbyshire, were greeted by a sign on the front door. It read: 'I must ask anyone entering the house never to contradict me in any way, as it interferes with the functioning of my gastric juices and prevents me sleeping at night'. Sir George had seven rooms he used as studies, where he occupied himself writing such profoundly obscure epics as *The History of the Fork*, *The Black Death at Rotherham*, *The Use of the Bed*, *My Advice on Poetry*, *The History of the Cold* and *The Errors of Modern Parents*. Other proposed works had titles such as *Wool-Gathering in Medieval Times and Since*, *Lepers' Squints*, *Domestic Manners in Sheffield in the Year 1250* and *Acorns as an Article of Medieval Diet*. The only one that found a publisher was *On the Making of Gardens*, which appeared in 1909. His advice to his readers was not always entirely practical: 'The great secret of success in garden-making is that we should abandon the struggle to make nature beautiful round the house and should rather move the house to where nature is beautiful.'

Landscape gardening was also one of Sir George's main preoccupations. He employed 4,000 men at one time to dig him an artificial lake in the grounds, with wooden towers sticking out of the water from where he could survey his various epic and expensive projects, most of them never finished. Lawns were raised or lowered, lakes appeared then disappeared, large trees were relocated. To improve the view from his study window he had Chinese willow patterns painted onto his herd of white cows. His landscaping ambitions were extended to the homes of his children. 'I don't propose to do much here,' Sir George announced when visiting his son Sacheverell's house in 1924, 'just a sheet of water and a line of statues.'

Sir George also turned his hand to inventing. There was a musical toothbrush that played 'Annie Laurie' and a small revolver designed for shooting wasps. He also discovered a way of making knife handles from condensed milk, prompting an enquiry from his faithful family butler Henry Moat, 'But what if the cat gets them?' There was also a Sitwell Egg comprising a yolk of smoked salmon embedded in a white of rice in a synthetic shell. He thought that it would be a boon to explorers because it would never go 'off'. Whether you were in the desert or at the North Pole, all you would have to do is boil it for a few minutes and a nourishing meal would be yours. One day, Sir George arrived unannounced in the office of Mr Gordon Selfridge, founder of the Oxford Street store, and declared: 'I'm George Sitwell and I have my egg with me.' Mr Selfridge's response can only be guessed at, because plans to market the egg were quietly shelved and it was never mentioned again.

Sir George had only a passing acquaintance with the conventions of modern life. He tried to pay Sacheverell's school fees at Eton in pigs and potatoes. His method of calculating Osbert's allowance, meanwhile, was based on the amount that a forebear paid his eldest son at the time of the Black Death. A friend of Sir George had told him that he would 'give him a ring on Thursday'. Sir George waited and then complained bitterly about his friend's lack of consideration: 'Such a pity to promise people things and then forget about them. It is not considerate – really inexcusable.' Sir George had been expecting to receive a piece of jewellery.

He travelled extensively around Europe, always accompanied by his butler and an enormous collection of self-medication, deliberately mislabelled to stop anyone else using it. He also took with him his latest invention, a self-erecting mosquito net. It was slung over the bed and rose when weighted ropes attached to it were thrown out of the window, provoking complaints from people walking by who were struck on the head by the flying weights. To save money he and his butler often dossed down with tramps in dormitories. He lived on a diet of roast chicken which he liked to eat alone, despite always donning full evening dress for the purpose, no matter how primitive the surroundings.

Sir George's wide-ranging interests left little time for his beautiful, equally eccentric wife, Lady Ida. Her father, Lord Londesborough, who amassed a fortune through banking, was a stranger to moderation. On their family holidays he had a mile of red carpet laid from their villa to the sea at Scarborough and gave his servants cheque books so they didn't need to bother him with requests for money. Hopelessly extravagant, Lady Ida once spent the equivalent of about £8,000 on a 'lucky' piece of hangman's rope which she attached to her bed, and lavished a small fortune on her 'psychic' pig. However, her extravagance led her into debt and the clutches of a blackmailer, and her efforts to extricate herself from the situation resulted in a three-month sentence for fraud in 1915. Sir George could have bailed her out but chose not to, to the disgust of their children.

Sir George's children were a disappointment to him. When he found out that Osbert was writing a novel he advised him: 'You'd better drop that idea at once. My cousin had a friend who utterly ruined his health writing a novel.' He told Edith to give up her literary ambitions and take up gymnastics instead. 'There's nothing a man likes so much', he confided to her, 'as a girl who's good on the parallel bars.' The junior Sitwells were so anxious to avoid their father that they invented an imaginary round-the-world cruise on a yacht called the *Rover*, then had some fake headed notepaper made up on which they wrote to him explaining that the yacht's itinerary had yet to be finalized so they couldn't provide a forwarding address at which they could be contacted. All the while they were living in London, confident their ruse wouldn't be rumbled because their father was unable to recognize his own children when he passed them on the street.

## Mad, bad and dangerous to know

William, the fourth Lord Byron, great-uncle of the poet, was known as 'the Wicked Lord' because of his reputation for settling disputes violently. In 1765, he killed his cousin William Chaworth in a duel fought over a difference of opinion on how to correctly hang game. Byron was convicted of manslaughter; after his release, he mounted the sword he used to run through Chaworth's stomach on his bedroom wall. On another occasion, Byron had a disagreement with his coachman and shot him mid-journey. He dragged the man's body into the coach next to his wife and took the reins himself.

## Filthy rich

Eighteenth-century English nobility, when faced with newfangled ideas about disease and personal hygiene, clung to the belief that washing was strictly for the working classes. A duchess at a society dinner once sat down to eat with noticeably filthy hands. When the grubbiness of her fingers was remarked upon, she replied, 'Madam, you should see my feet.' When Queen Victoria inherited Buckingham Palace in 1837, it didn't even have a bathroom; her predecessors, the Georgian royals, believed it was 'sweat, damn it, that kept a man clean'.

The expression 'filthy rich' most appropriately described Charles Howard (1746–1815), eleventh Duke of Norfolk, who was said to be the richest and smelliest man in England. Howard was one of Regency London's most epic inebriates. He had an astonishing capacity for alcohol and was said to be capable of drinking five or six times more than any normal person – including his good friend the Prince Regent, who was not afraid of knocking back the odd gallon of cherry brandy. The Duke and the Prince were often seen together staggering around the streets of London, blind drunk.

The Duke was also a dedicated glutton and in old age became so massively obese that he couldn't get through a standard door frame. A bigger problem for his servants was the Duke's detestation of soap and water. When his body odour became unbearable they would wait until he was drunk then wash him while he lay comatose on the floor. In his later years he also suffered terribly from rheumatism. He complained to a friend, Dudley North, that he had tried everything to relieve the pain without effect. 'My Lord,' enquired North, 'did you ever try a clean shirt?'

## Peer pressure

John James Hamilton, the Marquess of Abercorn (1756–1818), was so overbearingly aristocratic that it was said even the King was afraid to speak to him. Hamilton wore his ceremonial Blue Ribbon of the Knights of the Garter everywhere he went, even when he was hunting. Servants were required to wear white kid gloves when they changed his bed linen and his footmen had to dip their hands in a bowl of rose water before handing him a dish. The novelist Walter Scott once came across a procession of five carriages with twenty outriders; it turned out to be Hamilton, off for a spot of lunch at the local inn.

In 1816, Hamilton's youngest daughter died of consumption. He was grief-stricken, but too proud to admit that a member of his family had died of a disease associated with poverty and the working classes. He begged his doctor to write a letter to *The Times* announcing that the death had been caused by something 'less common'.

## High-class hooligan

Henry Beresford, the third Marquess of Waterford (1811–59), was a notorious ne'er do well and upper-crust delinquent; the *Oxford Dictionary of National Biography* describes him as a 'reprobate and landowner'. Waterford took part in various orgies of drunken exhibitionism and random pugilistic encounters. He also made wild bets and got involved in destructive practical jokes, and spent most of his inherited fortune paying for the damage he caused. The origin of the phrase 'paint the town red' is said to date from 1837, the year when Waterford and a group of friends ran amok in the Leicestershire town of Melton Mowbray, daubing red paint over the town's toll-bar and several buildings.

One day on a whim he bought several large casks of gin and stood in the Haymarket in London, serving it free to passers-by in half-pint mugs. Within an hour he was besieged by every vagrant in London and a drunken riot ensued. The police were only able to extricate Waterford from the fracas by arresting him. He was later summoned to appear before Marlborough Street magistrates after driving his horse and carriage through a crowded street at high speed. Waterford arrived at court mounted on his horse and demanded they both be let in. As his horse was a star witness for the defence, he said, it should be cross-examined, for 'only he knows how fast he was going'. The judge, who knew a top-drawer fruit-cake when he saw one, elected to wash his hands of the case as quickly as possible and acquitted him.

On another occasion, Waterford hired eight cabs and a troupe of musicians to sit on the cab roofs, playing while they were driven round the streets at high speed. Waterford himself took the reins of the leading cab and drove so recklessly he was almost killed. After surviving this and many other dangerous pranks, he broke his neck in a hunting accident and died from his injury, aged forty-eight.

## Small deposit

In 1995, Lord Erskine of Rerrick (1926–95) bequeathed his testicles to the Bank of Scotland which had declared him bankrupt, because it had 'no balls'.

## The burrowing duke

The fifth Duke of Portland, William Cavendish-Bentinck-Scott (1800–79), was the strangest product of one of the English aristocracy's most ancient families. As a young man the Duke was a fairly 'normal' member of the British aristocracy and even served as an MP for several years. He was also fond of the opera. His problems began after he made his one and only proposal of marriage to the Covent Garden singer Adelaide Kemble. She turned him down – not unreasonably, as it turned out, because she was already secretly married, but the Duke took rejection badly and retired to his bedroom more or less permanently.

His bedroom was fitted with two letter boxes, one for incoming and one for outgoing correspondence. His valet was the only servant allowed near, in order to serve him daily a whole roast fowl. When the Duke fell ill the doctor was required to stand outside his bedroom while the servant took his master's pulse and reported his condition. On the rare occasions when he left his room and ventured outside, his staff were instructed to ignore him 'as they would a tree'.

Anyone who crossed the Duke's path was immediately impressed by his eccentric style of dress, especially his trousers, which were tied above the ankle by pieces of string, and the very tall hat perched on top of his long brown wig. He usually carried an umbrella which he used to ward off the gaze of any curious onlookers. Not that there were very many, as the Duke made it his business to avoid people as far as possible. He only travelled at night and was always preceded by a woman holding a lantern, who had strict instructions to keep fifty paces in front of him and never to turn round, on pain of dismissal.

The Duke's passion for privacy led to wild rumours. Some thought that he had become afflicted by a disfiguring skin disease; others were certain that was raving mad. The other main local source of gossip was the Duke's eccentric building operations. Over a period of twenty years he built a vast network of tunnels and underground chambers beneath his country estate at Welbeck Abbey, including a huge ballroom, said to be the biggest room in Europe. There was also a massive library and a games room big enough to take a dozen snooker tables. In all, there were about 15 miles of tunnels running underneath his home, linking the subterranean rooms with the Abbey and with each other. One tunnel was a mile and a quarter long and led directly to the local railway station at Worksop, allowing him to travel unseen when he ventured out to catch a train to London. The tunnel was wide enough to take two carriages and was lit by hundreds of gas jets. All of the underground rooms and passages were painted pink.

By the time the Duke died in 1879, Welbeck Abbey had fallen into a terrible state of neglect. When his cousin arrived with his family to take up his inheritance he found the grounds overgrown and strewn with rubble. Forcing the front door open, the new Duke was astonished to discover that the floor was missing from the main hall. The only habitable rooms were the four or five used by the fifth Duke in the west wing, all painted pink, with little or no furniture apart from the odd commode in the corner. One of the rooms was lined with cupboards that were filled with green boxes, each containing several dark brown wigs.

The fifth Duke's seclusion also resulted in a bizarre legal battle over his will. In 1896, a Mrs Anna Druce made the astonishing claim that her deceased father-in-law Thomas Charles Druce, a dealer in second-hand furniture at the Baker Street Bazaar in London, was actually William John Cavendish-Bentinck-Scott, fifth Duke of Portland. She claimed that the fifth Duke had tired of his self-enforced seclusion and invented an alter ego in the shape of Thomas Druce so he could experience the simple life of a tradesman.

The Jekyll and Hyde existence, she claimed, was maintained via a secret tunnel from the Duke's house in Cavendish Square leading to Druce's furniture shop, allowing the Duke to swap identities whenever he liked without fear of discovery. The story was the media sensation of the day, especially when her son George arrived in England from Australia to claim the Portland estate. The case to claim the Portland inheritance dragged on for years, long after Mrs Druce was admitted to a mental home in 1903. A company was set up to support the case with a capital of over £30,000, subscribed by the public in expectation of huge profits. In the end the authorities called their audacious bluff. The Druce coffin was finally opened in 1907 and was found indeed to contain the body of T. C. Druce. One of the difficulties in disproving the claim was the lack of visual records of the Duke of Portland, a recluse who had shunned public contact. A photograph of a bust was finally submitted as evidence of his appearance, which in one important respect was unlike Druce, who, according to the testimony of those who knew him, had two large warts on his nose.

## Sold short

The tenth Duke of Hamilton, Alexander Douglas (1767–1852), outbid the British Museum in 1842 when he paid £11,000 for a magnificent ancient tomb originally made for an Egyptian princess, and housed it in a fabulous mausoleum at his ancestral home, Hamilton Palace. The Duke frequently visited his magnificent sarcophagus and imagined himself in it. He even bought the spices he was planning to have himself embalmed in. There was, however, one small problem: the sarcophagus made been made for someone much smaller than the Duke, and as it had been made from a piece of rare Egyptian marble, could not be altered. It wasn't until his death in 1852 that it was discovered that he was too tall to fit inside it; the only way they could get his lordship in was by sawing his legs off and placing them in the coffin beside him.

## Mitford family values

David Bertram Ogilvy Freeman-Mitford (1878–1958), second Baron of Redesdale, was head of one of the oddest households in England. Redesdale was a brave army officer who fought with distinction and lost a lung in the Boer War. His career took an unexpected sideways move when he became editor of the upmarket women's weekly *The Lady*.

This came as a surprise to many, not merely because he took his mongoose to work to catch rats, but also because he was an avowed chauvinist and also semi-literate, having hardly ever read a book in his life. When his wife read *Tess of the D'Urbervilles* to him he found it so upsetting she had to explain that it was a work of fiction. Redesdale was dumbstruck. 'What! The damned feller made it up?' he shouted. The writer in the family, his brother Clement, was the author of one book, a privately printed volume of his letters to *The Times* and other publications, mostly on the subject of manure; the greatness of Elizabethan England, it appears, was due to the widespread use of sheep droppings in producing an organically based diet and therefore a sound society.

Lord Redesdale moved his family several times from one large residence to another, finally settling permanently at Swinbrook, near Chipping Norton. His family renamed it 'Swinebrook' because it was cold, draughty and had a plumbing system unimproved since the Black Death. It was built as a fortress, according to his daughter Jessica, to keep out 'Huns, Frogs, Americans, blacks and all other foreigners'. Lord Redesdale was truly xenophobic. 'Abroad is unutterably bloody and foreigners are fiends,' he said. 'I loathe abroad, nothing would induce me to live there. As for foreigners they are all the same, and they all make me sick.' He made no distinction between race or colour. When one of his nephews married an Argentinian of Spanish origin he remarked, 'I hear that Robin's married a black.'

'Farve', as Lord Redesdale was known to his six daughters and one son, had some novel ideas about bringing up children. He was an enthusiastic huntsman and occasionally used them as quarry. He had little time for any form of education. His son Tom was sent to school, but his daughters received no formal education at all. Lady Redesdale, meanwhile, held strong opinions about health and diet, believing that the body would heal itself more effectively without the intervention of doctors or medicine, especially vaccination, which she described as 'pumping disgusting dead germs into the good body'. Lady Redesdale once met Hitler and lectured him at length about the health benefits of wholemeal bread, while her daughter Unity translated. She refrained from sharing her other dietary rules with the Führer; although neither she nor Lord Redesdale practised the Jewish faith, the Mitford children were not allowed to eat pork, rabbit, hare or shellfish, 'as dictated by Moses in the Old Testament'. School meals were a great relief to Tom, who wrote home from Eton: 'We have sossages every day.' One day the children burst into the morning room where their mother was writing letters to inform her: 'Diana says she's going to jump off the roof, she's about to commit suicide!' Lady Redesdale replied without looking up: 'Tell her it's her favourite pudding for luncheon, that's sure to get her down.'

When Lord Redesdale died, *The Times* noted with delicate understatement that he 'adhered to somewhat old-fashioned views with tenacity and boisterousness'. His fame was eclipsed by that of his six variously gifted daughters, collectively known as the Mitford sisters, of whom only two inherited their father's right-wing politics to an extreme. Unity Mitford became a friend – and possibly a lover – of Hitler, who described her as 'a perfect specimen of Aryan womanhood', while Diana Mitford married the fascist Sir Oswald Mosley.

## Taking the plunge

Charles Radclyffe, fifth Earl of Derwentwater (1693–1746), was a gamomaniac – an obsessive whose disorder is characterized by persistent proposals of marriage. He proposed on fifteen occasions to the reluctant Charlotte, Countess of Newburgh, who became so annoyed by the constant harassment that she bolted herself into her home and gave her servants instructions to throw him off the property on sight. The Earl finally found a way into her house by climbing onto her roof and lowering himself down the chimney into her drawing room where, black from soot, he made his sixteenth marriage proposal. His persistence paid off and they were married at Brussels on 24 June 1724.

## Gerald's japes

Gerald Hugh Tyrwhitt-Wilson, fourteenth Lord Berners (1883–1950), inherited his title in 1918 along with his fortune and his estate, Faringdon House in Oxfordshire. As a child Berners showed early signs of eccentricity when he threw his mother's spaniel out of the bedroom window. He explained later that he heard someone say that if you threw a dog in water it would instinctively learn to swim and wondered if a dog thrown from a window would instinctively learn to fly.

In adulthood he acquired a number of idiosyncrasies, not least of which was his habit of dying the doves at his home in various pastel shades and dressing his whippets with diamond collars. He also painted pictures of his horses as they posed for him in the drawing room and had a harpsichord fitted into the rear compartment of his Rolls-Royce. Meals at Faringdon were served colour coordinated. For example, if Berners's mood was pink, lunch would consist of beetroot soup, lobster, tomatoes and strawberries.

In 1935, he built the Faringdon Folly, a 140-foot tower. When he sought planning permission some of the public objected and Berners was asked to justify his project. He explained, 'The great point of the tower is that it will be entirely useless.' The authorities were satisfied and the plans were approved. When his folly was finally built he put a sign on it which read: 'Members of the public committing suicide from this tower do so at their own risk'.

Berners was a great practical joker. On train journeys he made sure that he had a compartment all to himself by wearing a black skull cap and comedy black glasses, then leaning out of his carriage window and beckoning fellow travellers to join him. Anyone brave enough to take up the challenge soon left; Berners liked to check his temperature every few minutes with a rectal thermometer. During the Battle of Britain, he sent a spoof invitation to Sybil Colefax, a famously shameless social climber. It read: 'I wonder if by any chance you are free to dine tomorrow night? It is only a tiny party for Winston and GBS [George Bernard Shaw]. I think it important they should get together at this moment. There will be nobody else except for Toscanini and myself.' Cruelly, both the address and the signature were illegible.

## Flight of fancy

Benjamin O'Neale Stratford, sixth Earl of Aldborough (1808–75), was the last of a long line of oddballs. His great-grandfather, the first Earl, created a bogus family tree claiming descent from William the Conqueror, then took to introducing himself as the Earl of Aldborough in the Palatine of Upper Ormonde. Sharp-eyed students of heraldry noticed that there was no such place and that his family coat of arms was identical to that of Alexander the Great. Having gone to the trouble of establishing his fake pedigree, he died four months later. The second Earl was famous for throwing lavish house parties. He left fifty-four wills, having died in the middle of a party during which he was planning to have each of his one hundred guests married to each other. The third Earl was a much less gregarious type. He anticipated the arrival of visitors to his home by hiding all the fruit from his garden to stop them from eating it and would greet each guest with the enquiry: 'What time do you leave?'

The sixth Earl was a prototype Howard Hughes. He dedicated his life and his considerable fortune to constructing the world's biggest hot air balloon. Highly reclusive and rarely seen outside his family estate, he worked on his fantasy dirigible in absolute secrecy in the grounds of Stratford Lodge in a vast hangar. He toiled for twenty years on his all-absorbing ambition, so fearful of rivals stealing his design that he kept only one servant and refused even to employ a cook; he had meals-on-wheels delivered daily by Royal Mail coach.

The Earl planned to pilot the balloon himself on a grand inaugural flight across the Channel to France. In anticipation he purchased an acre of land on the banks of the Seine where he confidently expected to be greeted by swarms of cheering Frenchmen. One Sunday morning in 1856, however, tragedy struck when Stratford Lodge went up in flames. Lord Aldborough, who was much less interested in the fate of his historic family home than saving his precious airship, ran around the blazing estate urging onlookers, 'Save the balloon house.' Although hundreds of buckets of water were flung over the great hangar, the balloon could not be saved. Lord Aldborough was a broken man. He moved to Spain where he lived reclusively in hotels. He had meals sent up to his room, but wouldn't allow anyone to remove the used dishes. When his suite was full of soiled crockery he would simply move to another. When he died, filthy and neglected in a hotel room littered with dirty cutlery and old crockery, the earldom expired with him.

## Lady light fingers

Mary Monckton (1746–1840), wife of the seventh Earl of Cork, was a popular Regency period host to some of the most famous people of the day, including Dr Johnson, Lord Byron, Sir Walter Scott and the Prince of Wales. The diarist Fanny Burney described her as 'very short, very fat but handsome, splendidly and fantastically dressed, rouged not unbecomingly yet evidently and palpably desirous of gaining notice and admiration'. Lady Cork continued to entertain in style at dinners and receptions until she was well into her nineties. The favour was seldom returned, because she was also a rampant kleptomaniac. Her 'tendency' was so widely known that her hosts anticipated her visits by hiding their best silver and replacing it with pewter utensils. It made little difference; Lady Cork scooped it up and hid it in her muff anyway. When she got home her servants would gather together any items they didn't recognize and send them back with an apology. It wasn't just cutlery that Lady Cork stole; she once made off with a live hedgehog in her handbag.

## Love me, love my dogma

Francis Henry Egerton, the eighth Earl of Bridgwater (1754–1829), was a miserable recluse who preferred the company of his dogs to that of people. The Egerton dogs lived like aristocrats in his family mansion, Ashridge House in Hertfordshire. Every night he dined with a dozen canines at his table, each dressed in the latest fashions including little hand-made leather boots. Each dog wore a linen napkin, ate off silver dishes and had its own footman.

Another of Egerton's obsessions were his boots. His footwear was used, in effect, as a diary. He had a different pair of shoes for each day of the year and every night he would remove his shoes and place them next to the pair he had worn the day before, until he had rows and rows of shoes removed in chronological order. The shoes were never cleaned and left exactly as they were. He could work out the date and the weather conditions on any particular day by observing the state of the shoes.

Egerton spent the last years thirty years of his life living in Paris, a city he said he despised. During all this time he didn't manage to pick up a word of French. He missed home, especially the English hunting and shooting season, and made up for it by recreating it in his Paris garden, staging miniature hunts and keeping it stocked with partridges and pigeons with their wings clipped so that, in spite of his failing eyesight, he could shoot them for 'sport'. At great expense he also hired one of France's top chefs who was instructed to cook him, to the chef's disgust, boiled beef and potatoes. On one occasion, Egerton set off for the country for the summer, complete with full retinue of thirty servants and sixteen carriages full of luggage. He returned after a few hours because he couldn't find a restaurant that served boiled beef and potatoes.

The misanthropic Earl died in Paris in 1829, unmarried and surrounded by soiled footwear and pampered cats and dogs. There was, however, one more unusual legacy – his lengthy and constantly changing will. He used to cheer himself up by having his secretary read aloud extracts from it. The Earl was one of many Creationists who were alarmed by the heretical new theories being advanced by the new science of geology, so in his will he left £8,000 to the Royal Society to fund the writing of a book that would 'prove the power, wisdom and goodness of God manifested in the Creation' – the so-called Bridgwater Treatises. Accordingly, eight sympathetic 'experts' were chosen from various branches of British science to write an essay proving the case for intelligent design. They were mocked by Darwin and his supporters as the 'Bilgewater Treatises'. The Egerton dogs were not mentioned in the will.

## Too posh to park

Like many of her class, Lady Diana Cooper (1892–1986), the famous socialite and muse of Evelyn Waugh, was a stranger to life's practicalities. She once contacted the War Office during the Blitz advising them to place large magnets in London's parks to attract Hitler's bombs. In later years she became even more detached. At the dinner table Lady Cooper liked to warm her plate, and everyone else's, by holding them over her breasts. During the day she wore a large hat concealing a set of rollers and carried with her everywhere a small dog in a basket. If she went somewhere where dogs were not allowed, she smuggled it in, concealed inside a large muff.

Lady Cooper's driving skills were legendary. She regularly ran red lights and abandoned her car wherever she liked, leaving a message in her windscreen which read: 'Please have pity on a poor blind lame old lady'. At a reception honouring the musician Sir Robert Mayer on his 100th birthday, the elderly Lady Cooper fell into conversation with a friendly woman who looked vaguely familiar. Her failing eyesight prevented her from recognizing her fellow guest, until she peered more closely at the magnificent diamonds and realized she was talking to the Queen. 'I'm terribly sorry, Ma'am,' said Lady Cooper, breaking into a curtsey, 'I didn't recognize you without your crown on.'

## Degenerate Douglas

William Douglas, fourth Duke of Queensberry (1724–1810), was the richest and the dirtiest old man of his generation, known to most of his acquaintances as 'Old Q'. In his prime Douglas was famous as a successful gambler. His reputation was sealed after the famous 'chaise match' in 1750 when he bet 1,000 guineas that a carriage could carry a passenger 19 miles in one hour. Douglas stretched the definition of carriage to the limit with a purpose-built stripped-down vehicle shell made from lightweight materials and pulled by specially trained horses, and won the wager at Newmarket. Douglas regularly employed a 'running footman' to run messages and errands for him and to beat a path before him in heavy crowds. He interviewed prospective candidates by making them do a test run up Piccadilly, dressed in full ducal livery, while he watched from the balcony of his home overlooking the busy street. One candidate ran so quickly that Queensberry called down to him, 'You'll do very well for me!'

'And your lordship's livery will do very well for me', the man replied, as he disappeared from sight, not to return.

It is as a pursuer and seducer of the opposite sex well into his dotage that Douglas is chiefly remembered. The libidinous old Duke was a regular fixture on the balcony of his London house, No. 138 Piccadilly, where he spent his days ogling the women who passed beneath, occasionally despatching his runner to proposition any that took his fancy. Although he had lost the sight in one eye, was stone deaf, had hardly any teeth left and was severely arthritic, he chased after women of every size and shape 'and with so much ardour at fourscore as he had done at twenty', according to William Carpenter's *Peerage for the People* (1835).

The randy old aristocrat went to great lengths to maintain his sex drive with the help of a strict fitness regime. He employed the former physician to Louis XV, Père Elisée, who was paid a handsome bonus every time his lecherous patient could manage an erection. The Duke's death, it was said, was eventually hastened by eating too much fruit. Remarkably, he had managed to avoid venereal disease throughout his life – an exceptional feat for an eighteenth-century stud. Queensberry was known to bathe in gallons of milk, believing that it was good for his libido. J. H. Jesse, writing in 1843, thirty-three years after the Duke's death, recalled that in London there was still an almost universal suspicion of milk in case it been used in one of Old Q's baths.

## Sorry Sykes

Sledmore Hall in Yorkshire was home to two generations of wealthy eccentric landowners, both called Sir Tatton Sykes. Tatton Sykes senior (1772–1863) was a prominent sportsman and bully. A throwback to another age, he wore clothes that had been out of fashion for decades, ate mutton fat and fruit pies for breakfast and went everywhere by horse, refusing to use coaches or the newfangled railway system.

He founded a huge stud at Sledmere and at one time owned over one hundred mares. Despite his strange decision to never train any of his fillies, which led to many homebreds being useless, he was a popular racehorse owner and attended every St Leger for seventy-six years. He had a horse named after him, which in 1864 won the 2,000 Guineas and St Leger, but finished second in the Derby, which it might have won had the jockey not been drunk. At home Sir Tatton terrorized his family, including his wife, who spent most of her time hiding in her orangery whenever he was around. He believed that children had to be thrashed into shape and was once seen chasing his son and heir through the village, barefoot and screaming, with a whip.

When Tatton Sykes junior (1826–1913) inherited his father's title at the age of thirty-seven, he set about wiping out the traces of a disturbed and miserable childhood. He sold most of the prized racing stud and destroyed Sledmere Hall's carefully cultivated orangery, hothouses and flower beds. His obsessive hatred for flowers stayed with him for the rest of his life. He never allowed any of his tenants to grow flowers and made them grow cauliflowers instead. By day he could be seen wandering through the village, walking stick in hand, slashing the head of any stray bloom he came across.

He was obsessive about maintaining a constant temperature and whenever he went out he wore eight overcoats and two pairs of trousers, which were discarded along the way one by one as he got warmer. The abandoned clothing lay on the ground until it was retrieved by local children who followed in his wake when word got round that he paid a shilling for every garment returned. Another Sykes obsession was his hatred of front doors on houses. He disliked the sight of front doors so much that he had entire housing estates designed without them.

His marriage to Lady Sykes, thirty years his junior, was

not a happy one. He drove her to a life of drink and heavy gambling, earning her the nickname 'Lady Satin Tights'. When she ran up heavy debts he reacted by placing an advertisement in all the national newspapers:

> I, SIR TATTON SYKES, hereby give notice that I will NOT be RESPONSIBLE for any DEBTS or ENGAGEMENTS which my wife, LADY JESSICA CHRISTINA SYKES, may contract, whether purporting to be on my behalf or by my authority or otherwise.

His refusal to settle her debts led to an infamous legal dispute in 1897. When the case came to court, Lady Sykes's counsel revealed that Sir Tatton had once ordered his servants to hang his son's pet terriers by their necks from a tree in order to teach his wife a lesson for drinking and spending too much money.

Apart from the wearing of multiple layers of overcoats, Sir Tatton also thought that cold rice pudding was the key to eternal life. When informed that his house was on fire in 1911, he refused to allow the impending crisis to disturb his digestion. 'I must eat my pudding,' he told his rescuers, 'I must eat my pudding.' Following the death of his estranged wife in 1912, he became convinced that he was going to die at precisely 11.30 a.m. – a time when he normally went out riding. He would get ready to mount his horse, then lose his nerve and wave the horse away, muttering, 'No, no, can't ride, can't ride, going to die.' Death came for him in 1913, to the inconvenience of the Metropole Hotel in London where he was staying. The hotel manager was anxious not to upset the other guests by letting on that there was a corpse on the premises and tried to smuggle Sykes out inside a hollow settee. The plan was abandoned when Sir Tatton's son found out about it. 'However my father leaves this hotel,' he fumed, 'he shall leave it like a gentleman.'

## Cold comfort

The Camerons of Scotland, who fought on the side of Bonnie Prince Charlie in the Battle of Culloden, enjoyed a reputation for toughness. Sir Ewen Cameron of Lochiel (1629-1719) was said to have killed the last wolf in Scotland with his bare hands and was the last to hold out against Oliver Cromwell, having once bitten through a Cromwellian officer's windpipe. One winter's day Sir Ewen was out camping in the Highlands with his grandson, Donald. The weather took a turn for the worse and as night fell they elected to set up camp in the open. Sir Ewen noticed that his young companion had rolled a large snowball to make a pillow for his head. He quickly kicked it away, growling, 'I'll have no effeminacy here, boy.'

## Faulty towers

The most fantastic architectural folly ever attempted in Britain was the work of William Beckford (1760–1844), who inherited the greatest private fortune in England at the age of ten when his father, a Jamaican sugar plantation owner, left him £1 million and an annual income of £100,000.

Beckford's childhood and early teens were spent in extraordinary opulence; he was given piano lessons by Mozart when he was five, completed the Grand Tour when he was sixteen and had put together one of England's biggest art collections before his twentieth birthday. He caused a furore in 1784 when he was caught in compromising circumstances with a fifteen-year-old boy, William Courtenay, son of the eighth Earl of Devon. Beckford fled to the Continent and sat out the scandal in exile. He spent the next thirteen years wandering around Europe accompanied by a huge retinue including his doctor, baker, cook, valet and a small orchestra. He travelled everywhere with his own bed and had the walls of the hotel rooms he stayed in repapered with his choice of prints. On a trip to Portugal he took with him a flock of sheep, not to keep him supplied with English lamb, but so that the view from his window reminded him of home.

Beckford eventually returned to England but found himself ostracized, and his reputation was never fully restored. He withdrew to his vast estate near Hindon, Wiltshire, with his four dogs – Viscount Fartlebury, Mrs Fry, Nephew and Tring – plus a posse of servants including an Italian dwarf who allegedly lived on a diet of mushrooms. To prevent prying eyes, at fantastic expense he had a wall erected around his estate, 7 miles long and 12 feet high, topped by spiked railings. Beckford made up for his solitary existence by occasionally ordering a formal dinner for twelve; when the table was fully laid and the footmen in position behind the chairs he would sit down alone, sample one meal then retire to bed. The other meals were probably eaten later by his staff.

In 1795, Beckford embarked on the grandiose building project for which he is most famous: Fonthill Abbey, a huge, fantastic Gothic structure with a 300-foot central tower, making it one of the tallest buildings in England. Unfortunately Beckford's impatience to have the building completed quickly, plus his system of plying his workers with alcohol to make them work faster, ensured that a few corners were cut. In 1800, he insisted on sitting down to Christmas dinner at Fonthill while the cement was still wet. Just as his servants were carrying his food into the dining room the kitchen collapsed behind them. Luckily no one was killed and rebuilding resumed immediately afterwards. Six years after work commenced, the central tower was completed – and very quickly fell down. Beckford simply ordered the immediate construction of a new tower. This time his architectural folly lasted a couple of years, then it too collapsed in a heap of rubble. He was forced to sell Fonthill in 1822 after a crash in the sugar market, by which time three towers had fallen. Beckford retired to Bath. According to legend, he watched the tower fall a fourth and final time as he sat in his garden 30 miles away.

## Pride and prejudice

Charles Seymour, sixth Duke of Somerset (1662–1748), was known as 'the Proud Duke' because of his obsession with rank and protocol. He was such a snob that he refused to communicate with his servants except by sign language. Whenever he travelled from London to his country estates he sent outriders ahead of his carriage to clear the roads of riff-raff, and had a series of houses built at convenient points along the route so that he wouldn't have to stop overnight in a public inn and mingle with the lower classes.

Even members of his own family were not spared his imperious manner. The Duke always made one of his daughters stand on guard while he was taking his afternoon nap. He woke up one afternoon after falling off the sofa and was furious to discover that his daughter, Charlotte, had taken the liberty of sitting down. He promptly cut her out of his will. One day his second wife dared to tap him on the shoulder with her fan. He rebuked her: 'Madam, my first wife was a Percy, and she never took such a liberty.'

## Aladdin sane

Henry Cyril Paget, fifth Marquess of Anglesey (1875–1905), was born into an illustrious Victorian dynasty. His grandfather Sir Henry William Paget was a cavalry commander whose stoic bravery at Waterloo, when he lost a limb but insisted on carrying on until the battle was won, made him a national hero and earned him the family nickname 'One Leg'.

Henry Paget was raised an only child in a Gothic-style mansion in Anglesey, north Wales, with one elderly nanny and an army of pets for company. When he was 23, his father died leaving him a 30,000 acre estate with an annual income of £110,000, equivalent to £55 million today. He devoted his brief, extraordinary life to squandering his very large personal fortune, mostly on jewellery.

In 1898, he married his cousin Lily, a marriage of convenience to unlock restrictions on the family money. He was particularly fond of using his beautiful young wife to showcase his vast collection of gems, often all of it simultaneously. On their honeymoon Paget saw his new wife window-shopping in the jewellers Van Cleef and Arpels, so he purchased the entire window display, then made her wear all of it to the races. Marital relations were further strained when he took to waking her in the middle of the night, ordering her to strip naked and then covering her with gems. After two years the marriage was annulled on the grounds of non-consummation.

Henry Paget's other chief interest was the theatre. In 1901, he converted the centuries-old Paget family chapel into a playhouse and put on a series of expensive productions in which casts of up to fifty or sixty were dressed in fantastic jewel-studded costumes. At first his only audience were his servants, but later he persuaded a professional theatre company to travel to Anglesey from London bringing with them top actors with vastly inflated salaries. Paget always reserved a small but colourful part for himself. He was especially fond of *Aladdin* and played the part of the Emperor's daughter Princess Pekoe. During the interval he would perform his celebrated 'Butterfly Dance' wearing large gossamer-effect wings and huge clusters of jewels. In other shows he was Little Boy Blue, wearing diamonds from head to foot.

At huge cost, he took the company on a tour of Europe for three years, complete with an entire orchestra, a small army of dressers and five truckloads of luggage, costumes and theatrical paraphernalia. Paget meanwhile travelled in his own car with Louis XV-style decorations on the roof and a perfumed exhaust. In just four years he managed to blow his entire fortune on clothes, jewels and the upkeep of his travelling show. He owed a further £544,000, equivalent to more than a quarter of a billion pounds today.

Instead of cutting back, he went on spending, piling up debts until in 1904 he was declared bankrupt. Five months later he died of pneumonia at the Hotel Royale in Monte Carlo. The bankruptcy sale of his effects, including the world's biggest collection of jewel-encrusted walking sticks, lasted seventeen days. He was succeeded by his cousin, the sixth Marquess of Anglesey, whose first priority was to systematically destroy all evidence that Henry Cyril Paget had ever existed. His obituary noted: 'His example will remain one of the strongest arguments against our hereditary system that the most ardent revolutionary would wish for.'

## The quiet life

The socially phobic fourth Duke of Marlborough, George Spencer (1739–1817), went for three years at a stretch without uttering a single word. He was jolted out of his silence at the beginning of the fourth year by the imminent arrival of the Frenchwoman Madame de Staël; when informed of her visit he said simply, 'I'm off.'

## You ain't seen nothing, yeti

The death of the third Baronet Sir Hugh Charles Rhys Rankin on 2 May 1988 deprived *Who's Who* of its most entertaining entry. Born in the Tunisian desert in 1899, the son of a big-game hunter, as a teenager Rankin ran away from Harrow school to work in a Belfast shipyard. He later joined the British cavalry and became an accomplished swordsman, before receiving a disability discharge after being shot by an Irish sniper. Rankin travelled widely in the Middle East and briefly became a Muslim, assuming the forename Omar. In 1935, he became president of the British Muslim Society, but resigned after a few weeks because 'they were very rude'. By 1944, Rankin was a practising Buddhist.

In 1950, he was elected to Perthshire County Council, one of the most solidly Conservative areas of Scotland, after describing himself as 'a blood-red militant Communist in every possible way'.

In 1959, he and Lady Rankin had an unsettling encounter

with the Abominable Snowman during a trip in the Himalayas. On another occasion, while cycling through the Lairig Ghru Pass in Scotland, they suddenly felt 'the Presence' behind them. They turned and saw a big, olive-complexioned man dressed in a long robe and sandals, with long flowing hair. 'We were not in the least afraid,' Rankin said later. 'Being Buddhists we at once knew who he was. We at once knelt and made obeisance.' Rankin went on to explain that they had instantly recognized the hairy stranger as a Bodhisattva, 'one of five Perfected Men who control the destinies of this world, and meet once a year in a cave in the Himalayas . . . one of them lives permanently in the Scottish Cairngorms.' According to Rankin, 'the Presence' addressed them in a language he thought was Sanskrit and he replied politely in Urdu. 'All the time the Bodhisattva was with us (about ten minutes) a heavenly host of musicians was playing high up in the sky. Immediately the Bodhisattva left us the music ceased and we never heard it again.'

In 1965, Rankin claimed that he was 'the only baronet in the United Kingdom who is living on national assistance'. When asked what job he would like to do, he replied: 'Anything except being a butler. I hate snobbishness.' He listed his hobbies as 'golf, sheep shearing and crawling under fir trees'.

## Bad hair day

The first Marchioness of Salisbury (1750–1835) was a keen sportswoman and Master of the Hertfordshire Hounds. In spite of poor eyesight and failing strength she continued to hunt well into her seventies, although she had to be tied into her saddle and led by a groom. The Marchioness refused to grow old gracefully and still wore the fashion of her youth, with her hair piled high and decorated with feathers, into her eighties. She died when a fire ripped through the west wing of her home, Hatfield House. It was several hours before the blaze was brought under control, by which time all that remained of Lady Salisbury were her dentures and a few charred bones. At the inquest, it was established that the fire had started at the top of Lady Salisbury's head, when her hair caught in a chandelier.

# Eight
# MILITARY ECCENTRICS

*'Sir, I have just written you a long letter. On reading it over, I have thrown it into the wastepaper basket. Hoping this will meet with your approval. I am Sir Your obedient servant Lt. Col. A. D. Wintle'*

– LETTER TO *THE TIMES* FROM LIEUTENANT-COLONEL ALFRED DANIEL WINTLE (1892–1958)

## The Ironic Duke

Arthur Wellesley, Duke of Wellington (1769–1852), victor of Waterloo and later twice Prime Minister of his country, was a blunt man with a deadpan manner and little time for small talk. When an aristocratic lady enquired whether the great man had been surprised to discover he had won the Battle of Waterloo, he replied icily, 'Not half so much surprised as I am right now, Ma'am.' Wellington also had little time for music, especially anything remotely contemporary. In Vienna he sat stony-faced through a performance of Beethoven's *The Battle of Vienna*. When asked by a Russian diplomat whether the music was like the real battle, the Duke replied, 'No. If it had been, I should have run away myself.' At Waterloo in 1815 the British cavalry commander Lord Uxbridge had his horse shot from under him nine times. Eventually, as he was riding beside the Duke of Wellington, he too was hit by French grapeshot. 'By God, Sir, I've lost my leg,' he informed Wellington. The Duke momentarily observed the shattered limb. 'By God, Sir,' he replied, 'so you have,' then continued to survey the battlefield through his telescope.

## Wintle's war

With his ramrod straight back, neatly trimmed moustache, immaculate uniform and monocle held firmly in place by a determined squint, Lieutenant-Colonel Alfred Daniel Wintle (1897–1958) was every inch the quintessential English officer and gentleman. He served with varying degrees of distinction in two world wars. Wintle hated foreigners, but reserved a particularly intense dislike for Germans. He was delighted, therefore, to find himself at war with them in 1914.

Wintle joined the Royal Military and was sent to France with the Royal Garrison Artillery. On his first day at the front he walked into a heavy German bombardment and watched as the officer next to him was blown to pieces. Wintle was unscathed but forced himself to stand to attention for thirty seconds so he could 'again become an Englishman'. He had another misadventure at Ypres in 1917 when he trod on an unexploded bomb and woke up in a field hospital minus his left eye, one kneecap and several fingers. He wore his trademark monocle from that day on; he was only nineteen years old at the time.

His war was over, or so it was reasonably assumed, but Wintle simply planned his escape from the Southern General Hospital back to the front disguised in a nurse's uniform. Bizarrely, he decided to try out his deception by attending the nurses-only dance on the evening before his escape. Unfortunately the monocle was a dead give-away. Wintle slipped his nurse's outfit on again and at the second attempt escaped back to France by train. In November 1918, he was again in the thick of the action near Jolentz, where he single-handedly took thirty-five prisoners, a feat of bravery which earned him the Military Cross.

Armistice Day came and went, but Wintle's problem with Germans did not abate. He refused to believe that they had been defeated; the 'filthy Boche' had merely sued for peace in order to lull the rest of Europe into a false sense of security while they regrouped. On 19 July 1919, he wrote in his diary: 'Great War peace signed at last.' The following day's entry reads: 'I declare private war on Germany.'

Wintle was a keen horseman who believed that 'time spent dismounted can never be regained'. In 1921, he joined the Eighteenth Royal Hussars in India, where he spent his days playing polo, pig-sticking and drinking whisky, all the while dreaming of fighting Germans. His Indian career was suddenly cut short when he fell off his horse and broke his good leg. Recovering in Aldershot Military Hospital, he encountered a trumpeter with the Royal Dragoon Band called Cecil Mays who was suffering from mastoiditis and diphtheria and was expected to die. Wintle hobbled over to Mays on his crutches and demanded, 'What's all this nonsense about dying, Mays? You will stop dying at once, and when you get up, get your bloody hair cut.' Forty years later, Mays revealed: 'After that I was too terrified to die.'

Wintle continued to fulminate on the subject of Germans to anyone prepared to listen. 'They are like their dogs; they cannot be trusted. The wolf will out.' His opinion of the British War Office was even lower, staffed as it was by 'bloody traitors'. The only point of having a War Office, as far as

Wintle could see, was to look forward to and plan for the next war. It was a triumphant Wintle, therefore, who found himself vindicated in September 1939 when Britain was once again at war with the old enemy.

Impatient to resume hostilities against the Hun since 1918, Wintle decided to fly to France to destroy the French Air Force before it fell into enemy hands, and tried to steal an aircraft by impersonating the Air Ministry Director of Intelligence, Air Commander Boyle. When he was inconveniently intercepted by Boyle in person, Wintle waved a revolver in his face and told him, 'You and your kind ought to be shot.' Wintle was arrested and sent to the Tower of London, where he was allowed to live in some style, with his batman (an officer's personal servant), a private bathroom, access to a telephone and his daily whisky on the stroke of 12 noon.

One thing Wintle refused to let his captors do was clean his boots and uniform. 'Much as I admire the Guards,' he said, 'I do not feel they quite understand how to look after a cavalry officer's kit.' Nor were they allowed anywhere near his ubiquitous umbrella, bought for him by an aunt from the Army & Navy Stores when he was a boy, which almost never left his side. For several years he even went to bed with it. Wintle boasted that it had never been unfurled (because 'no true English gentleman ever unfurls his umbrella'), except for one occasion, to insert a note reading: 'This umbrella has been stolen from Colonel A. D. Wintle'. For Wintle the umbrella represented the natural superiority of the English. 'There are essentially only two classes of Englishman,' he once wrote; 'those who believe themselves superior to foreigners, and those who know they are.'

At his court martial Wintle continued to make a nuisance of himself by threatening to name everyone in Whitehall he considered 'ought to be shot' and was let off with a reprimand. In 1941, he was back in action in occupied France as an undercover agent, attempting to pass himself off as a local, with gold coins strapped to his armpits in case of emergency. As expected, a one-legged monocle-wearing man carrying an umbrella made for an unconvincing Frenchman. He was arrested almost immediately as a spy and thrown into prison in Toulon, where he denounced his captors as 'swivel eyed sons of syphilitic slime frogs'.

Wintle spent his time berating his French jailers for their poor deportment, slovenly appearance and their treachery in supporting the Vichy regime. He told them that if they didn't smarten themselves up he would starve himself to death. At one point his weight went down to seven stones. Unexpectedly, his French captors gave in to his threat to a man and smartened themselves up. He eventually escaped by burying himself in the contents of the prison refuse cart, and made his way home via Spain. In 1959, when the television programme *This Is Your Life* paid tribute to Wintle's extraordinary career, the Frenchman in charge of guarding him, Maurice Molia, revealed that because of Wintle's relentless abuse he and his entire garrison of 280 had later gone over to the Resistance.

After the war, Wintle stood for election as Liberal MP for Lambeth Norwood on the platform that he was the first person to want to enter the House of Commons with good intentions since Guy Fawkes. He received just enough votes to secure the return of his deposit. He reappeared briefly in the public eye when he was accused of kicking a ticket collector at Victoria Station; unable to find a seat in the train, he sat in the engine driver's cab and refused to move until they found him one.

The most widely publicized incident of his career came in the 1950s. Alfred Daniel was not the only eccentric in the

Wintle family. He had an unmarried cousin called Kitty Wells, a reclusive lady who sent herself letters comprising envelopes stuffed with old bus tickets. She saved them in dozens of handbags hidden under her bed. She had never read a newspaper and had no idea that there was a war on, despite living on the south-east coast of England. Wintle's sister Marjorie looked after her for twenty-five years, but when Kitty died in 1948 she left her only forty pounds. The rest of her estate, around £100,000, went to her 71-year-old solicitor, Frederick Nye, who had helped draw up her will. Wintle appealed to Nye to give Marjorie Wintle a better deal, but Nye ignored his requests. Wintle was outraged, denouncing the solicitor as 'a cad, a liar and thief and embezzler'.

He decided to take matters into his own hands. Posing as 'Lord Norbury' he lured Nye into an empty flat at Hove, then wrestled him to the ground and made him sign a £1,000 cheque for his sister. Wintle then forced Nye at gunpoint to remove his trousers, photographed him wearing a dunce's cap made out of newspapers, then released the trouserless solicitor onto the street. Photographs of the debagging were sent to the national press. The escapade cost Wintle a six-month prison sentence in Wormwood Scrubs for assault. He was triumphant, noting: 'It will be a sad day for this country when an officer and gentleman is not prepared to go to prison when he thinks he is in the right. One must expect some casualties.' He added: 'I was going to fly his trousers in triumph from my flagpole at home but unfortunately I was arrested before dawn.' Acting as his own lawyer, assisted by his old colleague Cecil Mays, Wintle took his appeal against the will right up to the House of Lords. After a famous six-day hearing the Lords gave a unanimous decision in Wintle's favour – the first ever victory by a layman conducting his own case in the House of Lords. The *Daily Express* noted admiringly: 'You may say or think what you like about Alfred Wintle, but here is an Englishman.'

## Whip round

Queen Victoria's father Edward, Duke of Kent (1767–1820), was a brutal and tyrannical disciplinarian, known as the 'Flogging Duke' for his fondness for thrashing his soldiers at the drop of a hat. His predilection was first noticed during his command in Gibraltar as Colonel of the Royal Fusiliers, where he flogged his men to the point of mutiny, then shot two of the ringleaders and had a third flogged to death. The added bonus for the Duke was that he was sexually aroused by the sight of men being whipped, which also caused him to wet his trousers. When news of the mutiny filtered back to England, the Duke was quietly removed and sent to Canada. He simply viewed his new posting as a fresh opportunity for more outrageous punishments and the number of floggings in the Duke's new regiment went up roughly in line with his laundry bill.

## True Brit

Lord FitzRoy Somerset (1788–1855) distinguished himself as the leader of the Household Cavalry Brigade at Waterloo, but at the expense of his right arm, which had to be amputated on the evening after the battle. After it was removed Somerset snapped at an orderly, 'You, bring that arm back. There is a ring my wife gave me on the finger.'

## Privates on parade

Orde Charles Wingate (1903–44) was a brilliant but unorthodox military leader in the Second World War. His three campaigns in Palestine, Ethiopia and as commander of the Chindits led Winston Churchill to call him 'a man of genius'. Wingate also had his share of detractors who thought him simply 'barking mad'.

His strict religious upbringing left him with an obsession with the Old Testament. He endured prolonged bouts of depression and thoughts of suicide by endlessly repeating the phrase 'God is good'. There were other personal habits described by colleagues as 'a bit outré', including his theories about achieving good health. Wingate believed that the best way to stay fit in the tropics was to eat half a dozen raw onions a day and drink tea strained through his socks. He stopped bathing because he believed it was bad for his health.

Even more baffling was his habit of strolling around in front of his fellow soldiers stark naked. Wingate got his kit off whenever, and wherever, the mood took him. He dictated letters in the buff and held interviews while lying naked on a bed and combing his body hair with a toothbrush. Wingate made a lasting impression on the future Israeli ambassador by giving him an hour-long lecture on Zionism while completely naked. He terminated the interview in his usual manner, by drawing attention to the miniature alarm clock strapped to his finger. His brief career was tragically ended, at the age of forty-one, by an airplane crash in Burma. No identifiable remains of Wingate were found, save for his trademark outsize pith helmet.

## Fighting mad

Sir William Erskine (1770–1813) was one of Wellington's senior commanders during the Peninsular War. As Erskine already had twice been confined to a lunatic asylum, Wellington received news of his appointment with stunned disbelief and wrote to the Military Secretary in London for an explanation. The Secretary wrote back, 'No doubt he is a little mad at intervals, but in his lucid intervals he is an uncommonly clever fellow, and I trust he will have no fit during the campaign, although I must say he looked a little mad as he embarked.' During one of Erskine's less lucid intervals he was found at dinner when he should have been defending a strategically important bridge. He eventually sent five men to defend it; when a fellow officer queried his decision Erskine changed his mind and decided to send a whole regiment, but pocketed the instruction and forgot all about it. He found the order later in his trousers when he was getting into to bed and passed it Colonel Bevan, who arrived at the bridge too late to stop the French and ended up taking the blame. Erskine's mental health wasn't his only problem; he was also said to be 'blind as a beetle'. His eyesight was so bad that before a battle he had to ask someone to point him in the general direction of the battlefield.

Erskine committed suicide by jumping out of a window in Lisbon. Found dying on the pavement, he asked bystanders, 'Why on earth did I do that?'

## The Battle of the Moselle

James Thomas Brudenell, the seventh Earl of Cardigan (1797–1868), who led the Charge of Light Brigade in the

Crimea, was subject to flights of extraordinary rage – the result, it was said, of a near-fatal blow on the head in a childhood riding accident. Cardigan was a stickler for 'proper form' and in 1840 he was embroiled in a famous Victorian officers' mess dispute known as the Black Bottle Affair – a difference of opinion over the correct receptacle for decanting wine. Cardigan had a fellow officer, Captain Reynolds, arrested because he had placed a black bottle of Moselle instead of a decanter on a table at the regimental HQ in Canterbury. When an account of the incident was leaked to the *Morning Chronicle*, Cardigan challenged its author, Captain Harvey Tuckett, to a duel on Wimbledon Common. Tuckett was injured and the Earl was tried in the House of Lords, but acquitted for lack of evidence. Tuckett conveniently failed to appear and, it was generally assumed, had been bought off. Ironically, having survived the most suicidal cavalry charge in British military history, Cardigan died from injuries caused by a fall from his horse while on his morning ride.

He was survived by his similarly eccentric wife Lady Adeline, who was often seen bicycling around the village wearing her husband's regimental trousers. When the Earl died, although she was comparatively young and outlived him by forty-six years, she had her own death mask made at the same time so she would be remembered as a beautiful woman. She kept her coffin in the house and would lie in it and ask people how she looked.

## Taiping test

Major-General Charles 'Chinese' Gordon (1833–85) became a national hero when he put down the Taiping Rebellion in Shanghai, then died dramatically at Khartoum after ignoring orders to evacuate. Gordon was fanatically religious and refused to take instructions from anyone other than God, or the prophet Isaiah, with whom he spoke regularly, and would often assail complete strangers in the street demanding to know if they believed in Jesus.

He also wrote a book, *Reflections in Palestine*, in which he claimed that he had located the Garden of Eden in the Seychelles. According to Gordon, the Earth is enclosed in a hollow sphere with God's throne situated directly above the altar of the Temple in Jerusalem; the Devil lives at the opposite point of the globe somewhere near Pitcairn Island.

## Friendly fire

Captain Frederick August Thistlethwaytes (1830–87) was a wealthy army officer and nephew of the Bishop of Norwich. In 1852, he scandalized polite London society when he bought a house in fashionable Grosvenor Square and settled down with his new wife, a former Irish prostitute called Laura Bell, known as 'the Queen of London Whoredom', who once charged Prince Jang Bahadur, ruler of Nepal, £250,000 for services rendered, allegedly the most expensive one-night stand in history.

The Thistlethwaytes' marriage ended tragically due to the Captain's habit of calling his valet by firing a revolver shot through the ceiling. On 7 August 1887, Thistlethwaytes was found dead in his bedroom with a self-inflicted shot wound after an unsuccessful attempt to summon his manservant.

## Reverse Buller

Sir Redvers Buller (1839–1908), commander of the British forces in South Africa during the Second Boer War, was the butt of many jokes among his troops, largely aimed at his expansive waistline, his habit of consuming large quantities of champagne whilst on campaign and a speech impediment, acquired when he received a kick in the mouth from a horse.

Buller brought a new level of incompetence to the Boer campaign. The British military commander Kitchener found that he waged war 'like a game of polo, with intervals for afternoon tea'. After one spectacularly ignoble retreat, Buller boasted to his superiors in London that he had accomplished his withdrawal without losing a man, a flag or a cannon. When James Whistler heard about this, he added, 'or a minute'. For his heroic actions, Buller was later awarded the Victoria Cross.

## Scouting for boys

Before he became a household name, Lord Robert Baden-Powell (1857–1941), heroic defender of Mafeking during the Boer War and founder of the Boy Scout movement, was chiefly known for his definitive book on pig-sticking and his fondness for skin-tight riding breeches covered in pearl buttons. He also raised eyebrows with his outspoken views about the evils of prostitution, which made him a highly controversial figure within a British Army that considered brothels essential for maintaining morale. In 1907, after returning to England from South Africa a national hero, Baden-Powell created the Scouts' Association. It was to be a 'safe haven' for boys and young men away from the 'depravities of women'; girls were 'dirty'

his latest mission he was given two small wooden boats formerly belonging to the Greek air force. When asked by his superior, British First Sea Lord Admiral Jackson to give the two ships' names, Spicer-Simpson called them *Dog* and *Cat*. Jackson asked him to come up with something more suitable – perhaps something slightly more warlike in the great naval British tradition. Spicer-Simpson renamed them *Mimi* and *Toutou*.

Against all odds, he managed to transport his little flotilla all the way to central Africa, accompanied by a crew of twenty-eight men, including an officer known as 'Piccadilly Johnny' who wore a monocle and had dyed yellow hair, and two Scots seamen who seldom spoke but never stopped eating and answered to the names Gog and Magog. Another member of the crew was addicted to Worcester Sauce and insisted that two full cases went with him on the mission so that he could drink it neat as an aperitif before every meal.

When they got to Lake Tanganyika the Germans took one look at Spicer-Simpson's ramshackle, ill-equipped fleet through their binoculars and fell about laughing. This inexplicable lapse in concentration gave the British an important strategic advantage. After two bizarre battles, thanks to a huge measure of good luck and foolhardiness, the pride of the Germans' African fleet was somehow sunk.

Not that Spicer-Simpson had very much to do with this unlikely victory. To begin with, none of his officers could understand his signals. During the first battle his attempt at semaphore was interpreted by a gunner as Spicer-Simpson having a fit. Throughout the second battle he strode around the deck barking orders, swishing his lion-handled fly-whisk, but because he refused to remove his cigarette holder from between his teeth no-one understood a word he said. When one of the German ships was holed, Spicer-Simpson was unable to stop and accidentally rammed it, holing his own vessel in the process. He celebrated his victory by cutting off the ring finger of a dead German seaman, pocketing the ring and then keeping the severed finger in a bottle. One of the German captains was so appalled at having lost to Spicer-Simpson that he contemplated suicide, as Giles Foden notes in *Mimi and Toutou Go Forth* (2004).

Spicer-Simpson's downfall came when he was told to liaise with Allied troops to finish the job. He flatly refused to take orders from a Belgian officer and simply pointed to his badge, which he believed outranked his ally. Spicer-Simpson was however wearing a skirt at the time, which, he was careful to point out to the Belgian commander, had been made for him by his wife. He was relieved of his command, citing 'acute mental debility'.

## A Bailey's too far

Major Allison Digby Tatham-Warter (1918–93), World War II Company Commander of the 2nd Battalion Parachute Regiment, won a DSO for his part in the Battle of Arnhem in 1944, when he and his men stubbornly held on to the north end of a road bridge, although outnumbered and short of ammunition, food and water. During the heavy fighting that followed, Tatham-Warter led a bayonet charge equipped with an old bowler hat and a tattered umbrella. When a fellow officer pointed out that the umbrella would be useless in the face of the German artillery the major replied, 'But what if it rains?' He claimed later that he could never remember the password and it would be obvious to anyone that 'the bloody fool carrying the umbrella could only be an Englishman'.

Tatham-Warter was worried about the unreliability of the

radio sets and had trained his men in the use of bugle calls that were used by the British during the Napoleonic Wars of the early nineteenth century.

Although a fine company commander, he was less gifted at handling alcohol. He got into several wild drunken fist fights in the mess with his friends but remembered nothing of the incidents the following morning, although he would always return to his unit, fresh and impeccably attired.

## Master of deception

Lieutenant-Colonel Dudley Clarke (1899–1974) was expert at devising epic strategic bluffs to confuse the enemy about British plans during the Second World War. Described as 'a sharp little man with bright, quick eyes', in 1940 Clarke was posted to the Middle East under General Wavell's secret deception organization the 'A' Force, tasked with misleading the Germans about Montgomery's main thrust at El Alamein.

One of Clarke's most celebrated ruses was the creation of Monty's double; the lookalike appeared in the Mediterranean to distract the Germans' attention from the Channel shortly before D-Day. Clarke's most important contribution to the war effort, however, was the creation of a phantom army in south-east England, designed to convince Hitler that the Allied invasion was heading for Calais. The deception was maintained by phoney signals traffic, bogus supply dumps, cardboard tanks, plywood aeroplanes and canvas landing craft. To complete the illusion there were even genuine royal visits.

But some of Clarke's ideas to baffle the enemy were less effective. The removal of road signs caused such chaos on the home front that they had to be put back. Clarke's scheme to fool Mussolini into believing that Wavell intended to retake

British Somaliland in 1940 backfired completely. Far from reinforcing their position, the Italian army retreated into Eritrea, which was the real British target. The Luftwaffe once paid tribute to a Clarke design – a dummy railhead in Egypt – by dropping a wooden bomb on it.

The most notable hiccup in Clarke's career came in 1941 when he was arrested in Madrid by Spanish police, who found him wearing women's clothes and full make-up, flirting with some German spies. The British intelligence services asked Lord Gort, Governor of Gibraltar, to interview Clarke to establish that he was sane. The cross-dressing Colonel claimed he was trying out the costume for a secret mission.

## The full Monty

The British Allied Commander Field Marshal Bernard Law Montgomery 'of Alamein' (1887–1976) boasted that he was one of the three greatest military commanders of all time, along with Alexander the Great and Napoleon. Monty was renowned for his arrogant, autocratic manner. His Chief of Staff Sir Alan Brooke confided to King George VI, 'Every time I meet him [Monty] I think he's after my job.' 'Good,' replied the King, 'I thought he was after mine.'

Monty's odd behaviour at the front often left his long-suffering chiefs of staff scratching their heads. One day in France in 1944, a young officer returned from hospital after being wounded. Monty summoned the young man to his caravan and ordered him to strip. The puzzled officer did as he was told. Monty peered at him for a while, then ordered him to dress: 'I wanted to assure myself that you are fit for duty. You can go now.' In 1967, Montgomery urged the

House of Lords to throw out a bill to legalize gay sex, warning that it would be a 'charter for buggery . . . this sort of thing may be tolerated by the French, but we're British – thank God.' In 1985, when *Monty at Close Quarters* was published, a collection of anecdotes by men who served under Monty during World War II, it was known in the trade as 'Monty at Hind Quarters'.

## The iceman cometh

During World War II the Allies called upon their finest scientific minds to give them a competitive edge. The British government's secret weapon was the tall, skinny, goatee-bearded Geoffrey Nathaniel Pyke (1893–1948), civilian adviser to Combined Operations, a special wartime unit headed by Lord Mountbatten. Pyke was already a household name in England long before he joined Mountbatten's secret think-tank.

When war broke out in 1914, Pyke, then a Cambridge graduate, somehow persuaded the editor of the London newspaper the *Daily Chronicle* to send him to Berlin as their war correspondent. The newspaper gamely agreed to pay his expenses to Germany so long as they were not responsible for his safety. After bluffing his way across Europe on little more than a false passport and a cod German accent, Pyke was spotted by the German authorities eavesdropping on conversations in a cafe and was lucky not to have been shot as a spy. He spent four months in a freezing concentration camp at Ruhleben instead.

While his fellow mostly starving British prisoners kept themselves alive by recreating productions of *The Mikado* from memory, Pyke concentrated on hatching escape plans. After compiling statistics of failed escape attempts, he noted that they had all taken place at night and concluded that his best chance of escape was during the day. Amazingly, he escaped in broad daylight and made a dash across the German countryside to the Dutch border. Pyke returned home at the age of twenty to find that the *Daily Chronicle* had been serializing his adventures and he was a national hero. He cashed in by writing a book, *To Ruhleben – and Back*, and travelled the country giving lectures.

After the war, Pyke decided to play the stock market after spending a day watching people walk in and out of the London Stock Exchange and noticing that 'all of them appeared ineffably stupid and many of them were my relatives'. Pyke rode the futures market brilliantly and made a fortune by seizing control of a third of the world supply of tin. He spent a large chunk of his new-found wealth founding a private school where children aged four to ten were taught physics and chemistry before they could read or write. The school was forced to close in 1929 when its founder was ruined by a massive financial reverse. At the age of thirty-four, Pyke was a bankrupt. Deeply depressed, he grew a long beard and spent the 1930s as an eccentric hermit, living on herring and broken biscuits scavenged from a local bakery, and occasionally publishing warnings of Nazism.

In 1939, dressed in an old threadbare suit, a rumpled pyjama top for a shirt and a bootlace for a tie, Pyke turned up at the office of his old friend Lord Mountbatten, chief of the newly created Combined Operations unit. 'You need me on your staff,' the shabbily dressed visitor told Mountbatten, 'because I'm a man who thinks.' Mountbatten offered him a job on the spot. Pyke was to be civilian adviser to Combined Operations, his brief to think up new and original ideas for defeating the enemy. Within a matter of days he was hatching the first of a series of truly eccentric plans that were to earn him the nickname 'Professor Brainstorm'.

Pyke devised a plan to avert World War II by presenting the results of an opinion poll to Hitler showing that the majority of Germans wanted peace. Hitler would see the results, become discouraged and call the whole thing off. As Pyke had correctly assumed that the Fascist dictator was probably dead against people carrying out opinion polls *per se*, he planned to flood Germany with students disguised as golfers, carrying clipboards in one hand and golf clubs in the other. Although Germany had plenty of bunkers it was not at that time known to be a nation of golf enthusiasts. Nevertheless he did persuade a few students to dress up as golfers and travel to the Third Reich. Hitler was not convinced and invaded Poland anyway. Fortunately, the students were able to flee before the Gestapo spotted them.

Although he enjoyed Mountbatten's support, the military brass were convinced that Pyke was unhinged. He certainly did a convincing impression of a mad scientist, especially with his alarmingly dishevelled appearance. He once introduced himself to the Canadian Prime Minister Mackenzie King with his flies open. Pyke often worked from his bed because he couldn't be bothered to get up and put clothes on. He summoned military chiefs to conferences in his Hampstead flat, where they found him lying naked in bed surrounded by piles of papers, bottles, cigarette ends and other debris. He wrote obsessively, furiously scribbling ideas in his notebook.

Periods of manic hyperactivity, especially feverish writing, were interspersed with periods of depression. He signalled warning of an impending black mood to his secretary by humming, then would shut himself away or vanish for days without explaining to anyone where he had been. He once phoned Combined Operations headquarters at five in the morning and insisted that a junior officer take dictation from him for a memo to Mountbatten. Much to the officer's fury, Pyke was still dictating an hour later.

Pyke's ideas for defeating the enemy, however, flew thick and fast. He dreamed up the 'weasel', an amphibious jeep that could move easily through mud in Nazi-occupied Norway. None was ever used in Norway, but after the war the weasel played a vital part in polar exploration. The unique selling point of the weasel was that it could also jump sideways to avoid dive bombers. When he was asked to come up with a plan for the destruction of Romania's oil fields, he recommended sending in St Bernard dogs carrying brandy, so that the Romanian guards would get drunk before the British attacked. He later improved on his plan by suggesting that women should carry the brandy instead of dogs; this, he explained, would be more distracting for the guards. When neither idea found much favour with the military he came up with a new ploy. British spies could start a few small fires, then the British commandos could simply drive about the oilfields dressed as Romanian firemen in replica fire engines. Instead of putting out fires, the 'firemen' would stoke them up by spraying them with water mixed with fused incendiary bombs.

Pyke's next project was a motorized sledge to aid travel in occupied Norway. It was controlled by a man walking behind, holding reins, so that if the sledge fell into a crevasse, the driver did not – unless he forgot to let go. When the sledges were trialled the drivers were so completely exposed to gunfire that most preferred to ride inside and take their chances with crevasses. A refinement to this idea was Pyke's 'torpedo sledge'. The sledge was to be driven slowly up a slope to tempt the Germans into giving chase. Halfway up the slope the torpedo was to be released to roll down onto the Germans and blow them up. In case the equipment fell into enemy hands it was to be marked with a sign in German: 'DANGER – SECRET GESTAPO DEATH RAY'. Alternatively, Pyke suggested, the sledges could be marked in German: 'OFFICERS' LATRINE FOR COLONELS ONLY'. The Germans, Pyke explained to his patient employees, were a very obedient race.

Pyke's most inventive contribution to the war effort was the *Habbakuk*, a huge aircraft carrier, half a mile long, made entirely of ice reinforced with wood shavings – a material he called 'Pykrete'. This material had extraordinary properties, including remarkable strength, as strong as concrete but lighter. Pyke's ship was to be fitted with self-refrigerating apparatus to keep it from melting. As the hull was 30 feet thick it would be virtually impregnable. Pyke theorized that huge ice ships, clad in timber or cork and looking like ordinary ships but much larger, could serve as transport and aircraft carriers, while smaller ships would be adapted to attack enemy ports. The plan was for them to sail into the port and capture enemy warships by spraying them with super-cooled water, encasing them in ice and forcing them to surrender. Blocks of Pykrete would then be used to build a barrier round the port, making an impregnable fortress. From there, special teams would spread out into the countryside, spraying railway tunnels with super-cooled water to seal them up and paralyse transport.

Surprisingly, Mountbatten warmed to Pykrete. He liked Pyke's plan so much that he interrupted Churchill's ablutions one evening by dumping a lump of Pykrete into the great man's hot bath to prove it would not melt. Churchill was suitably impressed. He fired off a memo to his War Cabinet stamped 'MOST SECRET': 'I attach the greatest importance to the prompt examination of these ideas. The advantages of a floating island or islands, even if only used as refuelling depots for aircraft, are so dazzling that they do not need at the moment to be discussed.' Mountbatten ordered Pyke to produce some Pykrete samples for trials, which were secretly carried out in a refrigerated meat locker in a Smithfield Market butcher's basement. Pykrete was finally unveiled to a wider audience in Quebec in August 1943 at a tense meeting of the Allied chiefs of staff at the Château Frontenac Hotel. Mountbatten demonstrated the strength of Pykrete in front of a group of unbelieving generals by drawing his revolver and firing at it – the bullet ricocheted off the solid lump and zipped across the trouser leg of Fleet Admiral Ernest King. Mountbatten had made his point; Churchill and Roosevelt agreed that Pyke's ship should be built. Pyke, however, was conspicuously absent from all of these high level meetings. He had been stunned to discover that he was cut loose from his own project after sending a telegram marked 'Hush Most Secret' to Mountbatten. It read: 'CHIEF OF NAVAL CONSTRUCTION IS AN OLD WOMAN. SIGNED PYKE.'

Although a prototype *Habbakuk* was actually built on a Canadian Lake – and lasted an entire summer without melting – the Allied invasion of Europe was already too advanced for it to be put to practical use. Pyke was later granted the rights to patent Pykrete, but he never got around to filing for them. In fact very few projects inspired by Pyke ever got off the ground and he ended his war embittered and disillusioned.

His postwar years were similarly unhappy and traumatic. At first he addressed his imagination with usual manic intensity to writing articles about the fledgling National Health Service, and made radio broadcasts. Pyke's bed, which had figured so largely in his daily routine, now became his permanent workplace. As he scribbled away, piles of detritus – papers, medicine bottles, cigarette ends and food wrappers – littered the floor around him. He went on faddish diets, eating nothing but herring for months on end, then would binge on loaves of bread. Years of frustration and mockery at his ideas had taken their toll on his health. In 1948, aged fifty-four, ill with leukaemia and depressed, he shaved off his beard and said farewell to an unappreciative world by overdosing on barbiturates.

# Nine
# MEDICAL ECCENTRICS

*'Men will always be mad and those who think they can cure them are the maddest of all.'*

– VOLTAIRE (1694–1778)

## The usual pus specks

The famous Scottish surgeon John Hunter (1728–93) was an obsessive collector of anatomical artefacts. Over the course of his lifetime he amassed over 65,000 items, everything from teeth, fingernails and splinters of bone to gunshot wounds to aborted foetuses, corpses and human and animal skeletons. Like many of his fellow anatomists he also collected the corpses of executed criminals for dissection. His prize exhibit was the body of 7 ft 8 in. Charles Byrne, 'the Irish giant', which he acquired in spite of stiff competition. Byrne had lived in a dread fear that he might end up in a museum and made special arrangements to be buried at sea in a lead coffin. When he died of tuberculosis Hunter simply bribed officials to fill Byrne's coffin with rocks and gave them £500 for the corpse. The surgeon was intensely proud of his latest plaything and propped the corpse up beside him on his coach while doing his rounds. Eventually he took it home and boiled it in a large vat to separate the flesh from the bones.

Hunter's wife Anne complained only once about her husband's homework, and that was when he arrived on the doorstep with a stuffed giraffe which was too tall to fit inside his house, so he shortened it by hacking the legs off below the knee and placed it in his hall. Mrs Hunter also lived to regret another line of her husband's research, which had life-changing results. Hunter injected pus from the weeping sores of a gonorrhoea-infected prostitute into the glans of his own penis to find out how the disease was transmitted. Unfortunately for Hunter, the prostitute he chose to take his sample from also suffered from syphilis; a rare combination, and a mistake from which he never completely recovered. It was also bad news for venereology, because Hunter mistakenly concluded that syphilis and gonorrhoea were stages of the same infection, setting back the study of both diseases for many years.

Hunter had a quick temper and suffered from angina, which was characterized by painful spasms whenever his blood pressure was high. He was giving a lecture about King George III's 'madness' when someone in the audience challenged his theory that the King was genetically blighted; Hunter was so furious that he had an apoplectic fit and fell dead. His huge collection of specimens now forms the basis of the Royal College of Surgeons' Hunterian Museum in London.

## Where there's a will

The London dentist Martin van Butchell (1735–1812) studied anatomy under the great John Hunter but decided to take up dentistry when he found out he could charge eighty guineas for a set of false teeth. Van Butchell prided himself on his orthodontic skills, assuring the wary that 'gums, sockets and palate [could be] formed, fitted, finished and fixed without drawing stumps or causing pain'. It was a bold claim given that he was working in the pre-anaesthetic age and his technique amounted to hitting a prospective patient over the head with a large stick, or blowing a trumpet in his unsuspecting ear seconds before a tooth was to be pulled. Van Butchell did not confine himself to dentistry. As a sideline he made surgical trusses and specialized in the treatment of haemorrhoids. According to his promotional flyers he could also cure 'Wens, Carbuncles, Mattery Pimples, Inflammations, Boils, Ulcers, Aching Legs, Tumours, Abscesses, Strictures and Ruptures, without Confinement, Burning or Cutting'.

Van Butchell was also a notably eccentric character about town. He was a little man with a long white beard and always wore white, from his white bowler hat down to white stockings. He rode through the West End of London on a small white pony which he painted in various colours. One day it was painted entirely in purple, the next it was black with red spots. In his hand he carried a large animal bone, tied to his wrist by a piece of string, with which he threatened to whack anyone who came near him. His lasting claim to fame, however, came not through his dexterity with the pliers, nor his skills at self-promotion, but through his unorthodox devotion to his late wife.

Just before Mrs van Butchell died on 14 January 1775, she decided to repay her husband for years of marital misery with a spiteful will which decreed that her fortune pass to a distant relative 'the moment I am dead and buried'. The resourceful dentist found a loophole in the will by simply keeping her body well above ground. He persuaded William Hunter, brother of John, to fit her out with a new pair of glass eyes and fill her veins with oil of turpentine and camphorated spirit of wine.

She was then dressed, propped up in the drawing room and put on public display from 9 a.m. to 1 p.m., from Monday to Saturday. The rush to see the corpse was so great that van Butchell was forced to restrict viewings to private appointments only. A notice in the *St. James's Chronicle* of 21 October 1775 read:

> Van Butchell (not willing to be unpleasantly circumstanced, and wishing to convince some good minds they have been misinformed) acquaints the Curious, no stranger can see his embalmed Wife, unless (by a Friend personally) introduced to himself, any day between Nine and One, Sundays excepted.

When van Butchell remarried, his second wife, Elizabeth, took an instant dislike to the ex-Mrs van Butchell and ordered her out of the house. Reluctantly, the dentist gave the mummy to Hunter to put in his collection. A century later, the mummy had disintegrated into a 'repulsive looking object'. It was only in 1941 – 166 years after her death – that she was finally laid to rest by a German incendiary bomb.

## Bite the bullet

Dr Messenger Monsey (1673–1788) held the post of Resident Physician to the Chelsea Royal Hospital, London, until his death at the age of ninety-five. His will, an epic nineteen pages long, described with elaborate and graphic detail how his body should be dissected and the remains thrown into the Thames. Monsey was also famous for perfecting a highly original method of tooth extraction. He took a strong piece of catgut, wound one end around the patient's tooth, threaded the other end through a specially prepared bullet with a hole drilled through it, then loaded the bullet into his revolver and fired it.

## The shock of the new

Britain's most inventive quack, James Graham (1745–94), was also the proprietor of London's first ever sex clinic. The son of a Scottish saddler, Graham was born in Edinburgh and studied medicine at the local university. Although there is no evidence that he ever graduated, he appropriated the title 'Doctor' and set off for America, where he settled in Philadelphia, advertising himself as an eye specialist. It was there that he was introduced to the new and mysterious phenomenon of electricity. Graham soon became an enthusiast of the curative properties of 'electric medicine' as an alternative to the conventional remedies of the day, which still relied on leeches and blood-letting.

In 1775, at the first sign of trouble in the American Revolution, Graham crossed the Atlantic to England, where he opened clinics in Bath and Bristol, before settling in London. He opened a large new practice called the Temple of Health just off the Strand, where he promised a cure for impotence via jolts of electricity delivered through various chairs and headsets. For an entrance fee of one crown, paying customers could wander through elaborately furnished, heavily perfumed rooms, take massages, inspect the 'electrical apparatus' or hear Graham, attended by sundry black servants, delivering lectures on the sexual healing properties of electricity.

The centrepiece of the Temple was the Celestial Bed, a bizarrely ornate piece of furniture decorated with cherubs and standing on eight brass legs, attached to about 15 cwt of compound magnets. According to Graham, for a fee of £50 childless couples who spent a single night on the Celestial Bed would be 'blessed with progeny'. While the couple watched themselves copulate in the mirror on the bed's canopy, 'magnetic fire' was pumped into the room accompanied by soft lights, soothing music and random appearances by scantily clad Greek goddesses, among them sixteen-year-old Emma Hart, later to become mistress of Horatio Nelson. On the way out, customers could also purchase a range of Graham's special erotic products including the 'famous aethe-rial and balsamic medicine' and his 'elixir of life', which promised to sustain an erection indefinitely. Among the many famous celebrity guests who came to marvel at Graham's Temple were the Prince of Wales and Horace Walpole, who visited in 1780 and reported several astonishing experiences, including 'an invisible woman warbling to clarinets on the stairs'.

The Temple did a roaring trade for several years and Graham became a well-known dandy around town, with his white linen suits and his gold-headed cane. Eventually, however, it went out of fashion, mostly because Graham's methods didn't actually work, and he fell into debt. He returned to Edinburgh where he had a change of direction. Renouncing all his old theories about magnetism and elec-tricity, he announced his discovery of the true secret of immortality: mud baths. All the nutrients necessary to live a long and healthy life – anything up to 150 years – could be absorbed, he claimed, by simply bathing in mud. He said he had survived two weeks immersed in mud with no nourish-ment except for a few drops of water.

Graham's mud crusade took on a religious bent when he founded the New Jerusalem Church, with himself the only member, and began signing all his letters 'Servant of the Lord, O. W. L.' (Oh, Wonderful Love). He urged prospective followers to 'abstain totally from flesh and blood, from all liquors but cold water and fresh milk, and from excessive sexual indulgence' and said that most human ailments were due to wearing woollen clothing. At this time Graham's behaviour was becoming increasingly erratic. He took to removing his clothes in the street and giving them away. In 1794, he was found wandering the streets of Edinburgh naked and was arrested. His final work was a book titled *How to Live for Many Weeks or Months or Years Without Eating Anything Whatsoever*. He took his own advice, but after fasting for fifteen days wearing nothing but grass turf, he died, aged forty-nine.

## Small bier

Dr William Price (1800–93) was one of the oddest people to emerge from the valleys of Wales. Born in Rudry near Caerphilly, the fifth child of the Revd William Price, he was in conflict with authority from an early age, when he took to wandering the countryside naked. On completing his schooling, he worked as a doctor's apprentice in Caerphilly, then studied medicine in London. Five years later, he went home to Wales and became a doctor in the mines of the Rhondda Valley, where he allegedly performed one of the first skin-graft operations on an injured worker. He also agitated among the miners on behalf of the Chartist reform movement and after a failed workers' uprising in 1839, he fled to Paris.

Price returned to Wales seven years later and began a medical practice in Pontypridd, moving later to Llantrisant. Nude rambling aside, his was a peculiar practice, to say the least. He appointed himself Archdruid of Wales and took to wearing a fox skin hat over his long plaited hair and a white tunic, green trousers and a scarlet waistcoat. He dispensed herbal remedies, throwing in Druidic incantations for good measure. Price gained a reputation as a brilliant surgeon, but he only operated when he was short of money. He opposed vaccination, refused to wear socks on hygienic grounds and washed every coin that he handled. He was also a strict vegetarian and refused to treat patients who smoked.

Dr Price was also an advocate of free love and was against marriage on the grounds that it enslaved women. At the age of seventy-nine, he impregnated his nineteen-year-old housekeeper, Gwenllian Llewellyn, who gave birth to their child, whom he named Iesu Grist – Welsh for Jesus Christ – much to the fury of the local clergy. Price believed the child was the fulfilment of a prophecy and would restore the lost secrets of the Druids. Unfortunately, the infant Iesu Grist died aged just five months. What happened next secured Dr Price's place in history. Watched by a large crowd of curious onlookers, he took the dead infant onto the hilltop of East Caerlan, poured a container of paraffin oil over the body and then set fire to it. The improvised cremation caused a riot and the crowd dragged the corpse from the flames. The police were called in and Price was arrested for illegal disposal of a body. His case was heard at the Cardiff Assizes in 1884, where the judge ruled that cremation was legal, as long as it was done without nuisance to others. A year later, the first officially sanctioned cremation in Britain took place.

Price went about his business as usual. He was well into his eighties when his housekeeper bore him two more children, one called Penelopen and another Iesu Grist II (later renamed Nicholas). He was still walking to visit patients, in his usual regalia, when he was ninety. He took a fall on

23 January 1893 and uttered his last words: 'Give me champagne.' His own cremation, for which he left a set of instructions, took place on the same hilltop, with 20,000 people watching. A carnival atmosphere prevailed and the twenty or more pubs in Llantrisant ran dry during the height of the day-long festivities.

## Hair of the doc

The distinguished Scottish physician Dr George Fordyce (1736–1802) followed the same regime for twenty years. Every day at four o'clock he went to Dolly's Chop House in London and ate one and a half pounds of rump steak and half a broiled chicken or a large plate of fish, washed down by a tankard of strong ale, a bottle of port and a quart of brandy. He then made his way to the nearby Chapter Coffee House where he drank a glass of brandy and water, had a second glass at the London Coffee House and a third at the Oxford Coffee House. The refreshed Dr Fordyce then went back to work. One evening the doctor was summoned to the home of a rich patient who was suddenly taken ill. Fordyce struggled to locate his patient's pulse. Eventually he gave up, muttered to himself, 'Drunk, by golly,' and wrote a prescription. The next day he received a letter from his patient. Fordyce opened the envelope warily, expecting to find a rebuke for his negligence. The note read: 'I, too, am aware of the sorry state I was found in yesterday evening. I am sure that you will keep your evaluation confidential.' Also enclosed was a £100 note.

## Sexual healing

Charles Darwin's grandfather Dr Erasmus Darwin (1731–1802) was considered a leading expert on the treatment of the mentally ill. He had whirling beds and gyrating chairs fitted into most of the country's lunatic asylums so that patients could be rotated until blood poured out of their ears, eyes and noses. In his spare time, Dr Darwin was also a prolific inventor of steam-driven cars, wire-drawn ferries, horizontal windmills, mechanical birds, copying machines and speaking machines. He also fancied himself as a poet. In 1789, he published *The Loves of the Plants*, an epic 2,000-verse work about reproductive systems in vegetation. Many thought Dr Darwin was odd, and not only because he wrote poems about the sex lives of plants. His approach to medicine veered from the conventional. He prescribed sexual intercourse as a cure for, amongst other things, hypochondria.

Dr Darwin had a pronounced stammer, was heavily pockmarked and was so fat that he had to cut a half-moon section in the family dining table to accommodate his stomach. Nevertheless, he was very successful with women. His first wife Mary died early through drink and opium, leaving three sons. At forty-nine, after getting the family governess pregnant twice, Darwin seduced a married patient, Elizabeth Pole. When her husband died he married her and moved his whole family, legitimate and otherwise, to her Derbyshire mansion, where they raised a total of ten children. Charles Darwin later tried to restore his grandfather's reputation in *The Life of Erasmus Darwin*, but got his own daughter, Henrietta, to edit all the bits she thought were too racy for a Victorian audience – in all, nearly 20 per cent of the book.

## Nazi habits

Dr Marie Stopes (1880–1958), pioneer of birth control and sexologist, was the first person ever to write about the female orgasm. Given her area of expertise, Dr Stopes was curiously under-qualified. She received her very first kiss at the age of twenty-four and did not share a bed with a man until her thirties, when she married Reginald Ruggles Gates. Three years later, after consulting some foreign books in the reading room of the British Library, she was shocked to discover that she was a virgin. The marriage was soon annulled. Dr Stopes finally surrendered her virginity to her second husband, Humphrey Roe, aged thirty-eight and, shamed by her earlier ignorance, decided to write a sex manual, *Married Love*. The book dispensed practical advice on a variety of sex-related issues, including 'a husband and wife should spend as much time apart as possible – if they can not afford separate bedrooms at least share a room divided by a curtain', and 'never put anything in your vagina that you would not put in your mouth'. She was also the first person to assert the woman's need for orgasm, although she offered no clue as to how this might be achieved. Such was the British public's thirst for advice about bedroom matters, however, it was a runaway publishing success, quickly branded 'obscene' by the Anglican Church and banned in the US. Dr Stopes, meanwhile, also made up for lost time by sleeping with a succession of younger men.

Some of her lesser-known ideas trod a wobblier path. She took 'coal baths' by sitting naked in front of coal fires because she believed that they gave off beneficent rays. She was also a fanatical believer in eugenics and an ardent fan of Adolf Hitler. In 1919, she campaigned to prevent people who were poor, handicapped or 'prone to drunkenness or bad character' from having children. She boycotted the wedding of her own son when she discovered that the woman he was marrying was short-sighted.

This was not the only indignity Harry Stopes had to endure at the hands of his eccentric mother. Convinced that 'all men should wear kilts because the rubbing action of trousers can damage their testicles', she made her son wear a skirt. In 1939, just a month before her country went to war with Nazi Germany, she sent some love poems to Hitler with a note: 'Dear Herr Hitler, Love is the greatest thing in the world: so will you accept from me these poems that you may allow the young people of your nation to have them?'

## Bare necessity

The Scottish doctor Robert Broom (1866–1951) was a respected expert in midwifery. At an age at which most other people retire, the sixty-eight-year-old doctor started a second career as a full-time palaeontologist. He made a spectacular discovery in 1938, when he found the partial skeleton of an early hominid, *Australopithecus robustus*, including evidence proving that it had walked upright. Regardless of whether he was delivering babies or collecting fossils, Broom always dressed formally in a dark three-piece suit and starched collar and tie, unless it got too hot, in which case he would strip completely naked. In 1951, after writing the finishing lines of his paper on australopithecines, he said, 'Now that's finished, and so am I.' He died seconds later, at the age of eighty-five.

## Kill or cure

Although the position of Royal Physician is one of the best-paid medical jobs in Britain, it hasn't always necessarily attracted the best people. Ever since the Hanoverian kings created the post it has been held by some colourful and frequently controversial characters. King George II was attended by the mysterious John Taylor (1703–72), a student of St John's Hospital, London, and the most notorious oculist and eye surgeon of his generation. Taylor's real talent lay in self-promotion.

The self-styled 'Chevalier' and 'Opthamister' to the Pope and 'every crowned head in Europe' was as famous for his womanizing as for his knowledge of ophthalmology, but most famous of all for his habit of prefacing every operation he performed with a monologue in praise of his own skills, composed in what he claimed was 'the true Ciceronian'. His entire career, noted Dr Johnson, was 'an instance of how far impudence will carry ignorance'. Although Taylor was qualified, ophthalmology was still in its infancy and his clinical abilities were limited. He relied on a crude technique for the removal of cataracts known as couching, an invasive procedure using unsterilized instruments by which the opaque lens was displaced from the eye. The immediate results were good, but the operation was inevitably followed by serious infection. Taylor's two most famous victims were Johann Sebastian Bach and George Frideric Handel. Bach suffered agonies from repeated incisions into his eyes followed by treatment with mercury ointment, his death hastened as a result of the operation, without ever regaining his eyesight. Handel, at least, was spared septicaemia from Taylor's dreaded couching needle, but lost his eyesight completely and consequently suffered from terrible depression. In both cases Taylor claimed 100 per cent success.

Queen Caroline's decidedly strange personal surgeon William Cheselden (1688–1752) threw up before every operation he undertook and armed his assistant with a watch to try to keep his operations down to less than three minutes. When Cheselden was appointed, one of his first tasks was to find a cure for Caroline's profound deafness. He attempted to secure a human guinea pig in the form of a convicted criminal named Rey: the deal was that Rey would go free, and in return Cheselden would be allowed to do unspeakable things to Rey's ears, i.e. deafen him, then bore holes in his ears to find out if perforation would be of value to the royal earhole. There was a huge outcry by right-wing Hanoverians, but not on humanitarian grounds. They argued that vivisection was too good for Rey and he shouldn't be allowed to cheat the gallows: in any case, Rey might escape while he was in Cheselden's custody. The authorities bowed to the pressure and Cheselden was ordered to confine his experiments to the dead. The surgeon may yet have had his own way: he eventually helped establish the Company of Surgeons, whose headquarters were suspiciously located next door to Newgate Prison.

The prestige of the Royal Physician reached a new low in Queen Victoria's reign. The Queen, an avid fan herself of such dubious commercial remedies as Wordsdell's Vegetable Restorative Pills and Congreve's Balsamic Elixir, not to mention the odd drop of cocaine for colds and toothache, was a raging hypochondriac: one of her long-suffering medics was surprised one day to receive a telegram from Her Majesty informing him: 'The bowels are acting fully'. In 1887, at the age of sixty-eight, she had a particularly nasty axillary abscess drained. It was reported that when she came round from the chloroform she opened her eyes and said, 'A most unpleasant task, Professor Lister, most pleasantly performed,' proving perhaps that royal patients are not only a lot braver than the rest of us when they have to go under the surgeon's scalpel, their breeding also makes them slightly more courteous.

Queen Victoria spent much of her reign attended to by the mysteriously incompetent Sir James Clark (1788–1870), a man described by Lord Clarendon as 'not fit to attend a sick cat'. Clark was involved in a court scandal known as 'the Flora Hastings Affair'. In 1839, one of the Queen's unmarried ladies-in-waiting fell ill with a swollen stomach, convincing several people, including the Queen herself, that she was pregnant. To prove her innocence, Miss Hastings agreed to a humiliating internal examination by Clark. He produced a baffling medical statement which concluded that although Flora Hastings was still a virgin, it didn't necessarily mean that she was not pregnant; he had come across a few cases in his time, he explained to the young Queen, of pregnant virgins. The truth became horribly evident a few months later when Flora Hastings died in agony from a tumour on her liver. The court physician's career should have been terminated, but the Queen retained his services, so that when Prince Albert first fell seriously ill in November 1861, the trusty Dr Clark was again at hand to give both the Prime Minister Lord Palmerston and the Queen his personal assurance that the Prince Consort was merely suffering from a nasty cold – there was absolutely no cause for alarm.

Throughout Albert's protracted decline over a period of four weeks, Clark repeatedly gave hopeful prognoses, even encouraging him to leave his sick bed and get some exercise. As the wraith-like Albert wandered the freezing-cold stone halls of Windsor Castle in his dressing gown and all-in-one woollen sleeping suit, Clark continued to issue cheerful health bulletins. Finally the doctor conceded that he might have made a mistake. A week later Albert was no more. Clark belatedly volunteered that he thought he recognized typhoid symptoms. He was probably wrong about that as well, as retrospective diagnosis suggests that the cause of the Prince Consort's death was more likely stomach cancer. The Queen proved a grateful patient to the useless Clark, who upon his retirement was given Bagshot Park as a grace-and-favour residence until his death.

The above two cases are nothing, however, quite like the curious case of the regicidal doctor, Lord Dawson of Penn (1864–1945) who served as royal doctor to four kings: Edward VII, George V, Edward VIII and George VI. Dawson's esteemed position led to much professional jealousy. One of the more scurrilous stories spread by fellow physicians had it that he once treated a man for jaundice for several weeks until he noticed his patient was Chinese. His most famous patient at the time, King George V, was, like his father before him, a lifelong smoker and suffered from recurrent respiratory illnesses. The seventy-year-old King had been ill for several weeks, having suffered a series of debilitating bronchitis attacks, when Dawson was summoned to Sandringham on 17 January 1936. Dawson reassured the King that he would soon be away on his holiday to convalesce, a suggestion that provoked the notoriously salty-tongued Sailor King's final utterance, 'Bugger Bognor.'

Over the next three days George became steadily weaker, gradually slipping out of consciousness, and on 20 January he lapsed into a coma. Dawson took pen and paper and on the back of a menu card composed the line: 'The king's life is drawing peacefully to its close . . .' Then, shortly before midnight, to make absolutely sure his prose wasn't premature, he slipped a hypodermic syringe containing a lethal mixture of cocaine and morphine, now commonly known as a whizzball, into the King's jugular vein. Dawson's medical notes confirmed that he had not terminated the King's life to end his suffering – the King was unconscious and not in any pain. It was done simply for the sake of the morning papers. The moment of death was deliberately timed to ensure that the news, in Dawson's words, 'received its first announcement in the respectable morning papers, rather than the rather less appropriate field of the evening journals'. Dawson even phoned *The Times* to warn them to hold the front page and to expect an important announcement shortly. For his troubles the regicidal doctor received a Viscountcy later in that year's honours list.

# Ten
# UNSTRUNG HEROES

*'I'd recognize him straight away. He was in a green Barnado's plastic bag. Dennis was a bloke in a million'.*

– SIXTY-FOUR-YEAR-OLD WIDOW JEAN CARBERRY SEEKING PERMISSION FROM HER LOCAL COUNCIL TO SIFT THROUGH HUNDREDS OF TONS OF RUBBISH ON THE LOCAL TIP AFTER ACCIDENTALLY PUTTING HER HUSBAND'S ASHES OUT FOR THE REFUSE COLLECTORS.

## Survival of the fetishist

The biologist and philosopher Herbert Spencer (1820–1903) was one of the most influential academics of the Victorian era, working in disciplines as wide-ranging as sociology, anthropology, political theory, philosophy and psychology, and coined the phrase 'survival of the fittest'.

The thing that Spencer was most passionate about was his pulse. It all started when he suffered from a spot of mild heart trouble after an energetic trip to the Alps when he was thirty-five. Soon afterwards, stung by some harsh words by the critics about his new book *Principles of Psychology*, Spencer experienced some sort of mental breakdown, citing a strange sensation in his head he called 'the mischief'. His doctors could not find anything wrong with him but Spencer knew better; hard work was the problem. He simply stopped doing everything and took to his bed.

After a year and a half of enforced idleness Spencer slowly returned to his writing, but for the rest of his life he was a neurotic, hypochondriac semi-invalid, spending most of his time in bed, working at half speed and never more than a couple of hours a day, meanwhile treating himself for a variety of illnesses, including insomnia, by smoking tobacco (which he considered excellent for his health), vegetarianism and heavy doses of opium.

Spencer was morose at the best of times, thanks to his puritanical background of sexual repression and religious zeal in a family of dour Derbyshire Quakers who frowned on all forms of enjoyment; as his uncle and mentor Thomas had put it, 'No Spencer ever dances.' After his health scare he decided to give up anything he thought might be exciting and therefore bad for his heart – reading novels, for example. Lively conversation was another thing he thought would be too much for his delicate health. On rare trips to his gentleman's club, if anyone tried to strike up a conversation with him he would shut them out by slipping on a pair of velvet earplugs.

Ugly or noisy people put him off his food; if he found himself sitting at a meal near someone whose appearance upset him, he would simply leave the table. He was once invited to join a faculty luncheon group and was seated next to the famous biologist D'Arcy Thompson, known for his booming baritone voice. As soon as Thompson began to speak, Spencer picked up his plate and cutlery and scurried off to a corner of the room where he stood and ate his meal alone.

Spencer lived alone for twenty-six years in a boarding house. He was a lifelong bachelor and a very choosy suitor.

One potential romance was terminated when he found the woman's profile was 'too nutcrackery'. As far as anyone can be sure, he died a virgin, 'Miss Right' perhaps put off by his habit of wearing around the house a one-piece brown woollen suit that looked very much like a bear costume, or his curious nightly ritual which involved soaking his head in brine, then putting two layers of headgear over his wet hair.

Spencer was also a very fussy traveller. On train journeys he always took with him his own chair, a large supply of rugs and cushions and a hammock, carrying his manuscripts wrapped in brown paper and tied to his waist with a piece of string. Then there was his pulse, which had to be checked at regular intervals with great ceremony. He demanded complete silence while pulse checking. If the urge struck while he was travelling around London by coach, the driver was expected to make an emergency stop in the middle of the road, even if he was in heavy traffic in Piccadilly or Regent Street, so that Spencer could feel his pulse to see if it was safe to continue. Once the vital measurement was taken, if Spencer didn't like what he found, the coachman was expected to speed him home.

Spencer's *Autobiography* dwelt extensively on his poor health. As well as offering a complete and detailed history of his teeth, it also advanced the scientific arguments in favour of relaxation and the dangers of hard work. In the end, he probably got it about right. After a long and distinguished career of doing not very much, hypochondria notwithstanding, he died alone in 1903, aged eighty-three.

## Remains to be seen

The philosopher and reformer Jeremy Bentham (1748–1832) hardly ever stopped writing. He wrote tens of thousands of pages, many of which were never published. Before finishing one work, he would start another one, constantly jotting his ideas down on scraps of paper pinned to walls or curtains or just left lying on the floor. Ideas came so thick and fast that he worked at times literally knee-deep in pieces of paper. He frequently lost track of what he had written; one day he came across his important paper on parliamentary reform. He wrote on the cover, 'What can this be? Surely this was never my opinion?' He also kept several pet rats, which he allowed to chew through his notes. After his death it was left to Bentham's friends and students to piece together and rewrite some of his most important works from the tattered remains of his rat-ravaged manuscripts.

Bentham was also a prolific inventor of odd devices. One of his strangest creations was the Panopticon, a type of model prison. It functioned as a round-the-clock surveillance machine comprising a circular building with an inspector at the hub who was able to see everything going on inside via a series of reflecting mirrors. Bentham hoped to sell his model prison to the Russian Empress Catherine the Great, but nothing came of it. In fact Bentham spent the next twenty years pursuing his Panopticon idea, at massive expense. Fortunately, an inheritance received in 1796 saved him from financial ruin.

Bentham rarely went out of the house and lived a mostly reclusive existence. He was so painfully shy he could never bring himself to meet more than one visitor at a time, and the thought of meeting a stranger for the first time filled him with dread. He even found contact with people by post difficult and often wrote letters to fellow philosophers which were never sent. He also gave names to inanimate objects. Rare visitors to the Bentham household were bemused to hear their host address his teapot as 'Dick'. But no one realized just how strange he really was until his death in 1832.

Bentham thought that burying dead people was a wasteful

business. He suggested an alternative. Every man, if properly embalmed, could be used as his own commemorative bust or statue: he called them 'auto-icons'. The possibilities, Bentham posited, were endless: portraits of ancestors could be replaced by actual heads, 'many generations being deposited on a few shelves or in a modest sized cupboard'. When Bentham died he put his money where his mouth was. He left everything to the University of London on condition that he was publicly dissected and flayed in front of his friends. His corpse was then stuffed, dressed in his best clothes and mounted in a chair and placed on display in a glass cabinet, 'that folks may see me still, a hundred years from now . . .'. And so it has been, ever since. Bentham's physician, Dr Southwood Smith, kept the body until his own death in 1850 when it was presented to University College, London, where his body is brought out once a year to preside over the annual meeting of university administrators, the minutes recording 'Jeremiah Bentham, present but not voting'. His head, however, had to be replaced by a wax version because his natural smugness had lost something during the embalming process; the real head is preserved in a mummified state in a box nearby.

## Bad vibrations

In order to demonstrate the 'cultural inferiority of the United States', the Pogues' lead singer Shane MacGowan ate a Beach Boys album.

## Access all arias

The opera impresario John Christie (1882–1962), founding father of the Glyndebourne Festival, was the only child of an eccentric county squire who left him a large country house, 10,000 acres of land, an organ-manufacturing company and a building works. Before he came into his inheritance, Christie spent sixteen years as a science teacher at Eton, where he developed a lifelong affection for rice pudding. Christie could never get enough of it; as an adult he could eat seven helpings at one sitting.

He also served in France in the First World War and proved an unflappable leader in the trenches. One day a soldier was blown to pieces by a shell only a few feet away from Christie and his men; he produced a copy of Edmund Spenser's poem *The Faerie Queene* from his pocket and read it aloud to restore calm. In 1932, Christie married the thirty-year-old opera singer Audrey Mildmay, who was twenty years his junior. On their honeymoon she was taken ill with appendicitis, so to keep her company he had his own appendix removed in the same hospital.

It was Audrey who spurred on Christie's operatic ambitions. When he suggested extending the organ room, she told him, 'If you're going to spend all that money, John, for God's sake do the job properly.' As a result Christie ploughed millions into building an opera house in his back garden.

The Glyndebourne Festival has been an annual English institution ever since, save for one lengthy interlude in the 1940s. On 15 July 1939, the final curtain fell on what was to be the last performance for eleven years. Christie stepped before the audience to announce that he had 'serious news'. They stirred in their seats uneasily; rumours of war were in all the papers. Christie cleared his throat; for the first time since 1908, he informed his public, the annual Eton–Harrow cricket match had been won by Eton.

Christie loved throwing lavish parties at Glyndebourne, where the lady guests were given knitting needles and balls of wool to give them something to do while the men talked. There was one item guaranteed to be on the menu at every Christie gathering: rice pudding.

His attitude towards money, meanwhile, alternated between moods of reckless extravagance and extreme caution. He spent a fortune on champagne and celebrated news of his wife's first pregnancy by buying her a diamond tiara, necklace and brooch once owned by Empress Josephine. Meanwhile, his house guests would freeze because he refused to switch on the heating. He was so afraid of wasting electricity that he employed a man just to turn the lights off around his house and he was often seen around London with a large hot water bottle sticking out of the back of his trousers. He always wore an old pair of tennis shoes, even in formal evening dress, although he also went through a 'lederhosen period' in the 1930s, when all of his visitors were required to follow his lead and wear leather shorts for dinner. One hot evening at the theatre at Glyndebourne, Christie walked over to his house during the intermission, took a pair of scissors to his full-dress jacket and shirt, cut the sleeves off below the elbows then returned to his seat.

Christie never travelled first class and refused to tip waiters, but always made a point of explaining to the disappointed waiter that tips were demeaning to the recipient. He was also a bulk buyer. He once acquired 2,000 pairs of cheap plastic dancing shoes because 'they might come in useful'. He then had second thoughts and tried to offload them onto members of Brooke's, his private club. Brooke's was littered with piles of unwanted plastic shoes for several months.

His most ambitious bulk purchase was in America when he acquired a ton of sugar and rice and went home with it on the Queen Mary. As this was the late 1940s and rationing was still in place, it was illegal for one person to bring such a large quantity of sugar and rice into the country. Christie got around the problem by persuading fellow passengers to smuggle small portions through Customs with them in their hand luggage. Once safely ashore, he retrieved it all and stored it under the floors at Glyndebourne.

Christie acquired a permanent limp from a riding mishap and lost an eye in a sporting accident. One evening he found himself sitting next to the Queen at a dinner party. He removed his glass eye, polished it with his handkerchief, popped it back in, turned to Her Majesty and enquired, 'In straight, Ma'am?'

## Shit hits fan

For the artistic double act Gilbert and George, every day is groundhog day. Every morning at 6.30 a.m. they put on their matching business suits and leave their home in Spitalfields, east London, to breakfast at the same tiny café. Every night at 8 p.m. they dine on lamb chops at the same Kurdish restaurant. In between, they create art. In 1995, they staged an exhibition at the South London Art Gallery under the title 'Naked Shit Pictures'. It comprised sixteen large glossy photos of the artists surrounded by a series of 'defecation motifs', including turd circles and turd sculptures. A critic described the work as 'almost biblical'.

## Thereby hangs a tail

The aristocratic Scot James Burnett, Lord Monboddo (1714–99) was reputed to be the most learned judge of his day. He spent his life convinced that babies were born with tails and that there was a universal conspiracy of silence among midwives who cut them off at birth. Monboddo's faith in his tail theory remained intact even after witnessing the births of his own children. He concluded that the crafty midwives had tricked him and destroyed the evidence. Monboddo frequently interrupted court proceedings at Edinburgh's Court of Sessions by sending notes of enquiry to witnesses who had recently returned from abroad to ask them if they had seen any foreigners with tails.

Monboddo was a practising nudist, very near-sighted and stone deaf. In 1785, he was sitting for the first time at the King's Bench in London, when part of the court roof collapsed, causing lawyers and judges to flee for their lives. Monboddo alone sat unmoved among the debris and confusion. When asked why he hadn't reacted, Monboddo replied that he thought he was witnessing some local court ceremony with which he was unfamiliar.

## Gallows humour

The Irish judge John Toler, first Baron Norbury (1745–1831) was described as 'fat, podgy, with small grey cunning eyes, which ever sparkled with good humour and irrepressible fun, especially when he was passing sentence of death'. Norbury was without mercy and his sentences were usually harsh; on a 'good' day he sent ninety-seven men to their deaths. His courtroom manner combined drollery with vicious dry wit. He sent men down with long rambling speeches peppered with quotations from Milton and Shakespeare and threw his wig in the air after he had passed sentence.

Towards the end of his career Norbury's performances in court became increasingly erratic. He fell asleep during trials and would awake in confusion without any recollection of the case or even where he was. He retired in 1827, aged eighty-two, after a complaint that he had snored loudly throughout an important murder trial.

Norbury was famous for one single act of clemency towards an alleged murderer. Although the evidence against the accused was clear-cut and overwhelming, he recommended the jury to bring in an acquittal, eliciting a gasp of astonishment around the courtroom. The crown prosecutor interrupted the judge to remind him that the sheer weight of evidence showed the man's guilt was undisputable. Norbury replied impatiently, 'I realize that, but I hanged six men at last Tipperary Assizes who were innocent, so I'll let this man off now to square matters.'

## Have I got noose for you

Justice Sir Melford Stevenson (1902–87) took part in some of Britain's most notorious trials, including that of Ruth Ellis, the last woman to be hanged in Britain. Stevenson was known for judicial toughness, a style hinted at in the name of his Sussex home, 'Truncheons'. He was also famous for controversial courtroom observations of a politically incorrect nature. He once referred to bookmakers as 'a bunch of crooks' and upset Mancunians when he commented during a divorce case that the husband 'chose to live in Manchester, a wholly incomprehensible choice for any free man to make'. He told a man acquitted of rape, 'I see you come from Slough. It is a terrible place. You can go back there.'

During a bribery case Stevenson described Birmingham as 'a municipal Gomorrah'. In 1945, he stood as Conservative MP for Maldon, Essex, saying that he wanted a clean fight and would not therefore under any circumstances mention 'the alleged homosexuality' of his opponent Tom Driberg. In 1967, Stevenson was reprimanded by the Lord Chancellor when he described the reform of homosexuality laws as 'a buggers' charter'. In a single day in 1976, Stevenson had a record three decisions overturned by the Court of Appeal, a setback which caused him to note 'a lot of my colleagues are just constipated Methodists'. Stevenson also presided over the trial of Britain's most notorious underworld figures of the 1960s, the Kray twins. He recalled later that the Krays had only told the truth twice; first when Ronnie described a barrister as 'a fat slob', second when Reggie complained that the judge was biased.

## Pervert in the course of justice

Justice Rayner Goddard (1877–1971) was one of the most enthusiastic hangers and floggers ever to have held the post of British Lord Chief Justice, an office he assumed at the age of sixty-nine – elderly even by the standards of the British legal system – and held for thirteen years. He presided over some of the most notorious cases in criminal history, including that of Derek Bentley, a nineteen-year-old with a mental age of eleven, sentenced to hang in 1953.

The writer and broadcaster Ludovic Kennedy, in his anthology of alleged miscarriages of justice *Thirty-Six Murders and Two Immoral Earnings*, describes the Lord Chief Justice's idiosyncratic approach to sentencing prisoners to hang:

> After Goddard's death his clerk to the court, Arthur Smith, told John Parris [Craig's counsel] that on the last day of a murder trial he would bring a fresh pair of trousers into the robing room, as Goddard was in the habit of ejaculating into his present pair when sentencing a prisoner to death.

## Taking liberties

Justice Michael Argyle (1915–99) was called 'the Domino Judge' because of his habit of handing down sentences of five and seven years, the maximum for most sorts of crime. Argyle was chiefly renowned for his controversial courtroom outbursts. He first came to the attention of the British public during the notorious *Oz* magazine 'School Kids Issue' obscenity trial in 1971 when he told a woman detective: 'You are far too attractive to be a police woman. You should be an actress.'

On the subject of the number of British immigrants in Britain, he once noted, 'I don't have the figures, but just go to Bradford,' while black British defendant was told to 'get out and go back to Jamaica'. Argyle was a big cricket fan and always kept a TV set in his robing room. In 1986, he told a jury at the Old Bailey that the lack of Test Match cricket on television was 'enough to make an Orthodox Jew want to join the Nazi party'.

## Tight genes

John Elwes (1714–89) was born into a family of notorious Suffolk misers. He inherited his fortune from his father, a brewer who died when Elwes was four; he acquired his parsimonious habits from his mother, who reputedly starved herself to death with several thousand pounds still in her bank account. The biggest influence in his young life however was his rich and equally miserly uncle Harvey. Hoping to secure a favourable result from his uncle's will, Elwes was a frequent visitor to his home. Before each visit, Elwes always took care to change into an old threadbare suit in case his uncle thought he was spendthrift and disinherited him. The two of them would spend the evening complaining about other people's wasteful spending habits over a single shared glass of wine. When Harvey died, Elwes came into possession of his entire estate with a net worth of £500,000 in today's money. He celebrated by wearing his new wig; more accurately, a wig he had recently found in the gutter.

Elwes was so tight-fisted that he refused to pay for the education of his own two sons, because education might give them ideas about spending money. He never polished his shoes in case he wore them out, rode his carriage on the grass verge to reduce the wear and tear on horse shoes and made long detours to avoid paying at toll gates. Elwes once broke both legs in an accident, but would only pay his doctor for one splint to halve the bill. His dietary habits were particularly repulsive. He ate meat that was so mouldy and maggot-infested that it moved on the plate. He once dined on a long-dead moorhen he found being gnawed by a rat. He died aged seventy-six in 1789, leaving his mansion in a state of semi-dereliction, and £75,000 – worth about £20 million today.

## Where there's muck

The miserly Daniel Dancer (1716–94) inherited his family estate, Harrow Weald, at the age of 20, including an 80-acre farm with an annual income of £3,000 and an estimated £15,000 in cash. Instead of running it profitably and enjoying the life of a prosperous Middlesex farmer, he let it run to ruin and dedicated the rest of his life to hoarding his wealth. Weald was a world-class skinflint. He lived with his sister, who also served as his housekeeper. The pair survived on one piece of beef and fourteen boiled dumplings a week, which were cooked on Sundays and then made to last, although they once got lucky and found a sheep which had expired from an unknown disease. They dined on mutton pies for a month.

A neighbour once took pity on him and sent him a dish of trout. He couldn't eat it cold because he had toothache, so he placed it between two plates, then sat on it until he considered it was warm enough to eat.

To save money on heating and maintenance Weald withdrew to an outbuilding and slept on sacking on the floor. He washed only in the summer, when he would wait for a sunny day, jump in a pond and then lie naked on the common until he was dry, or scrub himself down with sand. In winter he was conspicuous by his body lice. Infrequent fires in his home were fuelled by logs and sticks stolen from his neighbours. His sister died after a brief illness in 1766; Dancer had refused to call a doctor.

He was terrified that thieves would steal his inheritance, so he spent his days roaming around the neighbourhood collecting cow and horse dung, which he took home and built into a giant dunghill. When Dancer died in 1794, the results of a lifetime of dedicated parsimony were finally revealed. Hundreds of pounds were stashed away up chimneys, in jugs, teapots and stuffed into chairs. The single largest hoard, £2,500, was hidden where no burglar would look for it – inside the giant dunghill in his cowshed.

## High spirits

The London miser John Overs was known as 'the rich ferryman of Southwark' because he enjoyed the monopoly of the boat trips across the river Thames after buying the franchise from the City of London. Although he made a fortune, Overs lived mostly on mouldy bread and condemned meat and lived so frugally that, according to tradition, the rats left his house of their own accord. In a moment of madness, Overs hatched a far-fetched plan to save a day's food bill by pretending to be dead. He thought that his staff and servants would fast for a couple of days after the funeral, as tradition dictated, and thus reduce his food bill. The plan backfired when his overjoyed employees celebrated by throwing open the doors to their master's pantry. Overs rose from his deathbed to remonstrate with them, and thinking he was a ghost, a young employee clubbed him to death with an oar. An investigation into the killing cleared the employee and named Overs as an accessory to his own death, effectively amounting to suicide. As such, the Church considered the bitter old misanthrope unworthy of a Christian burial. His daughter Mary had to bribe a gravedigger to bury him in the grounds at Bermondsey Abbey while the Abbot was away.

## The Queen's miser

The most grossly misplaced act of generosity ever was the last will and testament of the London barrister John Camden Neild (1780–1852). Neild inherited a quarter of a million pounds and a huge house in one of London's most fashionable addresses at Cheyne Walk, Chelsea, but occupied only one room to save on heating bills. For years he slept on bare floorboards, although when he reached his late sixties he allowed himself the comfort of an old bed. He always wore the same old moth-eaten blue swallow-tailed coat and brown trousers, refusing to have his clothes even brushed in case it wore them out.

Neild owned properties all over south-east England and insisted on collecting the rents himself rather than pay an agent to collect them for him. On his trips around the country he cadged lifts on coal carts or farm wagons, and on overnight stopovers would always stay with his tenants for free. In 1828, while visiting a tenant in North Marston, Buckinghamshire, he attempted to take his own life by cutting his throat. He was saved only by the prompt attention of his tenant's wife, a Mrs Neale.

By the time of his death by natural causes in 1852, his incredible thrift had helped him double his inheritance to £500,000 – around £30 million by today's value. Inexplicably, he had left almost the entire fortune to Queen Victoria, 'begging her Majesty's most gracious acceptance of the same, for her sole use and benefit, and her heirs'. The Queen, who was already one of the richest women in the world, was naturally delighted. She and her husband Prince Albert spent the bulk of the windfall by purchasing Balmoral Castle, meanwhile continuing to harangue the British government for a bigger Civil List, thereby providing the platform upon which the present British royal family's personal fortune is now based. There was nothing in the will for Mrs Neale, who had saved Neild's life, although the Queen later granted her an annual pension of £100.

## A tale of two hermits

Charles Dickens based two of his characters on famous eighteenth-century recluses. Jane 'Lady' Lewson (*c.* 1700–1816) from Clerkenwell in London was the inspiration for the reclusive Miss Havisham in *Great Expectations*. 'Lady' Lewson shrank from all social contact after the death of her husband when she was only twenty-six years old. She occupied just one room of her large house and to the end of her days continued to wear clothes that were fashionable at the time of her wedding. She rarely washed, apparently for fear of catching a cold, and smeared her cheeks with a layer of pig fat, adding a touch of colour to each with rouge. She died in her home, according to tradition, at the age of 116, among the accumulated decades of dirt and cobwebs.

James Lucas (1813–74), also known as 'the Mad Hermit of Hertfordshire', was immortalized as Mr Mopes in Dickens's *Tom Tiddler's Ground*. Lucas was the son of a rich Liverpool businessman and sugar plantation owner. He became a complete recluse after the death of his beloved mother in 1849 and refused to have her buried, sitting by the coffin for four months, until the local magistrates ordered burial. The police had to break in, causing him lasting paranoia. Lucas never left the house again. He barricaded himself in his kitchen, armed to the teeth with shotguns and knives, and lived there for several years in appalling squalor. He wore only a horse rug and neither washed nor cut his hair for twenty-five years, until a thick, black, greasy layer of grime encased his entire body. As his fame spread he received an increasing number of visitors who came to catch a glimpse of Lucas through the bars of his kitchen window. In 1861, Charles Dickens went to see him, an unhappy encounter that ended with Lucas threatening the author with a shotgun. Dickens spitefully described his semi-fictional Lucas as 'a slothful, unsavoury, nasty reversal of the laws of human nature'. In 1874, twenty-five years after their first break-in, police forced entry into Lucas's home for a second time and found him dying from a stroke.

## The masked man of linguistics

In the early 1940s, the Cambridge academic, linguist and writer Charles Kay Ogden (1889–1957) hit upon the idea of creating a single universal language as a force for world peace. English was already in use by hundreds of millions of native English speakers and many more besides, but as a second language it took a long time to learn, so Ogden proposed a radical new solution. He took the 25,000-word *Oxford Pocket English Dictionary* and pared it down to 850 simple words, including just eighteen verbs. The result: a simplified form of English that the whole world could learn in a matter of weeks. He unveiled his new language in a book: *Basic English: A General Introduction with Rules and Grammar.*

Britain's Prime Minister Winston Churchill loved it. The widespread use of Basic English, Churchill announced, 'will be a gain to us far more fruitful than the annexation of great provinces'. It also fitted in with his plan for closer ties with the United States 'by making it even more worthwhile to belong to the English-speaking club'. In July 1943, Churchill wrote to the BBC urging them to 'teach Basic English every day' and a government-backed Basic English Foundation was established, with Ogden as chairman. For a while it looked as though Basic English would conquer the world, making its creator an international celebrity and a very wealthy man. Then, with fame and fortune beckoning, just when it seemed that Ogden couldn't fail, he somehow did.

Not everyone quite shared Churchill's enthusiasm. The US President Roosevelt promised him he would 'look into the matter thoroughly', but privately thought Ogden's scheme was a bit of a joke. He especially disliked the un-American spelling, which Ogden stubbornly refused to change. Roosevelt told Churchill: 'I wonder what the course of history would have been if in May 1940 you had been able to offer the British people only blood, work, eye water and face water, which I understand is the best that Basic English can do with five famous words.' The press also had fun with it. *Punch* translated the Churchillian classic: 'Never, in the field of human conflict, was so much owed by so many to so few,' into: 'Never, in the history of men's disagreement, did such great numbers have so great a debt to such small number.' In 1949, George Orwell savagely satirized the barely disguised Basic English as 'Newspeak' in his book *1984*.

There were other hindrances, most notably Ogden himself. Although a brilliant linguist he was also a bit of a fruitcake, a concept, incidentally, you would have struggled to put across in Basic English, there not being a word for fruit, or eccentric, or strange, or any other word that would come adequately close to describing Ogden's undoubted weirdness.

Ogden had been struck down by rheumatic fever at the age of sixteen and had to spend two years in a dark room. By the time he attended Cambridge University he was a full-blown claustrophiliac – he enjoyed being confined in small places. He thought that fresh air was dangerous to his health and kept his windows firmly shuttered. In his rooms he kept an 'ozone machine' that discharged 'healthful particles'.

He was also a chronic insomniac and walked the streets in the middle of the night, knocking on the doors of friends to see if any were still up. He had an intense, some thought unhealthy, interest in the philosopher Jeremy Bentham, whose stuffed remains were on permanent display at University College in London (see p.266–8). For Bentham's centennial, Ogden organized a change of underwear for his hero. For the last few years of his life, possibly as a tribute to Bentham, Ogden kept his own coffin permanently on display in his front hallway.

Ogden was also an obsessive collector of everything from music boxes to shoes. Then there was his huge collection of masks. During the press interviews to promote Basic English, journalists were ushered into Ogden's quarters and invited to sit on the floor to eat from saucers of sweets, nuts and bananas and to smoke homemade herbal cigarettes. Ogden would then put on one of his masks and invite his interviewer to do the same. This would, he explained to the bemused correspondents, help keep the conversation focused on logic, unhindered by personalities. Throughout the interviews he would pop in and out of the room, each time wearing a new mask. It made Ogden a laughing stock in the British press and did little to endear him to his financial backers.

With Churchill's departure the new Labour government was more concerned with social welfare than Ogden's universal language. The BBC was also relieved that they no longer had to promote it. An internal memo recommended that Basic English was placed 'on a high shelf in a dark corner'. The government paid Ogden off, giving him £23,000 to cover his costs. By the early 1950s Basic English had slid into obscurity, as indeed had its eccentric inventor.

## Give peas a chance

Stanley Green (1915–93) spent most his life warning his fellow man against the dangers of protein and lust. He was also against sitting, which was perhaps as well because he spent the best part of thirty years walking up and down London's Oxford Street with a large placard which read:

> LESS PASSION FROM LESS PROTEIN: MEAT FISH BIRD; EGG CHEESE; PEAS incl.lentils BEANS; NUTS AND SITTING PROTEIN WISDOM.

Green held a number of jobs before joining the Royal Navy in 1938. He began his campaign following his demobilization in September 1945. He told the *Sunday Times* magazine that, being 'a moral sort of person', he had been shocked by the 'passion of fellow sailors'. By 1958, Green had equated this passion, in both men and women, with a protein-rich diet. The solution, he decided, was a regime of moderation enshrined in the doctrine of 'less lust from less protein'. He began by printing thousands of leaflets entitled 'Eight Passion Proteins', produced on a noisy press in his council flat and sold at 12p each. Fortified by a diet of porridge, fruit, steamed vegetables, lentils, home-baked bread and barley water mixed with milk powder, he cycled the 15 miles daily from his home in Northolt to London's West End with his placard on his back. A favourite tactic of his was to accost queues of cinema-goers with the opening line, 'You cannot deceive your groom that you are a virgin on your wedding night.'

Green was such a regular fixture in central London that motorists sounded their horns and waved as they passed and whole coach loads stood up and cheered him. Not everyone was quite as appreciative. He was twice arrested for obstruction and wore green overalls as protection against spit. He never held grudges; people only attacked him, he said, because they mistook him for 'a religious nut'. He died unmarried at his home in Middlesex, leaving his message board, copies of his booklets and other papers to the Museum of London and Gunnersbury Park Museum, London.

## Live and let dye

Although he never recycled a bottle in his life, William Cope (b. *c.* 1770) was known as 'the green man of Brighton'. The local journal recorded that Cope always wore 'green pantaloons, green waistcoat, green frock coat, green cravat, and though his ears, whiskers, eyebrows and chin were powdered, his countenance, no doubt from the reflection of his clothes, was also green. He ate nothing but green fruits and vegetables, and had his rooms painted green and furnished with green sofa, green chairs, green table, green bed and green curtains. His gig, his livery, his portmanteau, his gloves and his whip were all green. With a green silk handkerchief in his hand, and a large watch-chain with green seals fastened to the green buttons of his green waistcoat, he paraded every day on the Steyne'. Nothing to do with his carbon footprint, then.

The newspaper went on to note: 'The Green Man continues daily to amuse the Steyne promenaders with his eccentricities.' But there was a sad footnote. In 1806, Cope jumped out of the window of his lodgings on Brighton's South Parade, ran across the road and threw himself off the cliff opposite. He survived the drop, but as the journal recorded, 'Mr. Cope, the Green Man, is pronounced out of danger from his bruises; but his intellects have continued so impaired as to render a straight waistcoat necessary.'

## The surreal McCoy

The millionaire arts patron Edward James (1907–84) was rumoured to be the illegitimate son of his godfather King Edward VII, which would have made him the natural great-uncle of Queen Elizabeth II. James randomly bankrolled dozens of painters and writers. He once met Salvador Dalí and was so taken by him that he agreed to buy everything Dalí produced for a whole year. He was already buying up all the Picassos and Magrittes he could get his hands on at the time.

An ungrateful Dalí later told Sigmund Freud that his rich patron was 'crazier than all the Surrealists put together. They pretend, but he is the real thing.'

James also wrote reams of terrible poetry, mostly under the influence of marijuana and magic mushrooms, which appeared in a series of 'vanity' publications over a period of thirty years. Although born into extreme wealth, he never threw anything away, even old matchboxes. He boiled up saucepans full of old paperclips, drenched in cologne, for re-use. Eventually his home became so full of bric-a-brac that every now and then he would have everything wrapped in tissue, packed in trunks and stored in a warehouse.

In 1945, James bought several thousand acres of Mexican jungle at Xilitla, where he built a series of fantastic concrete follies – simply, he explained, so that 'when archaeologists come and see this in two or three thousand years' time they won't know what to make of it'. Work began on Las Pozas in 1949 and employed as many as 150 workers at one time. By the time he died in 1984, James had sunk millions into the project. The follies had names: the House With a Roof like a Whale, the House on Three Floors Which Will in Fact Have Five or Four or Six, the Stegosaurus Colt, the Fleur-de-Lys Bridge and Cornucopia, the St Peter and St Paul Gate, the Temple of the Ducks, the House Destined To Be a Cinema. It is generally assumed that he got his ideas while under the influence of controlled substances.

He spent his afternoons strolling naked around his jungle estate assisted by two walking sticks, required partly because he never cut his toenails. He also kept a number of exotic pets, including a brace of boa constrictors, several parrots, kinkajous, ocelots, ducks, deer, peacocks, dogs, cats and four baby crocodiles. One evening he was staying at the Majestic Hotel in Mexico City with his snakes, when a live mouse escaped from his suite. A lady guest encountered the mouse and screamed that the hotel was infested with rodents. A maid reassured her, 'No, Señora, they are not the hotel's mice. They are food for the gentleman's snakes in the room next door.'

## Losing the plot (part one)

The incomparable Robert 'Romeo' Coates (1772–1848) was the worst actor ever to grace the English stage. Although minimal in talent, Coates was extremely rich thanks to his father, a rich sugar plantation owner in Antigua, who died in 1807, leaving him in possession of a huge fortune. Also nicknamed 'Diamond' Coates for his habit of dressing in furs and diamonds and driving in a bright pink chaise in the shape of a cockle shell, he was a late bloomer and first trod the boards at the age of thirty-seven. It was his debut performance in *Romeo and Juliet* in the spa town of Bath about a year later that earned him his first serious notices. From the moment he made his entrance as Romeo wearing a sequin-spangled cloak, vast red pantaloons and enormous plumed hat, it became obvious to all that they were witnessing a special talent. He forgot his lines, ad-libbed freely and brought the house down. When it was pointed out to him that he was straying from Shakespeare's text, he replied, 'Aye, that is the reading I know, for I have the whole play by heart, but I think I have improved on it.' A critic wrote: 'In the school of Coates, dignity is denoted by strutting across the stage in strides two yards long, agony by the furious stamp of the foot at the end of every line.'

Coates toured the British Isles in what was to become his signature role, creating mayhem wherever he performed. His tour de force was the Romeo death scene; no one ever died on stage quite like Coates. He would produce a silk handkerchief from his top pocket with a mighty flourish and proceed to dust the stage with it. He then carefully laid down the handkerchief, placed his plumed hat on it then arranged himself on top of the hat. If his death scene got a big reaction, Coates would leap to his feet, take a bow, then 'die' all over again. During one performance the audience sat open-mouthed as Romeo appeared wielding a crowbar, trying to open Juliet's tomb. Theatre-goers were prepared to travel great distances to see for themselves if he was truly was as bad as his notices. When Coates played the part of Lothario in *The Fair Penitent* at London's Haymarket Theatre, at least a thousand people had to be turned away and there were people standing in the wings. Not even the sound of his audience baying with laughter during a death scene could put him off his stride. At a performance in Richmond, Surrey, he caused several people to laugh so hard that they had to be carried outside and receive medical treatment.

Despite public ridicule and critical panning, he continued to perform on the stage until 1816, by which time the public had tired of laughing at him. He eventually fell into financial difficulties and retired to Boulogne. In 1848, having reached an arrangement with his creditors, he returned to England. On 15 February, Coates was leaving a concert at Drury Lane when he was crushed to death between two hansom cabs.

## Losing the plot (part two)

Over a long and distinguished career the roles played by the great British actor A. E. 'Matty' Matthews (1869–1960) evolved gradually from smooth romantic leads to crotchety old men. He was still acting right up to the time of his death aged ninety-one, making him Britain's oldest ever working thespian.

His stage performances became correspondingly erratic with age. He could only remember his lines if he had dozens of prompts concealed around the stage and in the wings, and he would often make unscripted exits to jog his memory. During one West End performance his memory deserted him at a particularly critical moment. Matthews played a pivotal scene which required him to answer a telephone onstage. When it rang on cue, he crossed the stage, picked up the receiver, then froze, having forgotten his line. He turned to another actor onstage and said: 'It's for you.' He put in a particularly eccentric performance during rehearsals for *The Manor Of Northstead*. 'Don't worry, chaps,' he reassured the worried producer and director of the play, 'I promise you, even if we had to open next Monday, I'd be all right.'

'Matty,' the director replied, 'we *do* open on Monday.'

In his nineties, Matthews made national news when he had a row with his local council over a concrete lamp-post they wanted to put outside his house and he staged a protest 'sit-in' on the pavement. Inspired by Matthews's protest, Spike Milligan wrote a *Goon Show* script, 'The Evils of Bushey Spon', about a council lamp-post, in which Matthews was given a part. The last five minutes of the show were completely ad-libbed because of Matthews's total refusal to stick to the script.

## Is this a lager which I see before me?

Although small, deaf and lame, Edmund Kean (1789–1833) was regarded as one of the greatest ever Shakespearian actors. His earnings were unprecedented for a stage performer, but more than matched by his expensive tastes, which ran from marathon backstage romps with actresses and prostitutes, before, during and after performances, to parading his pet lion in London's streets.

Kean's career was punctuated by many drunken absences. It was often necessary to hold his head under a cold water tap before he went on stage to try to sober him up. If that failed, he would sit on a bucket and drunkenly heckle his understudy from the wings. During a performance of *Macbeth* in New York, he somehow staggered through the first half, but at the interval the theatre manager announced that the performance would continue without Kean, who was suffering from malaria. A wag from the stalls shouted: 'I could do with a bottle of that myself.'

## Last orders

Oliver Reed (1938–99) spent much of his adult life being thrown out of pubs and hotels after marathons of bibulous excess he called 'tests of strength', generally followed by random displays of exhibitionism. In 1974, when he was filming *The Three Musketeers* in Spain, police were summoned to his hotel to arrest him for dancing naked in a giant fish tank. Later that year, Reed invited 36 rugby players to a party at his home and between Saturday night and Sunday lunchtime they consumed 60 gallons of beer, 32 bottles of whisky, 17 bottles of gin, 4 crates of wine and a bottle of Babycham. The party concluded with Reed leading the players on a nude dawn run through the Surrey countryside. One of his more regular pranks was to take out his tattooed penis, although to the relief of the BBC he never once managed this during his many appearances on *Parkinson*.

In 1985, he married twenty-one-year-old Josephine Burge after a five-year courtship. At his stag party, which lasted two days, Reed is said to have drunk 136 pints of beer. On one occasion he spiked snooker star Alex Higgins's whisky with Chanel perfume. Higgins reacted by squirting washing-up liquid in Reed's crème de menthe. In 1986, Reed dug up nine acres of his back garden after forgetting where he had buried his wife's jewellery.

He suffered a fatal heart attack in Malta during the making of Ridley Scott's film *Gladiator* after drinking three bottles of rum and then challenging a local fisherman to an arm-wrestling contest. Before he died, he arranged to have £10,000 out of his estate spent at his local pub, but only for 'those who are crying'. His views on how he wanted *not* to be disposed of were well documented. He didn't want to be laid out for days in his Sunday best in order to 'have people gawping at me to see what a dead hellraiser looks like', nor did he favour burial, due to his fear of 'maggots having a ball crawling up my nose and out of my mouth', or burial at sea: 'Who wants to be gobbled up by a big fish and become excrement that is swallowed up by a prawn . . . ending up as mayonnaise, being nibbled at by a pretty girl? I don't want to be permanent shit.'

## Torquay shoot

Donald Sinclair (1919–81), proprietor of the Hotel Gleneagles in Torquay, was the unwitting inspiration for the classic comedy *Fawlty Towers*. Sinclair was a former Commander in the Royal Navy who had been torpedoed three times. His wife Beatrice persuaded her husband to leave his senior position in the navy to help her run the hotel, which may help explain why he didn't seem to enjoy his role. John Cleese discovered Sinclair, whom he later described as 'the most wonderfully rude man I had ever met', when the *Monty Python* team stayed there in the summer of 1970 while they were filming in nearby Paignton. According to Michael Palin, Sinclair 'seemed to view us as a colossal inconvenience right from the start'.

He endeared himself to the Pythons by throwing Eric Idle's briefcase out of the hotel 'in case it contained a bomb'. When the American Python Terry Gilliam left his knife and fork at an angle, Sinclair leaned over him, put his knife and fork together, and said, 'This is how we do it in England'. On another occasion Sinclair threw a bus timetable at a guest who dared ask when the next bus to town would arrive. The rest of the Pythons relocated to another hotel, but Cleese and his wife Connie Booth remained, gathering material which would eventually come together in their creation of Basil Fawlty, the neurotic, eccentric and bad-tempered manager of *Fawlty Towers*.

According to Sinclair's former employees, Basil barely did him justice. On one occasion while guests were enjoying a drink after dinner in the bar, at 9 p.m. Sinclair suddenly pulled down the bar shutters and told everyone to get out because he was going to bed. When guests complained he told them it was 'tough' and called them 'a bunch of cowboys'. One evening Sinclair astounded guests when he suddenly cancelled a dinner dance he had advertised. When they complained, he dumped a record player in the middle of the dance floor and stomped off to bed. Sinclair once halted breakfast because a waiter had placed some teapots on the wrong tables, then went up and down the tables interrogating the guests for a description of the guilty waiter. One evening, around 10.45 p.m., a young mother was pressing the night porter service button at reception. After about fifteen minutes, Mr Sinclair appeared in his dressing gown. When the guest asked if she could have a flask of hot water to heat her baby's bottle, he berated her for getting him out of bed for such a trivial request.

Sinclair died in Canada in 1981 after emigrating in the 1970s. In 2002, his widow Beatrice Sinclair broke her silence to complain of *Fawlty Towers*'s unfair portrayal of her late husband, protesting that he had been 'turned into a laughing stock'. She agreed that her husband was a disciplinarian who did not suffer fools, but in no way was he a 'neurotic eccentric'.

## Duke of diplomacy

Prince Philip, the Duke of Edinburgh (b. 1921), has always done his bit for race relations. In 1986, he advised a British student in Peking, 'Don't stay here too long or you'll go back with slitty eyes,' later describing the city as 'ghastly'. Ten years earlier, on tour in Hong Kong and unaware that he was miked up, he told a Chinese photographer, 'Fuck off or I'll have you shot.'

At an official function in Chile he was introduced to Dr Allende, soon to become the country's President, and found fault in Allende's attire – he was wearing an ordinary suit instead of the required white tie and tails. Allende explained that his people were very poor and that as their representative it would be inappropriate of him to dress expensively. Philip replied: 'And if they told you to wear a bathing costume, I suppose you'd have come dressed in one.' On the same tour of South America he told the Fascist dictator of Paraguay, General Alfredo Stroessner, a protector of Nazi war criminals, 'It's a pleasant change to be in a country that isn't ruled by its people.' On a tour of Canada, Philip reminded his British Commonwealth hosts that 'we don't come here for our health, you know,' and visiting an Aboriginal cultural park in Queensland, Australia, demanded to know, 'What's it all about? Do you still throw spears at each other?'

Other victims of his 'dry sense of humour' include the

Dutch – 'What a po-faced lot the Dutch are'; the French – 'Isn't it a pity Louis XVI was sent to the guillotine?' and Panamanians – on a trip to Panama he shouted at his official police escort who had sounded a siren, 'Switch that bloody thing off you silly fucker.' He said of the Hungarians that 'most of them are pot-bellied'; and Scots that 'they drink too much'. At least the Duke is very even-handed; in 1966, he reminded his wife's loyal subjects, 'You know, British women can't cook,' and in 1995, enquired of a Scottish driving instructor, 'How do you keep the natives off the booze long enough to pass the test?' Philip is also known as 'the best argument for republicanism since George III'.

## Mean cuisine

Britain's original TV celebrity cook, Fanny Cradock (1909–94) was regarded by many as the saviour of postwar British cooking. She was credited with introducing a new wave of 'sophisticated' foods to Britain, including her signature dish, prawn cocktail.

Fanny's memory for detail was never very good. She was born either Phyllis Pechey, or possibly Phyllis Primrose-Pechey, either in the borough of Leytonstone, London, or in the Channel Islands. She often claimed her father was a wealthy gambler, or she sometimes described him as an author, but in fact he was most likely a corn merchant called Archibald Pechey. Having been expelled from boarding school at the age of fifteen for giving Ouija board readings to younger girls, she eloped at the age of seventeen with an RAF pilot named Sidney Evans, who died shortly afterwards, leaving her a pregnant widow. Within a year of giving birth to her son Peter, Fanny married again, this time to Arthur Chapman.

Another child was born, Christopher, but when the boy was four months old she abandoned him and Arthur for life in the West End of London. In September 1939, she married Gregory Holden-Dye, after forgetting to mention that she was still legally married to Arthur. The new marriage only lasted eight weeks. By that time she had already met Johnny Cradock, a Royal Artillery major who was married with four children. He left his wife and family for Fanny and stayed with her for the rest of his life.

In the late 1940s, she and Johnny joined the *Daily Telegraph* to write a cookery column under the nom de plume 'Bon Viveur'. They progressed to live cookery demonstrations, then stage shows, and from 1955 until the 1970s, a popular TV show. Johnny's role was that of subservient sidekick, good only for handing Fanny her rolling pin, knowing which wine to serve and the odd sign-off, most memorably in 1965 when he told viewers, 'I hope your doughnuts turn out like Fanny's'. Although she took Johnny's surname and they were regarded as husband and wife throughout their TV career ('living in sin' was a sackable offence at the BBC), it was not until 1977 that they actually married. It came as no surprise that at the registry office there was confusion over both her age and her name. She claimed to be fifty-five, even though her first son was by then fifty and her other son by her second marriage was forty-eight.

Fanny was as celebrated for her rudeness and bad tempered run-ins with the public as for her cooking. Her unpredictable behaviour was exacerbated by an addiction to appetite-suppressing and mood-enhancing amphetamines, known among her inner circle as 'Fanny's hundreds and thousands'. In 1964, she was charged with careless driving and fined £5 after the arresting officer described her as 'abusive and excited'. When he asked her to move her Rolls-Royce, which was parked across the flow of traffic, she called him a 'uniformed delinquent' and reversed into the car behind. On another occasion she was prosecuted for dangerous driving after she swerved across her lane and caused a collision. When the injured party attempted to remonstrate with her she said, 'How dare you hit my car,' and sped off. The other driver followed her for 15 miles and finally overtook her. When he stood in front of her car waving her down, Cradock ran over him.

Fanny had her finger in several pies. As well as her work as a high-profile TV chef, she wrote cookery columns, wrote erotic fiction under the name 'Frances Dale' and spent time communicating with the dead. She recalled, 'I was on intimate terms with the court of Louis XIV.' In 1964, she called upon her psychic powers to predict 'the end of the Chinese restaurant'.

By the early 1970s, neither her cookery nor her presentation style had aged well, especially her reliance on piping bags and vegetable dyes and her insistence on doing her on-screen cooking while wearing vast crinoline ball gowns. Cradock's legendary rudeness finally ended her career as a TV cook in 1976. A Cornish housewife, Gwen Troake, won a competition to organize a banquet to be attended by a number of VIPs, including Edward Heath and Earl Mountbatten of Burma. The BBC filmed the result for the TV series *The Big Time* and asked Fanny to comment on Troake's choice of menu. Fanny was seen mugging to the camera, pretending to retch and rolling her eyes. The BBC decided that while it was permissible to be rude to professional cooks, the public were off limits; Cradock was sacked. Fanny and Johnny however continued to be regulars on the chat show circuit and appeared on programmes such as *The Generation Game* and *Blankety Blank*. Her final BBC appearance was when she appeared alone on *Parkinson* with a co-star, the drag artist Danny La Rue. When it was revealed to her that La Rue was actually a female impersonator, Cradock stormed off set, never to return.

# SELECT BIBLIOGRAPHY

Avery, G., *Gillian Avery's Book of the Strange and Odd* (Penguin, 1975)
Barnes, A., *Essex Eccentrics* (Boydell Press, 1975)
Brookes, M., *Extreme Measures: The Dark Visions and Bright Ideas of Francis Galton* (Bloomsbury, 2004)
Buchell, P., *Great Eccentrics* (George Allen & Unwin, 1984)
Burgess, G., *The Curious World of Frank Buckland* (Baker, 1967)
Caufield, C., *The Emperor of the United States and Other Magnificent Eccentrics* (St Martin's Press, 1981)
Donaldson, W., *Brewer's Rogues, Villains, Eccentrics: An A–Z of Roguish Britons Through the Ages* (Weidenfeld & Nicolson, 2002)
Fleming, F., *Barrow's Boys* (Granta, 2001)
Gleick, J., *Isaac Newton* (HarperPerennial, 2004)
Goodman, M., *Suffer and Survive: The Extreme Life of J. S. Haldane* (Simon and Schuster, 2007)
Gratzer, W. *Eurekas and Euphorias: The Oxford Book of Scientific Anecdotes* (Oxford University Press, 2004)
Gribben, J., *Science: A History 1543–2001* (Penguin, 2001)
Hamilton, N., *Great Political Eccentrics* (Robson Books, 1999)
Jardine, L., *The Curious Life of Robert Hooke* (HarperCollins, 2004)
Masters, B., *The Dukes* (Pimilco, 2001)
Montgomery-Massingberd, H., ed., *Daily Telegraph Book of Obituaries Volume 1* (Pan, 1996)
Moseley, M., *Irascible Genius: The Life of Charles Babbage* (Hutchinson, 1964)

Nahin, P., *Oliver Heaviside: The Life, Work and Times of an Electrical Genius of the Victorian Age* (John Hopkins University Press, 2002)

Nicholas, M., *The World's Greatest Cranks and Crackpots* (Hamlyn, 1982)

Nichols, P., *Evolution's Captain* (HarperCollins, 2004)

Palling, B., *Book of Modern Scandal: From Byron to the Present Day* (Orion, 1996)

Pickover, C. A., S*trange Brains and Genius: The Secret Lives of Eccentric Scientists and Madmen* (Plenum Trade, 1998)

Porter, R., *English Society in the Eighteenth Century* (Penguin, 1982)

Regan, G., *Great Military Blunders* (Channel 4 Books, 2000)

Sitwell, E., *English Eccentrics* (Penguin, 1971)

Somerville-Large, P., *Irish Eccentrics* (Hamish Hamilton, 1975)

Swade, D., *The Cogwheel Brain* (Abacus, 2001)

Taylor, J., *The Voyage of the Beagle* (Conway, 2008)

Tibballs, G., *Great Sporting Eccentrics* (Robson Books, 1998)

Timpson, J., *Timpson's English Eccentrics* (Jarrold, 1991)

Uglow, J., *Lunar Men: The Friends Who Made the Future* (Faber and Faber, 2003)

White, M., *Isaac Newton: The Last Sorcerer* (Fourth Estate, 1998)

Wilton, I., *C. B. Fry: King of Sport* (Metro Books, 2002)

Wright Gillham, N., *A Life of Sir Francis Galton* (Oxford University Press, 2002)

Youngson, R. M. and Schott, I., *Medical Blunders* (Robinson Publishing, 1996)